The Unsung Family Hero

The Unsung Family Hero

The death and life of an anti-Nazi resistance fighter

Author: Paul Gardner

HYBRID
PUBLISHERS

Published by Hybrid Publishers

Melbourne Victoria Australia

© Paul Gardner 2020

This publication is copyright. Apart from any use
as permitted under the Copyright Act 1968, no part may be reproduced
by any process without prior written permission from the publisher.
Requests and enquiries concerning reproduction
should be addressed to the Publisher,
Hybrid Publishers,
PO Box 52, Ormond, VIC Australia 3204.
www.hybridpublishers.com.au

First published 2020

A catalogue record for this
book is available from the
National Library of Australia

ISBN 9781925736366 (p)
9781925736373 (e)

Cover design: Gittus Graphics www.gggraphics.com.au

Foreword

In this book, based partly on genealogical research and partly on rational reconstruction, the author tells the life story of Gerhard Badrian, a member of his mother's family. As told in the opening page, Gerhard was murdered in South Amsterdam in June 1944 by Nazi gunmen who had laid a trap for him.

The book then moves back in time and, like a verbal newsreel of many scenes, provides the frightening story of how this encounter with death finally came about.

Born in Germany as a Jew, Gerhard fled his homeland after Hitler's regime took over. But the apparent safety of the Netherlands evaporated after the German occupation began. Gerhard was forced underground where he used his photographic and other skills to produce convincing identity papers, essential to the survival of those in hiding and on the run. Gerhard's bravado saved many lives, including that of a nephew, Horst Kerpen, snatched from the jaws of death at Westerbork camp, a staging post for the one-way trains to Auschwitz and Sobibor.

Across the pages of this story scurry the heroes and villains of a fearsomely dangerous time. What is the value of such a book? In short, it converts the history of a global war and monstrous crimes against humanity into a personal story of courage, risk and heart-trembling fear. Before such stories are lost or forgotten, it is admirable that the author, whose family were among the few Jewish refugees that Australia accepted at the time, has pieced the story together so that readers can understand the impact of the Holocaust on those primarily involved. At a moment in history when shared global values are being questioned and challenged, it is admirable that this family story has been rescued from oblivion. It is presented as a gripping story of how extraordinary times converted ordinary people into heroes. And by presenting the story to today's generation, the author has ensured that we do not forget the wrongs and strengthen our defences against repeating them.

– **The Hon. Michael Kirby** AC CMG, past Justice of the High Court of Australia and Co-Chair of the International Bar Association Human Rights Institute.

"… According to some, a hero is someone who is not afraid, someone who is fearless in the face of danger. Hollywood reinforces this idea. On the silver screen you recognise heroes through their boldness. Gerhard Badrian of the *Verzet*, the anti-Nazi Resistance in Holland, would appear at first sight to be one of them. His biography reads like a ready-made scenario for an exciting film: great courage, spectacular resistance actions, a femme fatale. But unlike the clichés of the genre, the story contains no happy ending …"

> – **NIOD** (The Dutch Institute for War, Holocaust and
> Genocide Studies) from an entry in NIOD's
> "Hero of the Month" series, April 2012

"The story of the Holocaust is one of darkness and despair, questioning humanity itself. But the actions of those few who took great risks to help others are a reminder of the human capacity for love and hope."

> – **HRH Prince William**, Duke of Cambridge, reflecting on
> his visit to Yad Vashem, June 2018

History is "… a pattern / Of endless moments"

> – **T.S. Eliot**, from "Little Gidding" [1942]
> from his poem-cycle, *Four Quartets*

"Ordinary people believe only in the possible. Extraordinary people visualise not what is possible or probable, but rather what is impossible. And by visualising the impossible, they begin to see it as possible."

> – **Cherie Carter-Scott**

"There are no extraordinary men … just extraordinary circumstances that ordinary men are forced to deal with."

– **William Halsey**

"Good storytelling is viciously complicated. It's like juggling while riding a bike: one must control established facts while adding new, staying upright and moving ahead."

– **Anson Cameron,** *The Age* (*Spectrum*) 17 June 2017

"At the Anne Frank House there is a photo … of a raid at the Central Station in Amsterdam. Underneath it, it says, 'Dutch men and Dutch women, do not think this was only done by the Germans, by the foreigners, by the occupiers. This was done by Dutch soldiers, by Dutch storekeepers, by Dutch policemen, by Dutch citizens. We must look into ourselves to understand this, and not just blame others.' I think it is a good thing when countries can be self-critical."

– **The Honourable Justice Michael Kirby**
Australian Jewish News, 1 September 2017

Janusz Korczak, Polish educator and Holocaust victim, said that "Children are not the people of tomorrow, but are people of today. They have a right to be taken seriously, and to be treated with tenderness and respect. They should be allowed to grow into whoever they were meant to be. 'The unknown person' inside of them is our hope for the future." Approximately 1.5 million of the six million Jews murdered in the Holocaust were children. Tragically there were very few children who survived.

– **Yad Vashem Online Exhibition "Children in the Holocaust",** 2019

Contents

Gerhard Badrian

Prologue

Ordinary people faced with extraordinary situations can sometimes act in extraordinary ways. This book is about such a man, Gerhard Badrian, my mother's cousin. By all accounts, he was a gentle soul, quiet, thoughtful, artistic, compassionate. In a normal world, his passionate love affair with a beautiful young woman would have led to marriage and children, along with a successful career as an outstanding commercial photographer.

But the world of Nazi-occupied Holland was not a normal world. To cope with ruthless tyranny, his first reaction was a perfectly normal one. Keep your head down, don't draw attention to yourself, keep out of harm's way.

Yet as the Nazi screws were tightened, as the regime turned from inhumane to murderous, something inside Gerhard's brain snapped. He went underground, developed a false identity, joined the Resistance.

At first, his involvement was merely praiseworthy. He joined a team of men and women that prepared false identification papers. This saved the lives of hundreds of people. Good job, Gerhard. Well done. Worth an article in a newspaper. Doesn't warrant a book, though.

I first encountered Gerhard Badrian's name when I was young. Just an entry on my family tree, he was one of many of my extended family who died during World War II. In my middle age, a cousin showed me a photograph of a memorial plaque in the Rubensstraat in Amsterdam. The wording of the plaque plainly demonstrated that

Gerhard was an exceptional man. But it was not until my retirement that I had the time and the resources to discover what made him so.

I learnt about his exploits, pretending to be a Gestapo officer (Secret State Police) as he removed Resistance colleagues from custody and spirited them away to safety. In the archives, I found a Gestapo message to Berlin, gloating over the death of this "leading Jewish terrorist". I learnt about the event held in the Rubensstraat on Memorial Day – annually, 70 years later! – where relatives of colleagues still gathered to remember him. I listened to a recording of a radio broadcast made 30 years after his death, in which his lover remembered him as the love of her life.

In Amsterdam, I met the son of a policeman who was a close colleague of Gerhard's in the Resistance. The son told me that his father, since deceased, had kept a photo of Gerhard on his desk for the rest of his life. In Germany, I met the son of Gerhard's nephew whom Gerhard had saved from the Westerbork transit camp. The son had previously been unaware of Gerhard's involvement, as the nephew had hardly ever spoken about his wartime experiences. And back home in Australia, when I told friends about some of Gerhard's exploits, a common response was that Steven Spielberg could make a film about him.

Such a man deserves more than a newspaper article, more than a Wikipedia entry (yes, there is one). He deserves a book. Gerhard is not simply an unsung hero, he is the unsung hero of my family. This is my personal tribute to his memory.

Paul Gardner
November 2019

Introduction

1

The ending

Amsterdam, under Nazi occupation, 30 June 1944. A small café in the heart of the city.

Lunchtime. Five people are sitting around a table. One of the five, Gerhard Badrian, has invited the others. He's a man in his late thirties, medium height, well built, distinguished in appearance, and slightly balding despite his relatively young age. Next to him is Anne-Marie Deij, an attractive woman in her late twenties; they have been a couple for the past two years. The others are two of Gerhard's close associates, Frans Meijer and Frits Boverhuis, and another striking young woman, Bella Tuerlings, a more recent acquaintance.

Although there is not much to be cheerful about in wartime Amsterdam, the group is in good spirits. The Germans are heading for defeat. The Russians are pushing steadily towards eastern Germany, and the Americans and Canadians are advancing through parts of the Netherlands. But the main reason for the happy frame of mind is that Gerhard and Anne-Marie have been looking for a new place to live, as their existing apartment is no longer suitable. Their new-found friend Bella has offered them hers. She says she won't be needing it any more, as she's about to flee the country with false papers. Straight after lunch, they intend to inspect Bella's apartment.

It's time to go. Gerhard pays the bill. Frans excuses himself, saying he has to leave. Bella flashes a warm smile. "Oh, come along, you should see my apartment too!"

"Thanks, but no," Frans responds. "I'm off to get a haircut, and anyway, Gerhard's car's too small to fit the five of us comfortably."

The four of them drive the short distance to south Amsterdam, to an apartment block on the corner of Rubensstraat and Euterpestraat. A large, dark-grey building diagonally opposite the brown-brick apartment block was once a girls' secondary school before the occupation, but no longer serves that purpose.

Gerhard parks the car, a German-made Opel. It's not too hard to find a spot. Traffic is light in wartime Amsterdam. Few people can afford a car or the petrol to run one. The four of them emerge. Bella leads the group up a flight of steps to the first floor and invites them all in.

The apartment isn't empty. There are men inside: SS – *Schutzstaffel* – the Nazis' surveillance and terror organisation. Within seconds, Gerhard sums up the situation. It's an ambush. He pulls out his pistol and shoots one of the men, who falls, critically injured. Anne-Marie and Frits are arrested. Gerhard is quick. He runs out of the apartment and leaps down the stairs to the street. But as quick as he is, the SS has planned this operation. Other SS men are covering the street. One of them shoots Gerhard dead as he reaches the footpath.

This is a major triumph for the SS. Berlin is quickly informed of the successful elimination of one of the leaders of the *Verzet*, the Dutch Resistance in Amsterdam.

A van comes by to take the body away. It's 30 June 1944. This was the day that Gerhard Badrian died. This is his story.

Beginnings

2

Birth of a son

"Birth is a beginning, death is a destination, life is a journey."

– from the Memorial Service in the
Union of Progressive Judaism prayer book

Beuthen (pronounced Boy'ten), Germany, 13 October 1905

"*Mazel tov*, Frau Badrian," said the midwife, Frau Schlesinger. "You have a healthy baby boy! It'll be nice for little Erna to have a baby brother." She'd attended the birth of Frieda's first child. In the close-knit Jewish community of the Upper Silesian town of Beuthen, she was a popular midwife and she liked to keep in contact with the families whose babies she had helped to bring into the world.

The baby's father was waiting nervously out in the corridor. He'd heard his wife's screams of pain as she was giving birth and the later high-pitched cries of the newborn. He was desperate to know the result. Frau Schlesinger was an experienced midwife who was quite familiar with the anxieties of new fathers. She poked her head out the door. "Everything went well, Herr Badrian. Just wait for a few minutes while we get your wife and baby settled," she said gently, "and then you can come in and see your son."

A son! Hermann heard the word he'd been hoping for. Of course he was happy when their firstborn was a girl, and he loved his two-year-old daughter, but like most men in his community, he thought that a son was something special. A son could carry on the family name into the next generation. There had been a continuous line of male Badrians for more than a century.

He loved Frieda so much. He felt fortunate to have met her in Beuthen and won her love. Frieda Herrnstadt had been born in the distant alpine town of Hirschberg in Lower Silesia, while he came from a small and much nearer Upper Silesian village, Ornontowitz. Both had come from tiny Jewish communities. Had they remained there, they probably would never have met, but both had decided as young adults to move to Beuthen.

When each of them arrived in Beuthen, separately, as very young adults, without knowing each other, they were amazed, even overawed, by the town. It was, of course, just a provincial town of moderate size, one of many in late nineteenth century Germany, in no way comparable to the large European cities such as Berlin and Paris that, as children, they had read about in books. For Frieda and Hermann, however, both born and raised in small villages, Beuthen was magical – a paradise. The streets were paved and were lit at night. People lived in enormous apartment houses – three, four, even five storeys high.

Hermann, interested since boyhood in technical things, explored the environs of this industrial town, made rich through the centuries by its mines of iron, coal, lead and zinc. Frieda was more attracted by the commercial and cultural facilities of the city, its shops, its schools, its imposing Silesian Opera House. The numerous churches were impressive, but both were particularly pleased when they first saw the large and elegant synagogue, which was where they first met at a community social event. A synagogue that could seat a thousand people was almost beyond their comprehension.

Hermann had moved to be with his extended family. His parents had been separated for years. His father had died and his mother had moved to Beuthen to be cared for in her old age by her only daughter, Hermann's unmarried older sister, Minna. An observant Jew, Hermann was also attracted by the fuller community life, totally different from that of the tiny village where he was born. The splendid synagogue resembled a cathedral. A distinguished and respected rabbi led the congregation. The community ran a Jewish elementary school.

Hermann was also attracted to Beuthen by the better employment opportunities in a large town. His older brother had already shown the way. Louis had been apprenticed to a shoemaker, had shown great skill and set up his own specialist business serving clients who had deformed or crippled feet. He'd done well: he had a big workshop and store in Dyngosstrasse, lived in a large and comfortable apartment nearby and employed a maid at home. Louis was listed in the town's commercial directory; he even had a telephone, unheard of in the Badrian family.

Frieda's motivations were similar, but not identical. Young women were not expected to think of themselves as business people or professionals. Their education was aimed at preparing them to be wives and mothers. She learnt cooking and baking, and how to sew and knit. Along the way, she discovered she had artistic flair and found that she could design and make stylish dresses that other women in the family were pleased to wear.

For women, and especially for Jewish women, the conventional pathway to a satisfying life lay in landing a suitable husband. In the Jewish community of the time, that meant finding *einen netten jüdischen Junge*, a nice Jewish boy. Hard to find in tiny Hirschberg with its community of 35 souls. So with her parents' blessing, she set off for the large provincial town of Beuthen to find, if not fame and fortune, then a *sympathisch* Jewish man with a good head on his shoulders.

She'd met Hermann at the Beuthen synagogue. He was active on the committee that helped run the congregation. In his mid-twenties, of medium height and well-built, he had a pleasant face and manner. He invited her out for dinner and they talked – about their backgrounds, their families, their interests. He told her that his father had died a few years before in Sohrau. His elderly mother Johanna was still alive, here in Beuthen.

Frieda asked him about his work. He'd found employment as a salesman in one of the local stores. He told her that he was making a living, but found the work uninteresting and that he thought it didn't offer much of a future. He was thinking about setting up a small business, which he called a "Chemical Cleaning Plant". Most people washed their own clothes in coppers and troughs at home, or got their maid to do it, if they had one. His idea was that people would bundle up their clothing and laundry and bring it to his store, where it would be washed, dried and ironed, ready to be picked up the next day. Frieda was impressed; she'd never heard of such a thing. Hermann explained that he had once visited Berlin and, seeing such a business there, had thought it had possibilities.

They found themselves mutually attracted. They were shy young adults, both of them quite inexperienced in talking about their feelings. One evening, after a quiet dinner together in one of the town's small kosher restaurants, Hermann walked Frieda home. He found some newly discovered inner resolve and managed, with some hesitation, to tell Frieda that he loved her, then asked her if she would marry him. She took no time at all to say *yes*.

Their engagement was announced and in 1902 they were married. They moved into an apartment and their first child, Erna, was born a year later. And now they had a son as well.

3

A name for the boy

Beuthen, 21 October 1905

Eight days after the boy's birth, the family and friends, together with Hermann's associates at the synagogue, gathered at home early in the morning for the *b'ris milah*, the celebration of the boy's circumcision. It was a happy event, attended by the extended family. His older brother Louis was the *sandek*, given the honour of holding the baby on his lap while the *mohel* performed the circumcision. Louis' wife Emma, four months pregnant with their third child, came to the family celebration. The Badrian family of Beuthen was growing.

Yet there was a tinge of sadness, too. The older generation was missing. Hermann's father Joseph had died, only in his fifties. His mother Johanna lived long enough to see Hermann and Frieda married and share in the joy of seeing her first granddaughter. But she died in 1903, just a few months after Erna's birth.

It was customary to give a newborn son his Hebrew name at his *b'ris*, and not before. It was also a strong tradition in Jewish families, widely respected in the Badrian family for a century, to name a boy after a deceased grandfather. Near the end of the ceremony, Rabbi Max Kopfstein therefore invoked the traditional blessing and announced the name of the baby boy, *Yosef ben Chaim*, Joseph the son of Chaim.

Traditions were important, but these were also modern times. German Jews felt blessed. They were living in an enlightened age.

They were free to live wherever they chose, no longer shackled by the requirements imposed on them by the lord of the manor in a small village. They could rent apartments in cities, follow any occupation, vote in elections and become integrated into the life of the wider community. They spoke German as their mother tongue, not the Yiddish of their Polish co-religionists. They were proud German citizens, loyal supporters of Kaiser Wilhelm and the Second Reich.

And so, while they maintained the ancient tradition of giving their children Hebrew names, those names were reserved for ritual use in the synagogue. For half a century, out in the street, modern German Jews used conventional German forenames, added to the family surnames adopted in Napoleonic times. The adoption of German forenames was already well-established when Hermann was born. He'd been named "Chaim" at his *b'ris,* but in the spirit of the times, Hermann's father Joseph had given his youngest child the more Germanic (but still recognisably Jewish) name Haimann. Although that was what he continued to be called within the family and on official documents, in business and everywhere else in everyday life he adopted the distinctly German name of Hermann.

One generation on, the Jews of Beuthen had become integrated into German society. No need any more for this triple-name trick of a Hebrew name given at the *b'ris,* a German-Jewish name for use at home, and a wholly German name for use in business. Two names were enough for modern German Jews. And so, when Hermann visited the Beuthen town hall to register his son's birth at the *Standesamt,* he informed the official, who dutifully recorded in old German script on a blank printed form that his son, of the Mosaic religion, born on the thirteenth day of October in the year nineteen hundred and five, the son of the merchant Haimann Badrian and his legally wedded wife Frieda née Herrnstadt, was to be known as Gerhard Joseph Badrian.

4

The captain from Köpenick

Beuthen, 1913

The sky was a clear and bright icy-blue on a cool spring morning as young Gerhard left home for his daily ten-minute walk to school. He waved to his mother in the kitchen as he headed for the front door. Frieda was washing the breakfast dishes and flashed a quick smile. She loved her eight-year-old son and took quiet pleasure in his gentle manner and keen intelligence.

Gerhard skipped down the steps of the apartment building and out into the street. He hadn't seen his father that morning. Hermann had already left early for work at his commercial laundry business a few blocks away.

Gerhard looked up at the sky. It wasn't always this clear in this industrial town. Beuthen lay in the centre of a mining area, and sometimes the air was suffused with a thin, dusty fog.

He passed his Uncle Louis' shoe store in Dyngosstrasse on his way to school. His uncle and aunt had five children and he knew them all, but except for the latest baby, the boys were all older than him and they had their own friends. The only girl, Irma, was just a year younger, but they didn't play much together. Girl cousins weren't much fun. He preferred the company of his friends at school.

Gerhard was a bright child. Like most of his classmates he did what was required of him and behaved himself in class. Some of the schoolwork was boring, while other parts of the curriculum puzzled him.

The Hebrew lessons and religious studies that were a central part of the curriculum didn't excite him much, but he knew that his father was very involved in the town's Jewish community. The family observed Shabbat, ate kosher food and went to synagogue regularly. It was a simple fact of life.

At school, he had to master the totally unfamiliar Hebrew alphabet and later to learn how to read the *siddur*, the daily prayer book. Nobody he knew spoke Hebrew. His teacher, Reb Mordechai, was a friendly man, and one day after school, little Gerhard plucked up enough courage to ask him why he had to learn this. The old man had heard this question many times before. "Well, Yosef [he liked to call his pupils by their Hebrew name], you've been in *shule* and you've seen many older boys have their bar mitzvah when they turn thirteen. They have to read out loud from the Torah and say several prayers. It will be a very important day in your life and that's why in school we help you get ready for it. It takes a lot of time to learn to do it properly. You'll want your Mama and Papa to be proud of you on that day, won't you?"

He really enjoyed the lessons with two of his teachers, at least often enough to keep him reasonably content. Mr Yosl Alterman loved poetry. He not only read out poems in class, but he was an amateur poet himself. Occasionally, some of his verses were published in the daily *Beuthen Zeitung*. He also wrote for children, including silly nursery rhymes, and he would sometimes read them out in class as a kind of rehearsal. When Gerhard was much younger, his mother would sometimes read fables and sing songs at bedtime. One of his favourites was *Auf der blauen Donau, schwimmt ein Krokodil*. Inquisitive as ever, Gerhard would pepper Frieda with questions. Was the Danube River really blue? And he'd seen drawing of crocodiles in children's stories, but were there really any crocodiles in the Danube?

Class time in school was also made more tolerable through the efforts of another teacher. Mr Heinrich Glassman was a young, cheerful man who often made lessons interesting. Some of his colleagues on the staff sometimes looked askance at his unconventional teaching methods but he kept control of his class and his pupils were progressing well. The principal of the elementary school found no cause for complaint.

This morning's German lesson was a nice example of his style. Glassman told the class he was going to read them a story called *The Captain from Köpenick*. "It's not only a funny story which I think you'll enjoy, but it's actually a true story. This really happened," he proclaimed with a smile. He had an ulterior motive for telling the story: it raised ethical issues about the way a society ought to behave, and he thought stories like this might help his students think about such issues. Yes, grammar and vocabulary development were important, but literature could help educate young people to attain other valuable goals as well.

Glassman read the story aloud, from an article in a magazine. As a competent teacher, he knew that some of the words might be unfamiliar to his class of eight-year-olds, so he would stop to explain a point in his own words and ask the class questions to keep them engaged. The story, about a man named William Voigt, described an incident that happened in the township of Köpenick, near Berlin, in 1906. Voigt had a criminal record, but after serving his jail term he found employment with a shoemaker in the town of Wismar and gave up his criminal ways. But the Wismar police took no notice of his reformed behaviour and ordered him to leave town because of his criminal record. They had no right to do this. He had served his time and now had an honest job. The same thing happened to him in other towns.

So, Voigt thought, if they're going to treat me like a criminal I might as well be one. He obtained a captain's uniform, stopped ten soldiers, plied them with beer and ordered them to accompany him to the town hall of Köpenick. Brandishing a forged document, he then ordered the mayor, the police chief and other authorities to be jailed, demanded 4000 marks from the town's treasurer, sent the soldiers to escort the public servants to the police station in Berlin, and then disappeared with the cash.

The class loved the story. It sparked an idea in Gerhard's mind. A couple of weeks later, the school announced that it would as usual be holding its annual *Purim* celebration, and children should come to school in fancy dress. Most responded conventionally, and came dressed as King Ahasuerus, or Queen Esther, or the wicked Jew-hater, Haman. Gerhard didn't. He asked his dressmaker mother to whip up something different. Frieda smiled and felt a glow of pleasure of having a son with imagination. But she checked with her husband first to seek his opinion. Hermann saw no reason to object; in fact, he thought it was a brilliant idea. When the tailoring was complete, Gerhard tried on his fancy dress and performed a dress rehearsal, strutting up and down the hallway of the family's apartment, occasionally barking orders, mostly to himself.

And when Purim morning finally arrived, little Gerhard marched into school dressed (very approximately) as a captain of the Imperial German Army. He even confronted Mr Glassman and handed him a piece of paper demanding that the school pay him 4000 marks. Mr Glassman just smiled. He appreciated imaginative pupils, and wished Gerhard a happy Purim.

5

The Great War

Beuthen, 1 August 1914

Germany at War! Headlines of newspapers all over the country screamed the news in large bold font.

"We're fighting Russia," Hermann announced, grim-faced, at breakfast. "But why, Papa?" Gerhard wanted to know. He had never experienced such a thing in his short life, and not surprisingly, he had no understanding of what the news meant. He'd seen children fighting in the schoolyard, and he'd seen soldiers of the German Imperial Army in the streets of Beuthen, but the idea of countries fighting each other was beyond his comprehension.

Hermann had little idea about how to explain what it all meant. A month earlier, the Archduke of Austria had been killed by a Yugoslav, the Austrians threatened the Serbians, the Russian Tsar had mobilised his army and the Kaiser demanded that the Russians withdraw their soldiers. The Russians refused, and now German soldiers were fighting the Russians. Europe had gone mad. How does one explain this to a child, he wondered; he barely understood it himself. He had no personal experience of war. The last war that he had learnt about in school, when the Prussians had conquered the French, had happened before he was born.

And in the fortnight that followed, the madness grew in intensity. The French were allied to the Russians, and they used the opportunity to exact revenge against the Germans who had defeated them in 1870. France opened up a second front in the current crisis. Germany ignored an 1839 Treaty of London that supposedly guaranteed Belgian neutrality by invading the country in order to move its troops to the front with France. And that brought the British Empire into the war because of the Germans' actions in Belgium. Hermann naturally hadn't seen the British papers that had begun to call the episode "The Rape of Belgium".

The Badrian family was not immediately affected, although several sons of friends and neighbours, young men of military age, were conscripted or even volunteered to join local regiments.

Beuthen wasn't under direct threat. The Russian front was far away to the east, and the French were hundreds of kilometres away to the south-west. "All the news is terrible," Hermann confided to Frieda (although as a loyal and proud German, he hoped Germany would win), "but I don't think we'll be affected too much."

A sensible judgement, perhaps, but he was wrong. As well as the unsurprising decision of the British to send their troops to fight in France and Belgium, England made an unexpected move. It blockaded the Dutch port of Rotterdam to German shipping. As part of its war effort, it sought to cut off supplies to Germany. Rotterdam was a major port through which food (and other) supplies reached Germany before the war.

The Dutch were neutral. The Kaiser had no imperial ambitions to rule the Dutch: his argument was with the Russians, the French and now the British. The tight Rotterdam blockade began to shrink German waistlines. Germany wasn't self-sufficient in food production; it needed imports. Especially when hundreds of thousands of soldiers fighting on two fronts had to be fed.

6

Foster-parents

Beuthen, 1916

Nothing happened suddenly. It was a steadily declining situation that eventually turned dire.

Germans began to go hungry, especially those who were less well-off. Families all over the country were finding it hard to feed their children.

The Netherlands was also affected by the blockade, but to a lesser extent, as the British allowed non-German ships through, provided they sailed all the way around Scotland to reach Rotterdam.

Some German families, both Jewish and non-Jewish, had family, friends and business acquaintances in the Netherlands, and many took or sent their children across the border. Some German churches and synagogues had links with Dutch co-religionists and developed schemes to place children in temporary foster homes.

One day, in the middle of the increasingly disastrous war (for both sides), a dejected Hermann and Frieda decided that enough was enough. "We're eating turnips instead of potatoes!" he fulminated. "Today the bakery was completely out of bread!" (He didn't even bother to complain that coffee was unobtainable.) "Our children are continually hungry," he told a despondent Frieda. She wept as she nodded in agreement.

He sought Rabbi Kopfstein's advice. The rabbi told him of offers by numerous Dutch communities to place German children in foster homes. Hermann was very hesitant about sending either of his children away to some unknown family. The rabbi understood his concern, and responded that Bussum, a small town outside Amsterdam, was one of the communities involved. He knew the elderly rabbi there, Rabbi Yakov Kupfermacher, a former colleague of his, and offered to write to him. He could be trusted to ensure that a reliable family would be chosen. Perhaps if they took one child, there would be just enough food to feed the other child. If Hermann and Frieda consented, he would make enquiries.

The railway lines between Germany and the neighbouring neutral Netherland were still carrying trains and the postal system continued to operate. Letters were exchanged between the rabbis. A middle-aged Dutch couple, Jaques and Rachel de Vries agreed to take a child into their home and care for him. They preferred a boy.

That evening, after their frugal dinner when all of them still felt hungry, Hermann and Frieda sat patiently with tears in their eyes as they explained the plan to their ten-year-old. "We love you," said Frieda, "and we'll miss you terribly, but there isn't enough food and the war is dragging on and getting worse and worse and we're worried about you. We want you to grow up healthy and strong, and our rabbi has found a kindly couple in the Netherlands who will look after you and feed you, and care for you just like we would. We will, of course, write to you, letters and postcards, every week, and we will think of you all the time."

Gerhard took all of this in, in silence. He didn't know what to say. He didn't want to leave home. He didn't want to live with strangers in a strange country where he didn't speak the language. But he knew without saying the words that his parents loved him and wanted was best for him, and he also knew in his stomach and thinning body that he needed this move. Without any words, he looked at his parents, quietly said goodnight, went to bed and cried for several hours before eventually falling asleep.

The arrangements were made. Hermann and Frieda helped Gerhard pack his clothes and other belongings into two suitcases.

Hermann would accompany him on the thousand-kilometre trip across northern Germany to Amsterdam. They would catch the Prussian State Railways train to Berlin, wait there for a few hours, and then take the night train to Amsterdam where they would be met at the Central Railway Station by Jaques de Vries.

7

Preparations

Bussum, the Netherlands, 1916

Jaques and Rachel de Vries had no children of their own, but they were a kindly, loving couple who cared about other people and somehow knew instinctively what they needed to do to make this new addition to their family feel welcome. They asked Gerhard about his favourite food and toys and books. They reminded him regularly to write home to his family in Beuthen, and took an interest in his family's news. They took him for walks around the small town. Gerhard expressed surprise when he saw a canal for the first time. Rows of houses overlooking a narrow body of water didn't exist in Beuthen.

There was no Jewish school in Bussum – the community was too small for that – so they enrolled him in the local elementary school. They expected that he might struggle at first with learning Dutch, so they spent time with him at home, patiently helping him to develop his language skills. Many Dutch words were similar to German, but Dutch pronunciation was different. The couple were pleased to observe that the boy was a quick learner who was willing to meet new challenges.

Jaques was a regular worshipper in the small synagogue and took Gerhard along on Sabbath mornings. He introduced him to the elderly rabbi, who was warm and welcoming, not only to Gerhard, but to the small group of other German children who had arrived in Bussum to be fostered during the war. Rabbi Kupfermacher, himself of German background and education, was aware of the potential problems that these children might encounter. Most missed their parents. Some had trouble adjusting to their foster family. A few felt lost in their new and unfamiliar surroundings. No doubt Gerhard experienced some of these feelings, but the rabbi was impressed with the way the boy was coping with this major disruption in his life.

Late in the year, the rabbi invited Jaques and Gerhard to meet with him. The boy was now eleven years old, and it was time to begin his preparation for his bar mitzvah when he turned thirteen. Gerhard was invited to participate in the rabbi's regular Sunday morning class.

One of the first practical decisions to be made was the actual date of the ceremony. This required advance planning because the boy would be reading and singing in Hebrew the weekly portion from the Torah, a different one each week. That normally required a year or two of preparation. The date chosen was Saturday, 5 October 1918.

Gerhard was puzzled. "But my birthday is on the thirteenth of October," he exclaimed. "Why is it being held early?"

Rabbi Kupfermacher smiled. He'd heard other children ask this question before. "Bar mitzvahs are usually held soon after your date of birth according to the Jewish calendar," he explained. "I looked up your birthday. You were born on the fourteenth day of the Hebrew month of Tishrei in the year 5666. That was in October then, but in two years' time it happens to be in September. However, the fourteenth is always the eve of the week-long Succoth festival, and we never hold a bar mitzvah then, so we'll hold your celebration two weeks later, in early October."

Gerhard was still bemused. Why didn't the Hebrew and Dutch dates match? His inquisitive nature prompted his next comment. "I still don't understand why my bar mitzvah will be before my birthday."

The old rabbi chuckled. He appreciated teaching children who wanted to understand, and not just blindly accept what they were told. "That's because the Hebrew calendar is divided into lunar months. Each Hebrew month starts on the day of New Moon, so twelve lunar months is shorter than twelve months on the ordinary calendar. But to keep the Jewish calendar in line with the seasons, and with the ordinary calendar, an extra leap month is introduced from time to time. That means the Jewish date of fourteenth *Tishrei* moves around a bit from year to year on the Dutch calendar."

Gerhard already knew how to read Hebrew; he'd learnt that in elementary school in Beuthen. During his weekly lessons with the rabbi, he had quickly learnt to recite the blessings he would have to say. That was easy. More challenging was the task of learning to read the weekly section of the Torah. The portion was called *Bereishis* [In the beginning], the opening section of the Book of Genesis, always read immediately after the *Tishrei* holyday period.

The preparation demanded disciplined study, even for an able child. The Torah is written on a scroll of parchment without vowels or punctuation, and each word and phrase has an accompanying but unwritten set of musical notes which have to be memorised. Every boy finds the task challenging. Gerhard enjoyed the challenge and took pride in doing things well. And while perhaps he would not have been able to put it into words, he was motivated by the hope that his foster family should be proud of him on this special day of his life. Quite possibly, he had forgotten that his Hebrew teacher in Beuthen had said much the same thing several years earlier.

8

Bar mitzvah

Bussum, Saturday, 5 October 1918

The war was going badly for the Germans. The Kaiser's army was suffering defeat after defeat in the field. Jaques de Vries read his daily paper to learn what was happening, and kept Gerhard informed without going into unnecessary detail. Gerhard's main concern was for his parents and sister, but his worries were allayed by the regular delivery of postcards from Beuthen. His parents assured him that everyone was well and that Beuthen remained far from the battle-grounds. They avoided telling him of the severe shortage of food and other basic goods. Jaques tried to cheer Gerhard up by offering his opinion that the war would probably end soon.

It was an unhappy time for the Dutch, too. Although its citizens were untouched directly by the war, the partial blockade of Rotterdam had affected them as well. Not as badly, but still noticeably. Some foods were hard to get. Prices of basic goods had risen. Families on low incomes suffered. The De Vries family were not poor, but their standard of living was nonetheless affected. They had to manage their money carefully.

As the important day of the bar mitzvah approached, Jaques had taken Gerhard to a local store and bought him a new suit, shirt, tie and shoes for the occasion.

Finally, the big day arrived. It was the culmination of two years of study, a special day of celebration for Gerhard and the family circle. On the Saturday morning, the neatly attired lad impressed the congregation with his clear diction and pleasant voice. On that day, according to Jewish tradition, he would "become a man", not of course in the physical sense. From then on, Gerhard himself would be responsible for his own observance of religious ritual and proper ethical behaviour.

This was not the time for lavish family celebrations. The extended Badrian family from Beuthen were unable to attend. Jaques and Rachel organised a small afternoon tea the next day in their home, with just the rabbi, a few invited guests from the synagogue and Gerhard's small circle of friends.

When the party was over and the guests had gone home, the family gathered together and Jaques spoke to Gerhard. "We have something for you. Your parents sent me some money and asked me to buy you a present that they hope you will enjoy. We have combined with them, so this is from all of us. Open the box carefully."

Jaques handed over the neatly-wrapped gift, the size of a shoebox. Gerhard untied the string, unwrapped the paper, removed the lid and the packing. The box contained a shiny leather case. He opened it carefully. When he saw what it was, he gasped with astonishment and excitement.

It was a Rietzschel Tip, a folding camera. Inside the box lay a few rolls of film. Although Gerhard had seen a few of these new devices in shop windows and out in the street, he had not imagined that he would own one himself. He had never received so generous a gift in his life. With tears of joy in his eyes, he hugged Jaques and embraced and kissed Rachel on both cheeks.

9

The young photographer

Beuthen and Berlin, 1920s

The Great War ended and Gerhard returned home, with mixed feelings. He was naturally happy to be with his family again, yet there was sadness too at leaving his foster-parents. The couple and the boy had grown fond of each other. Gerhard promised to keep in touch.

He came home to find that major changes had occurred in his parents' life. A year before the end of the war, his Uncle Louis had died quite young. His parents had told him about that in a letter. His widowed Aunt Emma had been unable to sell the specialist shoemaker business in Dyngosstrasse and so the business was closed down. Hermann and Frieda had new business plans and offered to take over the rental of the property. He sold his dry-cleaning business and the couple began a new venture. Frieda's skills at dressmaking led her to open a ladies' fashion salon in the Dyngosstrasse storefront, while Hermann used the workshop at the rear to begin working as a tailor.

Gerhard noticed that during the two years of his absence, his sister Erna was beginning to show signs of becoming a young woman. The experiences of living in a country that had just lost a calamitous war had clearly affected her. She looked thin and drawn, no doubt the result of a shortage of good food. Now fifteen years old, she had completed her formal education and was looking without much success for a job. Although she and Gerhard had few interests in common, he did care about his sister and he spent many hours with her, listening to her tell about the events in her life while he was in Bussum, and sharing with her some of his experiences of living with a foster family in a strange country.

Gerhard naturally showed his parents his bar mitzvah gift and thanked them profusely for helping to make it possible. The gift had been a joint present from his parents and the de Vries family, but he suspected that his father was responsible for initiating the idea.

The camera was his prized possession, and it led to photography becoming his serious hobby. Both parents encouraged his interest. Frieda asked him to visit her new dressmaking business and take photos of models wearing her latest creations. She was delighted with the quality of the pictures. Hermann was a technically-minded man who encouraged his son to understand how mechanical things worked and how they might be improved.

Gerhard absorbed this positive attitude from his father. As he matured from boyhood into adulthood, he bought a more sophisticated camera. He read about technical improvements, took old cameras apart to study their inner workings, but not his old Rietzschel: that had sentimental value. He learnt to develop his own films and bought an enlarger. However the experiences in his mother's salon also influenced his thoughts about how photography could be used to create a lasting image, to convey a feeling, to tell a story.

He was acquiring an unusual combination of technical and artistic skills and took pleasure from this learning. From the positive responses he received from family and friends, he gradually came to realise that this was where his future career lay.

Many thoughts ran through his mind over a long period of time. Yes, he thought, I'm good at this but I really need top-level skills if I'm going to make a living from it. And, looking further ahead, Beuthen isn't the place to do it. Although it's nice enough, it's just a provincial industrial town. There's really no future for me here.

But where to go? The answer was obvious: Berlin. He'd been there once, with friends on a brief summer vacation. The nation's capital city had numerous colleges that provided advanced technical education. Its large and expanding businesses could surely use competent photographers. And, if reports from friends who were already living there could be believed, it offered an exciting social life.

Leaving home was not too hard; after all, he'd done it before as a child and now he was an adult. He wouldn't be the first of the extended family to move to Berlin. Louis' oldest son Walter had his apprenticeship in the shoemaking business cut short when his father died and the young man had gone to Berlin to work in a shoe store. Walter's sister Irma had moved to the capital to enhance her career in fashion retail. Relocating to Berlin didn't involve leaving the country: the big city was just a few hours away by train.

And so the mature young adult Gerhard made the move, caught the train, enrolled in an art photography course, found employment, rented a flat in the Wilmersdorf suburb, made friends and flourished. This was the life he wished for. Berlin was his new home. Who would want to live anywhere else?

10

Hans Kerpen

Beuthen, 1929

Hans Kerpen was Austrian, from Sankt Pölten, a pleasant city in the east of the country, 80 kilometres from Vienna. Founded in Roman times, it achieved city status in the twelfth century. The city's fine baroque buildings, a spacious town square and its location on a river made it an attractive place to live. The town had been the home of generations of Kerpens. Their small house was located in a quiet suburban street, close to the synagogue.

For Hans, despite the attractive environment, he felt that something was still missing in his life. He was almost 30, but in the small Jewish community he had not yet found a woman to share a life with him. He was employed as a tailor, but saw no future in that line of work, not in St Pölten anyway. Perhaps he could do better elsewhere.

He decided to move. His first attempt was quite conventional: young men everywhere would frequently leave small towns to go to a large city. He lived for some time in Vienna, but that resulted in neither marriage prospects nor more satisfying employment. He decided to look further afield. Austria was like an island surrounded by a sea of several European countries. Czechoslovakia was close by, immediately to the north, but his unfamiliarity with the language was a challenge that he was not prepared to meet. Further north, just a few hours away by train, lay the German towns of Silesia.

He visited a few towns with substantial Jewish communities. He displayed initiative: he would contact local rabbis, buy local newspapers and look up the city *Adressbuch* to locate potential employers. He eventually struck gold in Beuthen. The town's directory listed a Hermann Badrian, whose advertisement described his business as catering to elegant men of distinction. Even better, at the same Dyngosstrasse address, Frieda Badrian was the proprietor of a store selling ladies' dresses. He contacted them and made an appointment to meet.

The middle-aged couple impressed him. Hermann was a member of the local Jewish community, active in promoting technical education in the town. He encouraged young people wishing to train as apprentices and journeymen. His own business was growing, and he offered Hans a job as a tailor. Frieda was also interested in having an assistant in her growing business, and invited him to learn the particular skills of becoming a *damenschneider*, a ladies' tailor.

He could start immediately.

The Badrians invited Hans to their home for dinner, which is where he met their daughter Erna, in her mid-twenties, still unmarried. She had not yet found the right man.

They started going out together, and within weeks, Hans proposed and Erna accepted.

They were married in the Beuthen synagogue in February 1930. Their son was born in November.

They named the baby Horst.

Frieda wrote to Gerhard in Berlin that they were delighted to have become grandparents and that he had become an uncle.

11

Seize the moment!

Berlin, early 1930s

For all his skills, the Gerhard who left Beuthen was not a scholar of sociology, business or economics, and he may not have been aware then that his move occurred at a perfect time for a young man with his particular interests. Berlin had been developing for half a century as the centre of *Konfection*, mass-produced quality clothing. Seamstresses – 150,000 of them working from home, sweated labour, to be truthful – made clothing that could be afforded by the growing middle class. Fashion magazines – *Die Neue Linie, Die Dame, Der Silberspiegel, Elegante Welt* – reported on the latest trends.

The newest styles were not initiated by German fashion design-ers. Everyone knew that Paris was the world fashion centre. The big businessmen would send the heads of their fashion departments to France in an attempt to discover the next big thing. Paris excelled at *haute couture*, but Parisian originals were expensive. The Germans were superb at *Konfection* and grew wealthy by selling thousands of copies at affordable prices.

Newspapers, long accustomed to publishing advertisements us-ing only text, were beginning to recognise the American advertising maxim that one picture was worth a thousand words. Department stores – also a new idea – had substantial budgets for placing large illustrated ads in daily papers. It was a conjunction of trends and events that were made for the growth of advertising photography.

If he wasn't aware of all this when he left Beuthen, Gerhard certainly became aware of the fit between his capabilities and the Berlin business world soon after his arrival. He read the daily papers, studied the city's commercial *Adressbuch* and visited camera stores and commercial photographers. Fairly soon, he was employed by a firm that specialised in fashion photography, whose business was expanding rapidly. The major Hermann Tietz department store chain was about to launch its latest summer line, and Gerhard was sent by his boss to the palatial five-storey building, occupying an entire block on the Alexanderplatz, to photograph the models. He especially enjoyed this type of work assignment. Large department stores, widespread advertising – and photography – were all part of the economic success story.

Now in his mid-twenties, Gerhard had developed a high level of technical skill. He'd kept the first camera that he'd been given as a boy, but now it was just a much-loved souvenir, which he treasured in much the same way that a keen schoolboy footballer might keep the first trophy he'd received when his school team won the final. Of course, he didn't use the Rietzschel anymore, but it had taught him the basics about aperture and focal length and shutter speed. After he'd found work in Berlin, he spent some of his spare cash on yet another new quality camera. His latest acquisition was a 35 mm Leica, a masterpiece of miniaturisation which he could hold in one hand. Although he himself had no particular skills in engineering, he appreciated the complexity and precision of this beautiful piece of German industrial design.

He knew that he was competent and he took pride in his skills, although he kept his thoughts about that to himself. Gerhard was content to let others look at his work and make their own evaluation of it. His confident self-assurance, however, was not accompanied by complacency. He was open to learning new techniques that would take his technical ability to a new level. A good photographer needed more than an ability to master the intricacies of shutter speed and focal length: artistic flair was required as well.

A friend of his mentioned that the University of the Arts was offering a new course in Advanced Photography. It was part-time, just a few hours per week, and his employer encouraged him to participate. His working hours were flexible, anyway. Gerhard compiled a folio of work to accompany his application, and his boss provided a supportive reference. He was accepted into the course.

Gerhard found the course deeply satisfying. The lecturers were experienced professionals, knowledgeable about the latest equipment and how to use it. One of them introduced the class to the innovative Leica II, the very latest model of the range. It had interchangeable lenses that could be screwed into the body of the camera. Another presenter ran a session on the use of fast film in low light, and recommended cutting down on the use of flashbulbs, which were expensive, took time to replace each time a photo was taken, and were, in his opinion, impolite and intrusive. A third man specialised in fashion photography, demonstrating with samples of his own work how clever use of backgrounds and carefully placed furnishings could enhance the visual appeal of a model wearing a new designer dress.

Perhaps the most influential teacher was a young instructor, Herr Steiner, a cosmopolitan man who had studied and worked in London and Paris. He brought to life the idea that new technology brought new opportunities, fresh approaches. "We've all grown up with the idea that photography is just a modern version of portrait or landscape painting," Herr Steiner declared. "So for half a century, we've been mounting our large press model cameras on fixed tripod stands and carefully assembling a group of people into precise poses for their perfect golden wedding anniversary family portrait. Well, of course, there's a place for that sort of thing, I'm not against it, but you shouldn't let that kind of thinking restrict you. With this new Leica, you can go out into the street and take a picture without most people noticing. You can capture in an instant something that you might have missed seeing a moment earlier or a moment later. Learn to be alert! Seize the moment!"

12

An informal job offer

A few weeks later

"So, Gerhard, tell me, what brought you to Berlin?" his friend Marius enquired. They were enjoying a cup of good quality *Bohnenkaffee* and a slice of excellent *Apfelstrudel* in a coffee shop close to the campus where both were enrolled in the photography course. Marius Meijboom, a few years older than Gerhard, was from Amsterdam. He'd learnt German as a second language at school, and a year in Berlin had helped him polish his German as well as his photographic expertise.

"Not too hard to explain," Gerhard replied. "You know I was born in Beuthen and spent a few years in the Netherlands as a child during the war. I went back home afterwards and completed my education in the local *gymnasium*. Beuthen's not a bad town, but it's rather dull. I have a cousin, Irma, who used to live in Beuthen. We're not close, although she was good friends with my sister. My cousin worked as a junior salesgirl in a women's clothing store. We were talking one day at a family event and she told me she'd had enough of Beuthen. It was boring and she didn't want to spend years of her life in a job with no prospects. She was going to Berlin. That sounded to me like a very good idea."

"Did you go together?"

"No, I followed a few years later, but she had the right idea. Already in my teenage years I was taking pictures of women wearing dresses that my mother designed and I'd been told that the pictures were great. I thought I could turn my hobby into a career. But I wanted something more challenging than just taking photos of babies and weddings. So I came to Berlin and found work doing fashion photography for newspaper advertising."

Marius nodded. "That's what I'm going to do in Amsterdam. I've been working for other people for a few years, but as soon as I get back, I'm going to open my own business specialising in that. Of course, I won't knock back taking baby pictures, but that's just bread-and-butter stuff. You can come and work for me. How's your Dutch?"

"Pretty basic. I learnt a bit as a kid in Bussum but I haven't had much opportunity to use it since. Thanks for the job offer, but I don't think so. I'm German, and Berlin is really home for me now. I can't see myself wanting to move."

Gerhard had a small but comfortable rented apartment, a growing collection of quality equipment, links to some of the top fashion houses, and a circle of friends, including a few attractive young women. Why would anyone want to work in Amsterdam?

13

A sharp change in the political atmosphere

"Das war ein Vorspiel nur, dort wo man Bücher verbrennt, verbrennt man
am Ende auch Menschen."
(This was but a prelude; where they burn books,
they ultimately burn people.)

—Heinrich Heine (1820)

Berlin, the early years of the Nazi regime

Gerhard's attitude to living in Berlin changed dramatically, in ways that came as a great shock to him. He had been brought up in a home that was both devotedly Jewish and proudly German. He knew his history, that the Beuthen where he was born had been a German town for almost 500 years. A Jewish community had been settled in the surrounding region for two centuries. Their life choices were at first constrained. His grandfather would have had to seek the permission of the *Gutsherr* in charge of the estate in order to move to another village. In his younger years, Grandpa Joseph would have been limited in his choice of work, even having to seek the approval of the *Gutsherr* to marry.

In the century before Gerhard's birth, all that began to change. Germany became a modern, enlightened nation. Hermann needed no permission to move from Ornontowitz to Beuthen, to marry, to set up a business in whatever field he chose, to live anywhere in the town, to vote in elections. German was the community's mother tongue. The family knew that some people disliked Jews, but that could happen anywhere and it was much worse elsewhere than in Germany.

And here he was living in Berlin, a city of culture, of refinement – such a contrast to his provincial birthplace. The huge city, almost four million people, was one of the largest in the world. A sophisticated transport system moved everyone around: the underground U-Bahn, the S-Bahn railway, the electric tramway. Gerhard had marvelled at what the Jewish community had achieved: schools, a hospital, old-age homes, numerous synagogues. The main synagogue – which admittedly he hardly ever attended – resembled a cathedral. Many of his clients, businessmen in the fashion industry, were Jewish. Typical of the community's attitude towards the needy, and with the full support of the city council, an impressive orphanage had been built a generation earlier in the northern suburb of Pankow to house Jewish refugee children who had lost their parents in the Russian pogroms. Berlin was a civilised city.

But the glow of all these early impressions began to fade. Adolf Hitler and his Nazi party had gained power in 1933 and brought the ill-fated Weimar Republic and all semblance of democratic rule to an end. Hitler promised a glorious future for the new German Reich. Gerhard had read enough history to know that tyrants often used scapegoats to justify their political actions. Hitler blamed the Jews for all the ills of German society, and that problem would have to be solved by removing them. Slowly, slowly, one step at a time, Jews were targeted and oppressed. Shop windows were smashed. Thugs were bashing Jews in the street with impunity. Posters were mounted in public, proclaiming "Jews not wanted here". New laws deprived Jews of the right to work as public officials. Jewish professors, orchestra conductors and judges were dismissed from their posts. Newspapers, now entirely under Nazi control, were publishing vicious antisemitic propaganda, day in, day out. A friend told Gerhard that he had walked past the campus of the Friedrich Wilhelm University and had seen a hundred students gathered around a huge bonfire in the courtyard in front of the Law Faculty, gleefully throwing thousands of books from the university library into the flames.

As if all this was not bad enough, he was troubled even more by the mass rallies of cheering supporters, enthusiastically shouting *Heil Hitler!* with their arms raised skyward and straight. And, worst of all, he viewed with dismay the thousands of sullen, silent bystanders who stood there and did nothing. Gerhard didn't really blame them: anyone protesting would have been dealt with sharply by one of the thugs. But he observed all this and saw something desperately sick that was infecting the body of his country.

He was not the first in his family to see it. In 1933, the very first year of the Nazis' rise to power, Gerhard received a letter from his cousin Rudi in Beuthen. Rudi had witnessed the uncontrolled brutes in the streets of his home town and was wondering about the direction that all this hatred was taking. Rudi wasn't going to stay to find out: he was leaving by boat for Palestine. He was the first of the wider Badrian family to flee the country; he would not be the last.

What Rudi had foreseen in 1933 took Gerhard almost four more years to see. He realised that he'd been beguiled by the attractions of life and work in Berlin.

He thought about various possibilities, corresponded with his parents, visited various embassies in Berlin, investigated travel possibilities before deciding what to do. He made what would turn out to be a final visit to his home town to discuss his plans with his parents and sister.

He found that he didn't have to argue too forcefully to convince his parents that it was time to go. Hermann's attitude had changed quite markedly. "You know," he admitted to his son, "I have to say I was quite wrong. In the early days of Hitler, I was of course appalled by the man and his politics, but I thought that his government couldn't possibly last. I used to be proud of our country. We had been through so many bad times. The terrible war. The uncertainty of the Weimar Republic. The hyperinflation when money became worthless. We lived through all of that. I thought that this horrible man was just another passing phase that we had to live through. We're a decent country, sensible, educated … or so I thought. The German people will surely come to their senses and throw this nasty little dictator out. Well, I was wrong, terribly wrong. There is no hope for us here anymore. Absolutely none. We have to get out. As soon as we can. What should we do, my son? Where should we go?"

Gerhard had already outlined in his letters from Berlin what he proposed. Now he laid out his plans as something definite, to be initiated immediately, with no more discussion. "I'm going to Brazil. I already have a visa. I have a booking on a ship, which I still need to confirm and pay for, leaving Hamburg for Rio de Janeiro. I have some money that I've been saving for a long time, enough to last me for a few weeks in Rio. I'll rent a room, try to get a job and find you a place to live. If they want to, Erna and Horst can come with you. I suggest that you don't book a voyage until you hear from me, but in the meantime, get ready. Obtain visas, enquire about available ships. Go through your belongings. Sell whatever you can to raise money. Get ready to leave at short notice."

Frieda didn't participate in this conversation, but she listened attentively and nodded occasionally to indicate her agreement. She was proud of her practical son. Like Hermann, she had witnessed the ever-growing oppression and brutality, one more anti-Jewish law after another. Gerhard turned to his mother and asked her what she thought. "I agree with you," she responded without hesitation. "There is no future for us here, none at all. It's time to pack up and leave."

Gerhard caught the next available train back to Berlin, paid for his ship ticket, packed up his belongings, travelled by train to Hamburg and boarded the boat bound for Rio. The voyage of 7000 nautical miles south-west across the Atlantic took three weeks. Only once before, as a small child, had he ever left his German homeland, and that took him only as far as the neighbouring Netherlands. That was a temporary absence. This time, he mused as the boat sailed out of the port, he did not expect to see Germany ever again.

14

Erna, the single mother

Beuthen, 1935–37

Erna's world was falling to pieces around her. She had fallen pregnant on her brief honeymoon and she had brought a child into the world before she and Hans were really ready for it. Caring for baby Horst took up much of her time, and housework most of the remainder.

Quite early in her marriage, she reflected that she had few real interests, no sense of purpose, and very little to talk about with her husband. Her feelings of dissatisfaction led her to be envious of her parents, who clearly loved each other, cared for each other, and spent much time in the evenings in shared conversation. *Is there something wrong with me?* she wondered. *Am I failing as a wife?* She had no one to talk to, and decided against confiding in her parents, frightened that they would disapprove of her, blame her for having such thoughts, even turn against her. She had no income of her own and was completely dependent on what Hans earned.

Hans was equally unhappy and deeply conflicted. He, too, felt little joy from the marriage and would have left, but felt responsible for providing for his wife and son. It didn't help the situation that Erna's parents were not simply his in-laws, but his employers as well. For a young Jewish man, finding another job in Nazi Germany was virtually impossible.

They were just two lonely people brought together by chance. Marriage, they thought, might be a cure for their loneliness. They'd married too quickly without really knowing each other properly. They did what they needed to do to care for their infant son, but this was no remedy for an unhappy marriage.

The unhappiness simmered below the surface for a long time, but for both of them it was eventually tolerable no longer. One evening, after Horst had been put to bed, a minor argument over a trivial matter suddenly erupted into an emotional explosion. "I've had enough of this," said Hans, "I'm going to leave you." Erna broke down, in tears, but she was in no mind to disagree. She had seen this coming for years.

Over the following week, they worked out the details of what would happen next. The next morning Erna told her parents. Frieda, as ever the loving mother, comforted her distraught daughter and talked Hermann into agreeing that she and Horst should come to live with them in their apartment. Hermann, for his part, felt a confused mixture of emotions. He was saddened for his daughter. He felt irritated that after years of sharing a quiet life in his apartment with his wife, he now had two extra mouths to feed and care for. He was disappointed with Hans. He remembered the pride he had felt when, as father of the bride, he was there when his only daughter married a decent young man. He'd given Hans a job and encouraged him to develop new skills. Hermann, now in his early sixties, had thought that one day, Hans might take over the family business. But there was anger, too, and although he didn't state it explicitly, Hermann blamed Hans for not being a good enough husband to his daughter. The anger was kept hidden, but emerged a few days later when he told Hans that he was no longer welcome as an employee in the business.

Hans moved out, temporarily found accommodation in a cheap rooming house, and wrote to his parents in St Pölten to tell them he wanted to come home to Austria. Before he left Beuthen, he signed the necessary papers to initiate divorce proceedings.

15

Confiscation

Beuthen, 1937

A prominent advertisement was published in the daily *Beuthen Zeitung*, announcing that over the following month, all Jewish businesses were to be taken over and their administration would henceforth be in the hands of Aryan owners. An article alongside the notice explained that Jews, as everyone knew, were not loyal supporters of the German Reich, and that for far too long they had exerted excessive control over the German economy. The Reich was rectifying this situation by taking control of Jewish businesses and putting them in the hands of loyal Germans. The transition would be carried out in accordance with the law and owners would receive payment for their business. Business owners affected would still be permitted to work in their chosen occupations, but not as proprietors.

What the advertisement and the news item didn't say was that the compensation price would be determined by the Party and would be only a fraction of the true worth of the business. Nor did it say – it didn't need to, as this was already well known – that Jews were not permitted to be employed in Aryan businesses.

As promised, within a month, Hermann and Frieda were each sent documents of sale by the local Taxation Office, the innocuous name for the organisation responsible for administering the confiscation process. They were subsequently visited by Herr Gustav

Zweigelt, representing the Beuthen branch. A fervent member of the Nationalsozialistiche Deutsche Arbeiterpartei, he wore the prominent circular red, white and black NSDAP badge with the large swastika in the centre on the lapel of his jacket. He introduced himself, told them that he was a qualified accountant and explained politely that he was there to inspect the business premises, collect the account books and examine the stock.

"I was told that we would be receiving a payment for our businesses," Hermann asserted firmly, but equally politely.

"Quite correct," was Zweigelt's reply, "but first we have to make a complete inventory of all your stock and equipment, and look at your account books to assess the true worth of your businesses."

"How long will that take?"

"Difficult to say, but be assured, it will all be done as carefully and as quickly as possible. In the meantime, you are of course free to work as a tailor, or you [turning to Frieda] as a dress designer, as soon as you wish." Zweigelt pretended to be concerned about their welfare, not because he cared at all, but because it allowed him to deal with more cases efficiently in a day. Someone else in the Taxation Office would select the new owners and determine the (fake) sale price that this couple would receive. The difference between the real price and the fake price would be going straight into the coffers of the Party. It was, from the Reich's point of view, a very effective business model. It had a dual function: to help Jews get the message that they had no economic rights in Germany, and they would be better off by leaving.

Hermann and Frieda were fully aware that they were being swindled, and knew equally well that there was nothing they could do about it. They knew that their income was about to be sharply reduced. They gave up the lease on the comfortable apartment where they had lived for most of their married life, and moved to a smaller one in Tarnowitzerstrasse. They would try to make a living by working at home.

Hermann informed the Beuthen *Adressbuch* of his change of

address. In it he could describe himself only as a "tailor" instead of a "proprietor", the way in which he had been listed in previous editions. The *Adressbuch* in its residential section listed only heads of households, so Frieda was not mentioned there. No longer the proprietor of a ladies' fashion salon, she was not entitled to be listed in the commercial section. She placed a small ad in the local Jewish community newspaper, offering her services as a dressmaker.

All of this was in a sense temporary, in that most of them were already planning to emigrate. Deciding to leave was not difficult. The challenge was to find a desirable destination in a country that would allow them in. Gerhard was already in Brazil. He'd been there for a few months. Hermann and Frieda were awaiting word from Gerhard about whether Brazil was a viable destination. If so, they would emigrate, and perhaps Erna and Horst would travel with them.

Erna was impoverished, miserable, despondent, unsure of what she should do, but driven by one central thought. She had a young boy to care for, and she would do whatever she could to keep him safe.

16

Rio to Bussum, 1937

Gerhard knew that making a new home for himself and his family in Brazil would be challenging. He was aware that emigration for himself was much simpler than for the others in the family. He was unmarried, had no dependents, no real estate assets or business to be sold. The situation for his parents, sister and nephew was more complicated. He cared about his family circle, and his planning took their needs into account.

His choice of Rio was not arbitrary. A major attraction was that it was far away from the turmoil of Europe. But so were other countries. An equally important factor was the ease of obtaining a visa. He might have preferred the United States or Australia, but gaining entry to these countries was becoming increasingly difficult. Many countries were starting to close their doors to refugees. Several South American countries in contrast had virtually open doors. And living costs there were much lower: his savings in German Reichsmarks would last longer on that continent. Peru or Chile might have been equally suitable, but their ports were on the western side of the continent. Rio or Buenos Aires were closer. He'd seen photos of Rio in a Berlin library and it looked an attractive place. So he chose Rio. He'd previously obtained a German passport, took it to the Brazilian Embassy, paid a modest fee and obtained a visa the same day.

Rio, Gerhard soon discovered after his arrival in the middle of 1937, was a magnificent city. His first impressions were that he had made the right choice. He loved the high steep hills plunging dramatically into the sea, so different from the flatness of inland Berlin. Although it was the middle of winter in the southern hemisphere, the weather was mild, the sun was shining and the sky was blue. It certainly looked like a pleasant place to make a new home.

But pleasant only if one had money. Gerhard noticed that the rich lived in mansions, but most people were not wealthy and the living conditions of the poor were dreadful.

He wasn't there to be a tourist and quickly got on with what he had to do. He rented a small, bare room in a cheap rooming house close to the city. He'd brought his collection of cameras with him. He would naturally have liked to work as a photographer, but no one wanted to employ him. He would have taken other work, but there were many unemployed people in the city and he made no progress there. Social welfare support was virtually unknown. He visited the synagogue to see if the Jewish community could help him, but that led nowhere. He spoke no Portuguese, made no friends, found no employment opportunities. Weeks went by without success. His savings were running out. He realised that Rio was not going to be the answer. The idea of bringing his family here was unworkable.

He had arrived in Brazil with a spirit of optimism, but not with any feeling of certainty. In Berlin, he had already conceived a back-up plan. He deliberately hadn't told his parents about it. He wanted to keep their planning as simple as possible. They had enough to deal with; why burden them with unnecessary complications?

But now he was forced to adopt the alternative plan. He would go to the Netherlands. It failed entirely to meet the criterion of being far away from Germany, but it was a democratic nation, tolerant and peaceful, easily accessible, with a large and long-established Jewish community. He had contacted the local Dutch Consulate; the country was accepting refugees. Best of all, he had some knowledge of the country from his time there as a child and knew some people there. He even spoke – admittedly not very well – the language. He would go there first, and then ask his parents to follow.

Gerhard spent an evening carefully drafting and redrafting a long letter to his parents, explaining in detail what had happened in Rio and telling them about the new plan. Although personally dispirited about his failure in Brazil, he was careful not to over-emphasise his feelings. His objective was clear. It was to provide the best possible advice to his family circle about what was best for them, about what they should do to leave Germany quickly.

After the opening lines of greetings to the family and assuring them that he was perfectly well, he wrote *Ich kann meine Füße in diesem Land nicht finden*, I couldn't find my feet in this country. Without too much elaboration, he told them that he had not found a job, and without that it would be impossible for him to rent a house or apartment that could comfortably house the three of them, or the five of them if Erna and Horst were to come too.

He spelled out his alternative plan. He had already decided to leave Rio. He had obtained a Dutch visa from the local consulate. He had actually met the Consul who understood the situation precisely and was sympathetic and efficient. He had already booked a passage on a ship leaving Rio the following week, bound for Rotterdam. He expected to arrive there in October. He would contact them again as soon as he had found a place to stay, perhaps in Amsterdam, perhaps in Bussum. Once there, he would set about finding a job – he had some contacts – to earn some money. Then he would look for a place to rent for the family.

Although probably unnecessary, he spelled out that while he wished he could return to Beuthen to personally lead them out of Germany to their new home, that would be impossible. Once a Jew left Germany, he would never be allowed to return. In any case, it was clearly more practical for him to go the Netherlands first and find a suitable place for them and have it ready to welcome them when they arrived.

In the meantime, they should maintain their readiness to leave at short notice. They should ensure that they all had valid passports and obtain Dutch visas. He couldn't give them an exact date for them to emigrate, but estimated that it would be sometime in the early months of 1938.

He read and reread what he had written in order to check that it said exactly what he wanted it to say. The letter would probably take a month, maybe more, to reach Beuthen. He sealed it, addressed it, bought a stamp next morning at the local *correios* and posted it.

Gerhard bought a third-class ticket on the first available ship bound for Rotterdam. The trans-Atlantic voyage in the spring of 1938 on a slow and far from luxurious boat took almost a month. A cargo boat that also carried a few passengers, it stopped at several southern European ports to refuel, and load and unload cargo along the way.

On arrival in Rotterdam, he took the train to Amsterdam and spent a couple of days there, for a brief and warm reunion with his foster family. He had kept in touch with them ever since his boyhood. He knew that many years earlier, they had moved from Bussum to Amsterdam. Jaques and Rachel de Vries, now quite elderly, were overjoyed to see the teenage boy who had turned into such a mature and impressive well-built man.

While in Amsterdam, Gerhard telephoned his friend from Berlin days, Marius Meijboom. Initial calls were encouraging, and he arranged to go to Amsterdam to meet with him. Then he caught a local train to Bussum, the town he knew from his boyhood years. He had already decided in Rio to make Bussum his base as he planned for his parents' emigration. Accommodation was less expensive there than in the big city. He quickly found a place to live, in Tesselschadelaan, in a comfortable room in a house owned by David Goudsmit.

Gerhard's priorities were first to get himself settled and find a job. His second priority was to find a place for his parents to live. He scanned the local newspaper and contacted real estate agents, but nothing caught his eye as suitable. The cheap places were too small and unattractive; the pleasant houses were too expensive.

He eventually found a place by chance. When he had some free time, he liked to walk around the small town, reviving memories of streets he'd wandered along as a child, exploring unfamiliar areas, enjoying the parklands that lay on the edges of the small suburban area. One Sunday afternoon, he turned into Mecklenburglaan, just a few hundred metres from his temporary accommodation. He noticed a pleasant-looking two-storey twin maisonette. The left-hand of the pair was clearly occupied – some children were playing in the front garden – but No. 23a was vacant and bore a sign that it was available for rent. He noted the details and visited the agency. Yes, it was available. Yes, the rental was affordable. He signed a lease. He would write to tell Hermann and Frieda that they had a new home. He would move in with them temporarily until they were comfortable in their new surroundings.

17

Anschluss and its consequences

"It was the best of times, the worst of times ..."

– Charles Dickens, *A Tale of Two Cities* (1859)

1938–42

For Horst's father, Hans Kerpen, it was only the worst of times – four years of a lonely, miserable and frightened existence, ending in his death.

On 13 March 1938, Hermann brought in a copy of the *Völkischer Beobachter* to show Erna. The front-page headline, in huge bold font, proclaimed Anschluss! It announced that the *Führer* had the previous day annexed Austria and incorporated it into the German Reich. The paper praised Hitler's brilliance in bringing this about with the complete cooperation of the Austrian government and the united support of the Austrian people. The Austrians were proud Germans and the new Greater German Reich would allow the German nation to achieve its mission of becoming the leading nation of Europe.

Erna was concerned about Hans. She wondered what effect this would have on the life of her ex-husband. She didn't love him, of course, but she didn't hate him either. Although their marriage had failed, she certainly didn't wish him any harm. When, a few weeks earlier, he had left Beuthen to return to his parents' home in St Pölten, she had wished him well and hoped that he would find a better life in the land of his birth. At the time, Austria was still a free and independent nation.

And now, this. Hans had left Beuthen to get away from Nazis, and now the Nazis had followed him there.

After they had parted in Beuthen, she never heard from him again. No news about what had happened to him ever reached her or anyone else in her family.

Later that year, the Nazi leadership in Berlin established the Central Office for Jewish Emigration in Vienna, headed by Adolf Eichmann. She knew nothing about it; the name of the organisation and the identity of its leader would have meant nothing to her.

She never knew that the Kerpen family were forced out of their home in St Pölten and required to relocate to Vienna. Or that the Nazis were using the same tactics on the Jewish community in Austria as they were using in Germany, to motivate them to leave the country, leading to Hans being arrested in 1939 for failing to emigrate. He was then taken to the Dachau concentration camp for a few weeks, abused, beaten and starved, and released only after he agreed to leave Germany.

Or that he had fled to France in 1940, prior to the Wehrmacht invading the country, and that the French government, overwhelmed with refugees, had placed him in a refugee camp, where he remained for two years.

Or that, when the Nazis were ready to implement its *Endlösung*, the Final Solution to the Jewish Question, he was taken in 1942 to Drancy in Paris, and from there deported to Auschwitz. After that not only Erna but also nobody else ever heard from him again.

18

Farewell party

Beuthen, March 1938

Hermann and Frieda finalised their plans to leave. They had been talking about it for a year. They were not like the apocryphal frog in the pot of warm water that doesn't notice what's happening as the temperature gradually rises and dies when the water eventually boils. No, they noticed everything. The beatings in the streets. The smashing of Jewish shop windows. The relentless reduction of their personal freedoms.

Finally, they received the signal for action from their son that they had been waiting for. Gerhard now had a job in Amsterdam. He'd rented a house for them in Bussum. They were to come as soon as they could.

Brazil might have been preferable, Hermann mused, as it was a continent away from Germany. The Netherlands was, unfortunately, a close neighbour. Mind you, Austria was equally close, and Hitler had just acquired it peacefully; perhaps, Hermann thought, this would satisfy his lust for expansion. Hermann and Frieda had decided long ago to trust their son's judgement. "It will all work out for the best," said Hermann, and Frieda concurred. Their attitude was bolstered by the knowledge that they had sent their child there during the Great War. The peaceful, neutral Dutch had avoided being caught up in the German onslaught against France and Belgium. Perhaps that would happen again.

Hermann informed the congregation that he and Frieda would soon be leaving Beuthen. The synagogue was already planning its annual celebration of the festival of Purim, although celebrating an event that had occurred more than two thousand years earlier when the Jews of Persia were saved from the wicked plans of the evil Haman seemed strangely inappropriate at the present time.

Rabbi Dr Ludwig Golinski, Beuthen's senior rabbi, was deeply appreciative of Hermann's contributions to the life of the community, and immediately proposed that the annual Purim party, scheduled for the Saturday night two days after Purim, be expanded into a farewell event for the couple.

The well-attended evening event was hosted by the Jewish Community Association of Beuthen, of which Hermann had served in earlier years as chairman. The rabbi thanked Hermann for his 42 years of service, in particular his devoted work over several years as chairman of the association. Others spoke about his efforts in promoting craft work and technical education in the town. There was no need to explain why the couple were leaving Beuthen: everyone present understood the situation. Many in the crowd had been making their own plans.

Hermann and Frieda's departure the following month spared them the agony of witnessing the most woeful sight in the community's history. Almost seven months after they fled Germany, the Reich Minister for Propaganda, Joseph Goebbels, visited Beuthen and delivered a fiery tirade calling upon all good Germans to rise up and wreak vengeance against the Jews.

Two days later, on the infamous November night that would later be known in history as *Kristallnacht*, his SS and SA Stormtroopers obeyed his command. They set explosive and incendiary charges in place inside the synagogue. The community was forced to stand and watch as the building's tall Moorish towers collapsed, the stained-glass windows were blown out and the walls fell inwards while clouds of dust sprayed into the air. The community stood there, some in stony silence, others weeping, while a few of the elderly fainted from shock. All that remained of the elegant 1869 building was a blazing mass of rubble.

19

Marius Meijboom

Amsterdam, 1938

Gerhard's reunion with Marius Meijboom had gone well, in fact had exceeded all his expectations. On his first visit to the commercial photographer's office in Amsterdam, Gerhard had looked around at the size of the office and the number of people working there, and quickly told Marius how impressed he was with what he had achieved in the few short years since they were together in Berlin.

"Nice of you to say so," Marius responded, "but I'm happy to say it's going to get even better. This office is already too small for our needs: in a few weeks we're moving to a bigger place on the Keizergracht."

The two men spent some time reminiscing about Berlin. Marius told Gerhard that he had wildly ambivalent feelings about his time there. He valued the educational experience; he was influenced by the ideas that sprang from the minds of people such as Walter Gropius, who sought to unite the creative arts in a new way. Modern trends in art and design were influencing the thinking of engineers and architects.

Sadly, the creative ideas of the modernists were being stifled by the extreme right-wing views of the regime. According to the Nazis, art, like every other aspect of society, had to be kept under strict control; artists had to be guided into producing works that would further the aims of the Reich. And, almost by definition, any work produced by a Jew was decadent.

Marius found the Nazi ideology repulsive, and he wasn't afraid to say so, publicly, while he was a student there. He would not have been surprised if some informant had taken note of his views and passed them on to the authorities. Berlin was rapidly becoming that sort of place.

Amongst like-minded friends, he laughed at the stupidity of it all, although he knew that it wasn't funny at all. "You know," he told Gerhard, "they have no idea how moronic they are. They scream and shout about the awfulness of modern art and design, and then Hitler makes a speech about the wonders of the new autobahns he's building. The bridges are all based on Bauhaus principles! What an idiot!" Marius naturally saw through all this. Hitler actually had no objection to modern engineering design: it was the liberal democratic views of the Bauhaus proponents that he couldn't stomach.

Nazi views about art deserved derision, but what Gerhard had seen in the streets of Berlin, the growth of a violent tyranny continually abusing the human rights of minority groups and political opponents, frightened him. Marius had chosen to spend time in Berlin to learn from its culture. He returned home disgusted by it.

The reminiscences over recent times quickly gave way to serious discussion about employment. Gerhard's previous contacts with Marius by letter and telephone had all been positive. The face-to-face reunion simply confirmed what had previously been discussed. Gerhard had brought along a folio of some of his best Berlin work, and Marius politely looked through it, although his mind had been made up long before.

"As I mentioned," said Marius as he flipped through the folio while making appreciative comments, "we're planning on moving soon because I'm taking on several new staff. Advertising photography is booming, and I certainly have room for a capable fashion photographer. So, I'd like you to work for me. When can you start?"

Gerhard was overjoyed. He'd failed to find his place in Rio, but he'd certainly landed on his feet in Amsterdam.

Gerhard worked in the studio for three years. Marius regarded Gerhard as an amiable and competent colleague, who combined artistic talent with a sound head for business.

Later, others in Amsterdam recognised Gerhard's talents. He was invited to teach a course on photography as a part-time lecturer at the Amsterdam College of the Arts.

He was earning a decent salary, enough to help his parents to settle. He gave up his rented room in Bussum, moved in briefly with his parents, and then found a more convenient and comfortable little apartment in Amsterdam. He took out a substantial life insurance policy with a hefty premium, and he bought a car. Life in the Netherlands was treating him well.

After three years, Marius was about to offer him a partnership in the business.

And then everything changed.

20

From Beuthen to Berlin

Beuthen, 1938

Erna sat in her small rented room with Horst perched on the thread-bare rug on the floor, quietly playing with some toys. She was worried, uncertain about her next moves. She was reading a letter from her parents. It comforted her a little. Hermann and Frieda were now settled in Bussum. Gerhard had arrived in the Netherlands from Rio and had prepared the ground for them. He had a job in Amsterdam. He'd found a comfortable rented house for their parents. Hermann had written a few lines about the situation, all good news. The Dutch would take in several thousand more German refugees. Visas were being granted. A new camp was being built in the countryside to house the new arrivals. Parents and children would be housed together.

Her mother added a few lines. "Dear daughter," she had written, "we miss you and our grandson. Please come here just as soon as you can. Give Horst a kiss from us. All our love, *Mutti*".

Erna was perplexed. She certainly didn't want to stay in Germany, but equally she didn't like the idea of living in a refugee camp with Horst. Her parents had no income and she couldn't impose on them. Gerhard was already helping them with the Bussum rental and she wasn't prepared to ask her brother to support her as well. If she left for the Netherlands, she wanted a job, to earn her own money, to look after her boy. She wanted a place to call home, not a refugee camp.

She wrestled with these conflicting thoughts, not knowing how to resolve them, but one thing was certain. She couldn't stay in Beuthen. There was nothing for her and Horst here – she had no job, no income, precious little in the way of savings and no family to support her anymore. Nothing.

Since the failure of Gerhard's Brazilian endeavour, she knew that the Netherlands would have to be her eventual destination. But not just yet. Friends had told her that in the meantime Berlin, with its larger Jewish community, might provide some better opportunities. Perhaps she could obtain work and shelter as a live-in maid for one of the better-off families there. While there, she might earn enough to get by and buy some time while her folks in the Netherlands searched for places where she could live and work.

She was despondent, depressed, yet at the same time determined. A powerful source of motivation was the desire to protect her son, whom she loved deeply. She felt anguish when she saw the unhappiness in Horst's eyes, the dull tone in his voice. Life had been so unfair to her, but at least as an adult she had the capacity to deal with the recent calamities in her life. A failed marriage. Unemployment. Nazi oppression. Her brother had gone to Brazil; no good news from him; then he said he was going to the Netherlands. Her parents had left Beuthen to go there. She was alone and she was suffering. But why did innocent children have to be tormented as well?

She picked up her son from the floor and hugged him. "I've just had a letter from *Oma* and *Opa*," she told him. "They send you their love and kisses." Horst shrugged his shoulders, gave her a brief smile and went back to playing with his toys. The smile didn't last very long.

But she didn't have the mental energy to think about her unhappiness too much. She was too busy packing up her few belongings and those of her son. It was time to move to Berlin.

21

Erna in Berlin

Berlin: Teltow and Pankow, 1938–39

Rabbi Golinski had given her the names and addresses of community people in Berlin who might be able to offer some support.

So, here she was in the capital, the last adult in her immediate family still in Germany. Erna had no education beyond middle school. The added middle name of Sara on her ID card excluded her from employment in any business firm. (The government required Jews to identify themselves in ways that would permanently separate them from the rest of the German population; by 1 January 1939, Jewish men and women had to add "Israel and "Sara", respectively, to their given names.) She eked out a living as a housekeeper, maid or cook – whatever was required – working for the few Jewish families who still had enough money to employ her. Some required her to live-in, others not. But children were not welcome. Eventually she found live-in work in Teltow, on the southern outskirts of the city, but the family could not provide accommodation for Horst.

She had to work. No close relatives or friends were around anymore who could care for Horst. Her cousin and childhood playmate Irma used to live in Berlin, but had moved to Karlsruhe and married a man who had relatives in Australia. The couple emigrated there as soon as they could.

Erna took the only available option. With tears in her eyes, she accompanied Horst to the *Jüdisches Waisenhaus*, the Jewish orphanage in the northern Berlin suburb of Pankow, and gave up her son into its care. It comforted her somewhat that it was a pleasant building and that Nurse Hofstein, the senior nurse who welcomed them, was competent and caring.

Pankow and Teltow were on opposite sides of the city, more than an hour's train trip between them on the S-Bahn. Calling in regularly for a short visit at the end of a day's work was out of the question. She had explained all that to Horst beforehand, but as she said goodbye to him after he had been admitted, she hugged and kissed her little boy and promised that she would visit him as often as she could. Horst, now eight years old, reacted with dull acceptance. So many bad things had happened over the past few years, things he did not understand, things he had no ability to change. He'd learnt long ago that crying, screaming and being angry with his mother were all pointless and didn't make him any happier. Easier to bottle it up inside and say nothing.

After kissing her son goodbye, Erna wandered through the corridors of the large building and out into the Berliner Strasse towards the train station to begin the long ride back to Teltow. She suddenly burst into tears. Never in her life could she have imagined that the day would come when she would be leaving her beloved son to be cared for in an orphanage.

22

Kindertransport

Berlin, 1939

Devorah Hofstein, the head nurse, had worked at the orphanage for over 25 years, ever since the imposing new building had been constructed. A fire had destroyed the original edifice. She knew the history of the earlier orphanage, built to meet a sudden growth in demand in the previous century to care for Jewish children whose parents had been murdered in the pogroms of tsarist Russia. She also remembered the pride she felt when, as a freshly-trained young nurse, wealthy benefactors in the community had raised the funds needed to replace the original. She also knew that the city government back then had been fully supportive of this important charitable institution. How times had changed! Now some of the children in her care were themselves about to become refugees.

After dinner one evening, she spoke to Horst in the dining room and invited him into her office, as she had something to tell him. He was a good-looking little boy, well-behaved, but sad for much of the time, which was not unusual for children in an orphanage. She had done her best to keep up the children's spirits. Jewish children were no longer allowed to attend public schools, so she had arranged for volunteers to come in to run classes, read stories, play music. There was no shortage of unemployed members of the community with time on their hands.

"Horst, I have some good news for you." Nurse Hofstein believed in being truthful to children, but her years of experience told her that there was no need to overload their minds with unnecessary detail, or to tell them in advance about potential problems that neither of them could solve. "Before you go to sleep tonight, I would like you to pack up all your belongings carefully and put them in your suitcase, because early tomorrow morning, after breakfast you will be going on a big trip by train."

This sounded exciting. He hadn't been on a long train ride ever since he and his mother had left their home in Beuthen to come to Berlin. "Why? Where am I going?"

"Well, Berlin isn't a nice place to live anymore, and you're going to *Nederland*. You know, you've seen maps and pictures of it. It's right next door to Germany. It's got windmills and canals and it's a quiet and peaceful place."

"Are any other children from the orphanage coming with me? Are you coming too?"

"Not from the orphanage, no. But there will be a few other children from Berlin travelling on the train with you. You'll meet them after breakfast tomorrow morning. And yes, I will come with you on the train until we reach the border. Then I have to come back here to work."

Nurse Hofstein felt no need to go into details about how the orphanage had been cooperating with other groups in the community to organise a *Kindertransport*. She would hand over responsibility for the care of the refugee children to a nurse appointed by the Dutch government's Ministry of Internal Affairs. Many Berlin parents, unable to leave Germany themselves but desperate to ensure the survival of their children, had agreed to send them to safety in a peaceful neighbouring country. As soon as the plan was finalised, Nurse Hofstein had contacted Erna to suggest that Horst join the group. All these details constituted information that Horst did not need to know.

"Is my Mummy coming with me on the train?" He never mentioned his father anymore. Hans had disappeared from his life after the separation. He did not know, could not possibly know, that right now, his father was a prisoner in the Dachau concentration camp.

She'd expected this question. "No, she won't. She's not allowed on this train trip, it's just for children. But she knows about it, and she told me that she's happy for you to go. She is planning to come after you. As soon as she is allowed to go and finds a place to live, you will see her again there."

"When will that be?"

"I really don't know. It might take a while. But I know from her visits here that she loves you and wants to see you again just as soon as she can. You've been a very good boy all the time you've been here, and I know that you miss your mother a lot. Just try to be as good as you can on the train."

Nurse Hofstein knew that any of a number of things could go wrong, even disastrously wrong … She saw absolutely no point in mentioning any of the possibilities.

23

The quarantine station

Berlin to Rotterdam, February 1939

After an early breakfast on his last day in Berlin, Horst was introduced to the other eleven *Kindertransport* children: six girls and another five boys. The group included three pairs of siblings. They'd come from various Berlin suburbs, leaving their parents behind. None of these eleven knew it, none of them could possibly have known it at the time, but they were unlikely to ever see their parents again.

Nurse Hofstein took charge of the twelve of them as they boarded the small bus that took them and their pitifully small collection of belongings to the local S-Bahn station, where they caught a train to the central railway station. In her large handbag, she carried the collection of documents authorising each child's right to leave Germany. There were no passports in the bag: children of that age were listed on a parent's passport, and all of the parents were still in Berlin. She'd been informed that there would be no problem at the Dutch border. The authorities there had been advised beforehand of the arrival of the *Kindertransport* group. The Dutch already had experience in admitting German Jewish refugees. Thank God, Nurse Hofstein thought, that there were still civilised people in the world.

The orphanage had organised packed lunches for all the *Kindertransport* children; nothing elaborate, food was scarce, just brown bread rolls and cheese and a piece of plain cake. Water would be available on the train. The journey would take most of the day.

At the border station, Fräulein Hofstein was met by Mirjam van de Berg, a social worker employed by the Dutch Ministry of Internal Affairs. Nurse Hofstein handed her the folio of documents. She waved to the children as the train departed, and spent the afternoon and night in a cheap local hostel where the night manager wasn't interested in seeing any ID. She would return by train to Berlin next morning.

Late in the afternoon, around sunset on this late winter's day, the train arrived at Amsterdam Centraal. By now, the children were tired and hungry, but this wasn't the end of their travels for the day. A change of trains took them to Rotterdam Centraal, and then a local suburban train looped around the suburbs to take them to their destination, the Rotterdam Port.

They arrived at a formidable dark building on Quarantainestraat, on the edge of one of the port's canals. The building once housed a quarantine station, where sailors arriving from lands riddled with infectious diseases were kept until given a clean bill of health. To cope with the influx of refugees, the government had transformed the facility into a refugee absorption centre. The steady stream of refugees would soon become a torrent, as the Dutch government had decided that they would accept a further 8000 refugees, starting the following month.

The former quarantine station would be Horst's home for a few weeks, until other arrangements could be made.

Other arrangements, not permanent arrangements: nothing would be permanent in his life for many years to come.

24

Erna leaves Germany

Gouda, South Holland, April 1939

Erna was quite fixed in her mind that she would not join her parents in the Netherlands until Horst's safety and care were ensured. She therefore made no definite plans to emigrate until she knew that the *Kindertransport* children had arrived safely. Nurse Hofstein had contacted her at the earliest opportunity to tell her that she'd received word from the Dutch that everything had gone smoothly and that the children were now housed in a temporary refugee centre in Rotterdam, where they were being properly cared for.

Erna promptly began the process of preparing for her own departure. Money was tight, but she had been carefully saving from her meagre income to ensure that she had enough to pay the train fare and any exit taxes the Nazis charged. The Germans were keen to expel their Jews and limited their asset stripping to those wealthy Jews who could afford it. Their attitude to near penniless women who wanted to leave was, good riddance! They were not going to put obstacles in their path. The Dutch helped by issuing visas to thousands of German refugees. Erna's major concern was to find a job and a place to live, preferably with Horst.

The moment that Horst was known to be safe in Rotterdam, Erna wrote to her parents and her brother, asking them to help her find employment and a place to live. She made it clear that she didn't want to live in refugee camp.

This wasn't easy. Finding full-time employment with live-in facilities and accommodation for a young child was almost impossible.

Horst's stay in the Rotterdam centre was always going to be temporary. The Dutch Ministry of Internal Affairs social welfare department, despite being overwhelmed by the demand, succeeded in finding him a place to stay, in an orphanage in Gouda. He was taken out of the Rotterdam centre in April. Frieda wrote to her daughter saying that she had asked around and was assured that this was a good place. She expressed confidence that some work could be found, so that Erna should not delay any longer.

Erna accepted the advice, and arrived a month later. She was able to find some part-time work in Hilversum. Unfortunately, her employer expressed regret that she could not provide accommodation for her son.

—⁂—

No one would recommend orphanages as the preferred environment for caring for children, but the *Burgerweeshuis*, the municipal civil orphanage in the famous cheese-making town of Gouda, was probably a happier place than most. The orphanage was long-established, dating back to the seventeenth century, although most of its buildings were more recent. Its staff did their best to keep the children educated, entertained and fit.

After the children had been admitted and allocated a bed in one of the dormitories, a German-speaking nurse showed the new arrivals around the property and explained the activities that would be arranged for them.

The institution even had an open-air unheated swimming pool, although it was unlikely that Horst would be diving into it while the country was still emerging from the depths of winter. Informal lessons were organised. One teacher was assigned to teach the children basic Dutch. Other staff sought to find out what children were interested in and design some relevant experiences for them based on that. A few teachers were German, which helped. Some staff took groups of children for walks around the town. A playground allowed them to kick a football around and practise scoring (or saving) goals. Some of the older boys played in the town's junior soccer team. Most importantly, the teachers and nurses were well aware that many of the recent arrivals had recently suffered personal trauma and needed special care.

Horst had been lonely and miserable in the Rotterdam refugee centre, and was much happier in this new environment. Best of all, he received a letter from his mother. Erna had been informed of Horst's location by the Ministry, and she wrote to tell him that she would visit him just as soon as she had a free day.

At last she travelled by bus to Gouda to see her beloved son. When they met again for the first time together in their new country, there were not too many words at first – just hugs, kisses and tears of joy. Three months had passed since they had last seen each other in Berlin.

They were both safe and they were free.

Beuthen to Berlin to Rotterdam to Gouda: one might wonder what sense an eight-year-old boy might make of the numerous sudden changes in his life over which he had no control. And these dislocations were only the first of many that would occur frequently in the months and years ahead. Undoubtedly the decisions were made with his care and (later on) his survival in mind. That is beyond question. The unanswerable question is what thoughts passed through Horst's mind, as he spent the remaining years of his childhood in a world gone mad.

25

A mother's heartfelt plea

Hilversum, 22 May 1939

Erna was happy, most of the time. A month went by after Horst's transfer from Rotterdam to Gouda and her reunion with her beloved boy. She was gratified that she and her son were safe in a decent country, free from Nazi oppression. Horst was well cared for, and her job in Hilversum as a *hulp in de huishouding*, a housekeeper, provided an adequate living wage.

Yet there was a problem. Gouda was in South Holland, while Hilversum was in North Holland. The towns were 40 kilometres apart and travelling by public transport between the two was not easy. Moreover, for a woman earning only 25 guilders a month, it was expensive.

So she sat down and wrote a polite letter, in German, to the Ministry of Internal Affairs.

In her letter, she begs the Minister, from the bottom of her heart, that if it is at all possible, could her child please be moved to somewhere close to Hilversum or Amsterdam, as she couldn't visit her son as often as she would like? She didn't have enough money to cover the fares and her parents were living in Bussum and they unfortunately had nothing. She signed the letter in Dutch style, the hyphenated surname the conjunction of her married name (despite the fact that she was divorced) and her maiden name.

It took several months for the Ministry to act on her request.

In the meantime, other events were happening in the wider world.

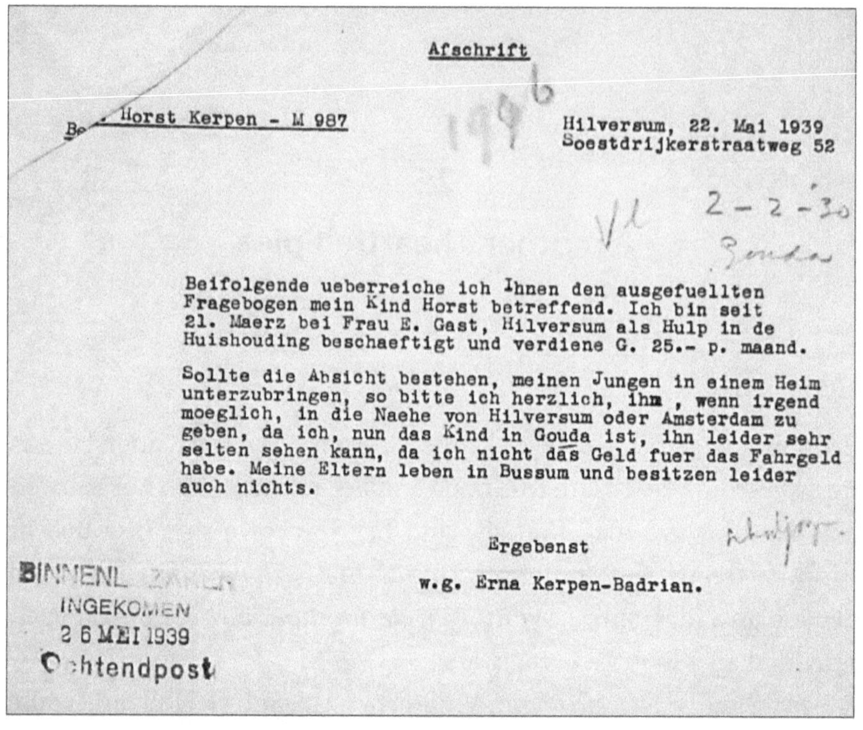

Afschrift

Betr. Horst Kerpen - M 987

Hilversum, 22. Mai 1939
Soestdrijkerstraatweg 52

Beifolgende ueberreiche ich Ihnen den ausgefuellten Fragebogen mein Kind Horst betreffend. Ich bin seit 21. Maerz bei Frau E. Gast, Hilversum als Hulp in de Huishouding beschaeftigt und verdiene G. 25.- p. maand.

Sollte die Absicht bestehen, meinen Jungen in einem Heim unterzubringen, so bitte ich herzlich, ihm , wenn irgend moeglich, in die Naehe von Hilversum oder Amsterdam zu geben, da ich, nun das Kind in Gouda ist, ihn leider sehr selten sehen kann, da ich nicht das Geld fuer das Fahrgeld habe. Meine Eltern leben in Bussum und besitzen leider auch nichts.

Ergebenst

w.g. Erna Kerpen-Badrian.

BINNENL. ZAKEN
INGEKOMEN
2 6 MEI 1939
Ochtendpost

Erna's letter to the Ministry of Internal Affairs.

War and Resistance

26

Street theatre

Western Europe, August/September 1939

A week is a long time in politics. It's a cliché. The last week of August 1939 provides a classic illustration.

On 23 August, Hitler and Stalin agreed on a non-aggression pact, for which Poland would bear the cost by being carved up by Germany and the USSR. Poland, needless to say, was not consulted.

Three days later, Hitler announced that he guaranteed the neutrality of the Netherlands and four other European nations.

On 28 August the Dutch demonstrated their level of trust in the *Führer*'s guarantee by mobilising their army. Next day, Queen Wilhelmina, in cooperation with King Leopold of Belgium, offered to intervene in the escalating political conflict over Poland. If Hitler actually heard of this offer, he and his circle probably had a good laugh. The Reich's major interest lay in causing conflicts, not resolving them.

Meanwhile, Hitler's most senior Nazis had already been hard at work, engaging in another quite different line of activity: playwriting. These cultural enthusiasts had a penchant for violent street theatre, and they were busy crafting a script for a short play that would have its German premiere (and only public performance) in Gleiwitz, an

Upper Silesian town close to the Polish border, on the night of 31 August 1939.

A small group of German operatives, dressed in Polish uniforms, seized the Gleiwitz radio station and broadcast a short anti-German message in Polish. It was a false-flag operation: the attack and the broadcast were intended to make the episode look like the work of anti-German saboteurs. The script included a bit part for a disposable political prisoner who would appear in the play as one of the men dressed in a Polish army uniform. He would be delivered, unconscious, to Gleiwitz, given a lethal injection and then shot to make it appear that he had been killed in the attack. A whole new meaning to the term *a one-night stand*.

Next day, 1 September, Hitler responded furiously, announcing that this was an act of war, and ordered the invasion of Poland.

It had certainly been a busy week, but there was more to come. Two days later, Great Britain implemented a guarantee made in March of that year that it would act if Germany attacked Poland; it announced that a state of war now existed with Germany. World War II had begun. In time, the Great War – Woodrow Wilson had called it the "war to end all wars" – would be renamed World War I.

On 4 September the Dutch government declared its neutrality. Hitler and his henchmen were no doubt pleased to hear this. It would give them a few months of breathing space while they proceeded to trample over their agreed half of Poland. The Dutch (and the Belgians and the French) would have to wait their turn. Stalin would have to wait a little longer. Non-aggression, Stalin would eventually learn, came in two German versions, temporary and permanent.

27

Hilversum

Hilversum, December 1939–May 1940

Seven months passed before the Ministry acted to accommodate the anguished mother's heartfelt request. If one's immediate reaction is to be disappointed with the painfully slow response by a government agency to Erna's reasonable letter, spare a thought for the hard-pressed public servants in the Ministry's social welfare department at that time. In Germany and Austria, the Nazis were ramping up their pressure on the Jews. Thousands more refugees were arriving. An epidemic of diphtheria forcing the closure of two outlying orphanages didn't help the situation.

In the months following the outbreak of war, the Netherlands remained at peace, neutral as it was in the Great War. Hitler informed the Dutch that he had no designs on their country, the aim, no doubt, being to lull the Dutch government into a false sense of security. No one in the government was actually fooled by Hitler's announcement.

Although the Ministry of Internal Affairs was overwhelmed by the challenges of the refugee crisis, it did eventually manage to meet Erna's request, with a short-term fix and then a longer-term solution.

On 7 December, Horst was transferred to the *Burgerweeshuis* in Amsterdam. Refugees and Dutch children were housed in separate sections. The building was four centuries old, the iron beds rusty, the dormitories gloomy, the walls in serious need of repainting, the food appalling, and the staff strict. Fortunately, Horst stayed there for only eleven days, before being moved again.

The longer-term solution offered the best possible placement for Horst since his arrival from Berlin ten months earlier. *Het Kindercomité* (the Children's Committee), with the support of the Jewish community, worked with the Ministry in helping to place refugee children. Their task was challenging, as among the tens of thousands of people who had sought safety in the Netherlands, two thousand children had arrived on *Kindertransports.*

The committee approached a Jewish family in Hilversum, the Frank family, a common Dutch surname (not the family of Anne Frank). The Franks didn't know Erna or Horst personally. David discussed the request with his wife Marianne, and mentioned it to their two boys, Jo David and Jacques. The older boy was of similar age to Horst, so there was the prospect of companionship. David and Marianne agreed to take Horst in and be his foster-parents. They were not a wealthy family. They informed the Ministry that they would of course pay for the additional expense of providing food, but they requested an allowance to cover the cost of the boy's clothing.

Erna, who lived and worked in the neighbourhood, met the family and was overjoyed that the disruptive period of Horst's life in orphanages appeared to be over. He would now be living in the home of a warm-hearted Jewish family in the neighbourhood and she would be able to visit him frequently. Foster care at the Frank home was, at the time, the best possible solution.

And it might have remained so, had the Wehrmacht not invaded in May 1940, six months after Horst's move to Hilversum. All of a sudden, order turned into disorder. Someone, perhaps several people in consultation, decided that Horst should move out of the Franks' home. Within a fortnight of the invasion, he was being cared for by his grandparents in Bussum.

For the next two years, Horst again led an unsettled life, even more disruptive than before. He spent three months with his grandparents. Then followed stays of varying length in Blaricum, Naarden, Hilversum again, Bussum again (but not with his grandparents) and Hilversum once more.

No one at the time could possibly have foreseen the consequences of the decision to terminate the foster-care placement, but it saved Horst's life. Sadly, the entire Franks family came to a tragic end. The Nazis captured David Frank and murdered him in Auschwitz in 1942. Marianne, Jo David and Jacques died in Sobibor the following year.

28

The Wehrmacht invades

The Netherlands, May 1940

For eight months after the outbreak of war in 1939, the Netherlands remained a peaceful place and continued to be a haven for the persecuted Jews of Germany and Austria. The flood of refugees continued. The reception centre at Rotterdam was hard-pressed to deal with all the arrivals. The government had already established a refugee camp out in the countryside at Westerbork. By May 1940, about 30,000 Jewish refugees had made their way to the Netherlands.

On 10 May, Hitler demonstrated that his promise of neutrality was worth precisely nothing. Early in the morning, German planes bombed various airports and triple-engine Junkers dropped paratroopers into the country. Dutch anti-aircraft batteries and a small number of Dutch fighters in the air managed to down a few of the Ju52s. Fighting on the ground resulted in the deaths of both Dutch and German soldiers.

But the Dutch were underequipped, underprepared and hopelessly undermanned. It was all over in four days. On 14 May the Luftwaffe mounted a terror raid and demolished the city centre of Rotterdam. Threats of similar treatment to other parts of the country had precisely the desired effect. The military surrendered the next day. The Dutch government and the Royal Family went into exile.

The Dutch were not the only victims. On 10 May, the Wehrmacht also launched attacks against Belgium, France and Luxembourg. Belgium took eighteen days to surrender, the French a few weeks.

29

The Nationaal-Socialistische Beweging

The Netherlands, 1931–36

In December 1931, two extreme right-wing activists, Anton Mussert and Cornelis van Geelkerken, together with ten other men, formed a pro-Nazi party, the Nationaal-Socialistische Beweging. The NSB garnered enough support to hold an assembly and publish a newspaper a year later, but failed to attract a widespread following, securing only 8 per cent of the vote in the 1935 election (and only half that subsequently). The NSB was strongly opposed by the Dutch government, who banned civil servants from joining it and issued a directive that paramilitary chapters of political parties must not outfit their members in uniforms. The two mainstream churches weighed in on the issue in 1936, with the Roman Catholic Church bishops and the Gereformeerde Kerken Synod both declaring that belonging to the NSB was incompatible with church membership. Later that year, Mussert visited Germany and held a secret meeting with Hitler.

On his return, Mussert met his little band of Dutch Nazis. The attendance was small enough to fit into the back room of a cheap local hotel. "Look, lads," he announced with pride, a feeling enhanced by his over-weening estimation of his own importance, "I've just come back from Germany. I met with the *Führer*. He told me he plans to make this country an important part of a much greater German Reich. This is exactly what we all hope for. He isn't ready to do this yet. It may take a few years. We have to be patient. But this is what we must do in the meantime. Keep talking to your friends and get them to join the NSB. We still have our NSB uniforms, but we won't wear them in public. We don't want anyone to get arrested. And if you happen to be a civil servant or a member of a church, just keep your membership of the NSB secret. There's no law that says you have tell anybody about it. Nobody needs to know. When the right day comes, everyone will know about it soon enough."

Mussert had told Hitler of the position of the Dutch government and the edicts of the mainstream churches. The *Führer* would not have worried too much about government opposition. The European nations that he had in mind to take over would either cooperate with him, or they wouldn't. It didn't matter too much, he would deal with either contingency. Cooperative countries would be taken over first. The rest would also be attended to, but not just yet. It would still take a few years for the armed forces to reach the required strength.

The church pronouncements, however, generated some discussion among the Nazi leadership. It was unexpected, as there was no united opposition by the churches in Germany. The Nazis filed away the information and it led to some policy decisions a few years later. The Dutch churches would be treated differently. With kid gloves, if necessary.

30

Kid gloves and iron fists

The Netherlands, 1940

Kid gloves were also used, at least initially, in dealing with Dutch society generally. After the terror bombing of the Rotterdam town centre and the swift capitulation of the Dutch military and the government, the invaders switched to a softer approach, designed to encourage quiet subservience as they established total command.

Normally, when an army invades another country, the defeated soldiers are imprisoned as POWs (or, in more violent cultures, executed). Not so in the Netherlands. An early edict went out to the military: just surrender your weapons and you will be free civilians.

Occupying rulers are often military governors. Not here, was the message: the country will continue to be managed by a civil administration. Civil servants could keep their jobs. True, but the kid glove could easily be replaced by an iron fist if necessary.

The original military governor, General Alexander von Falkenhausen, not a committed Nazi, was transferred on Berlin's orders to take charge of Belgium and France, because he was more interested in military tactics than in ruling a population with an iron fist. But in a nation whose military forces had been defeated and disarmed, military tactics were in fact no longer necessary. The governor was promptly replaced by Arthur Seyss-Inquart, who was appointed as Reich Commissioner. He was a ruthless Nazi administrator, briefly installed as Chancellor of Austria just prior to the

Anschluss (annexation of Austria) of 1938. He was a man dedicated to implementing Hitler's vision.

As to the civil service, there was just one minor detail. Seyss-Inquart issued an order: all civil servants had to sign a document that they were Aryans and would pledge their support to carrying out all the directives of the legitimate government. Jews, of course, need not apply.

And if there were to be vacancies in the future, why then, all Aryans would have an equal opportunity to join. However, as in any dictatorship, some people are more equal than others. Membership of the local Nazi movement, the Nationaal-Socialistische Beweging, provided a distinct advantage. Seyss-Inquart invited Mussert and Van Geelkerken to a meeting to tell them this. The NSB leaders swelled with pride when they realised that their vision was soon to be realised.

The Dutch police and the civil service generally cooperated with the new rulers. Further assistance came from various local pro-Nazi parties. After December 1941, however, the NSB was the only political party allowed under Nazi rule. It sought to unite the Netherlands and Flanders into a region called *Dietsland*, which would play second fiddle in a "Germanic League" orchestra in which Germany would be the concertmaster. Many citizens actually sympathised with this political position. Thousands joined the NSB in order to be appointed to civic positions and enhance their career prospects. Police Sergeant Spannenburg, a staunch member of the NSB, was pleasantly surprised when he was quickly promoted to the vacant position of captain of the Velsen police station near Haarlem. A few thousand ultra-loyal citizens even volunteered their services to the newly-formed Nederlandsche SS, with the finest recruits becoming Gestapo officers.

Business owners who employed Jews or who had Jewish clients were warned that they should not be too "Jew-friendly". These warnings proved insufficiently persuasive, so a law was passed forbidding Jews to work in non-Jewish enterprises.

Marius Meijboom had to let Gerhard go. "I'm desperately sorry, Gerhard," he told his trusted colleague and friend, "but I can't keep you here. It would be dangerous for both of us. I'd suggest you continue working as a freelancer, and I'll help you as much as I can." Gerhard took his advice, but business opportunities under the new laws were limited.

Marius also experienced the regime's displeasure. His "too-friendly" attitude towards Jews and political opponents was duly noted by the Gestapo, and in 1942 he was arrested and imprisoned in a detention centre until the end of 1943. Meanwhile, his wife Margreet, also a photographer, continued to run the business. After his release, he became involved with a group of photographers who surreptitiously took photographs documenting the Nazi occupation. The group became known as *De Ondergedoken Camera* (The Hidden Camera). Margreet kept in contact with Gerhard, helped him to obtain photographic supplies and gave him access to the Meijboom studio.

31

Jacob Lentz

In the late 1930s, a Dutch public servant named Jacob Lentz suggested that every Dutch citizen should have an identity card listing name, address, occupation, parents, spouse, children, occupation and religion. The idea was not original: Napoleon had, more than a century earlier, proposed a national registration system. There would be local registration centres and if a citizen moved from one town to another, the record of the card's contents would be moved as well. The initial pre-war government reaction was that the scheme treated every citizen as a potential criminal and it wasn't particularly interested in implementing the Lentz proposal. Not everyone was opposed to the idea however; some saw merit in that the system could provide a rational basis for apportioning grants to various religious entities on a per capita basis.

In 1938, the Nazis introduced such a system of ID cards, *Kennkarten*, in Germany, and then made wider use of the idea in the countries they subsequently conquered. After the Netherlands was invaded, Lentz was more than ready to assist, proposing that cards be printed with special inks on special paper, held together with special glue; a blank space was provided for fingerprints. The Nazis loved the idea. Lentz even suggested that Jews could have a "J" printed on their card "so that the Jews could be readily identified". The Nazis really didn't need his advice. Large lettering and colour coding of cards to identify ethnic backgrounds were already widely used elsewhere. But no doubt they praised Lentz and thought him a dutiful civil servant. The Nazis began implementing the scheme in January 1941.

It wasn't that Lentz was a passionate Nazi, just a devoted public servant who took pride in producing excellent professional work. Eager to help, he even compiled lists of Jewish surnames for his new masters to help them check whether everyone had registered.

32

Hiding

February 1941

Seyss-Inquart had taken up his new position in charge of the Netherlands fresh from his previous posting as a Minister Without Portfolio in the Generalgouvernement in Poland. The administration there had faced the challenge of recruiting Polish farm and factory workers to move to Germany. Hundreds of thousands of labourers were needed to make up the shortfall caused by military conscription and the losses of workers killed by Allied bombing raids. The problem was that voluntary recruitment had failed to provide the needed manpower (surprise!) and the solution was found by creating a new law, the *Arbeitseinsatz*, the (compulsory) "work assignment". Force would be applied to make it effective, if necessary. Work assignment sounds much nicer than slave labour.

There were already more than a quarter of a million unemployed in the Netherlands at the time of the invasion. Despite this, the Dutch were, not surprisingly, no more inclined to volunteer to provide Germany with workers than were the Poles, so Seyss-Inquart applied the Polish solution to the Dutch problem. Workers would be *invited* to volunteer. Those who were disinclined would be coerced with threats of punishment. Those who flatly refused would be incarcerated. Ordinance No 42, issued in February 1941, announced that unemployed labourers aged eighteen to 45 had to register to be drafted to work in Germany.

Gerhard discussed the ordinance with his friend Frans Meijer. They had been friends since Gerhard's arrival in 1938, brought together by a common interest in photography. Frans knew Gerhard's employer, Marius Meijboom well.

Gerhard had already thought about what he was going to do, soon after the edict was published in the daily newspaper. "Well, technically I'm not unemployed, as I'm working as a freelancer," he told Frans, "and in any case I doubt that the Nazis are going to transport Jews back to Germany, seeing that that they have gone to no end of effort to expel all of us. But there's a deeper issue."

"What's that?"

"I've been watching what's been going on since the invasion last year. It's basically a re-run of everything that happened in Berlin a few years ago. The gradual increase in oppressive regulations, one after the other. The Nazis are going to rule this country with a rod of iron, and woe betide anyone who disagrees with them. I've decided what I'm going to do. I'm not going to follow orders. I'm not going to register for anything. I'm not going to fill in any forms. I'm not going to register any change of address. To put it simply, Frans, I'm going to hide."

Frans took this in, thought about it for a moment, then asked, "Have you somewhere to go?"

"Nothing definite yet, but I have a couple of possible places in mind."

It was against the law to fail to register your address. So Gerhard became an *illegaal*. His first hiding place was only temporary, with a friend in Apeldoorn. Willem Harland was an anti-Nazi who worked at the Van Gelder Company, a leading Dutch paper manufacturer. The connection between the two would prove useful much later. However, Gerhard felt that he couldn't ask his friend to put himself in danger. Hiding an illegal was a criminal offence.

Gerhard's next move was to the countryside near Groningen. Other friends had suggested he visit a guesthouse there, owned and managed by a devout young Christian woman, Cornelia Dirksen.

Everyone called her Cokkie. She was appalled by the actions of the occupiers. As well as her "normal" guests – people with legitimate IDs and regular permanent addresses – who would be listed in the guest register, Cokkie had offered to provide temporary shelter to *illegaals*. They would be sequestered in unseen huts in the forest behind the guesthouse, their presence unrecorded.

Food during the war was rationed and buying food in a store required ration coupons. Out here in the country, that was less of a problem. Limited quantities could be obtained from sympathetic farmers in the region. The Nazis simply didn't have the manpower to count every sack of potatoes or crate of carrots grown in the country.

The rural solution was certainly safer, but it didn't work for Gerhard. He spent some time there, as if on holidays, reading, trying to relax, going for walks in the forest, taking photographs of trees and birds and landscapes. But soon he realised that he was unsettled, on edge, unhappy. He thought his presence there was a risk to other people. His restlessness grew into a feeling of serious disturbance.

He rightly judged Cokkie as being a sensitive and discreet woman to whom he could safely reveal his misgivings and his intentions. "I feel safe here and I'm very grateful for what you're doing," he told Cokkie, "but I also feel frustrated, completely useless. There are terrible things happening, and I think I should be doing something to help others. I have friends who are starting up a small Resistance group. If they'll have me, I'd like to get involved in their work. I know that's a risk, but I'd rather do something to fight against the Nazis than sit here doing nothing just to save myself. So, thanks for everything, but I've decided. I'm going back to Amsterdam. I'll keep in touch with you."

Not long after he returned to the city, his elderly foster-father died on 8 April 1941. Gerhard placed an ad in the *Joodsche Weekblad*, the weekly Jewish newspaper. He wrote:

I have the sad duty to notify the death of my foster-father Jaques S de Vries.

Those who knew him will realise what his loss will mean to me.

G Badrian

Gerhard may have been in hiding, but he had not yet completely disappeared from view.

33

The *Persoonsbewijzencentrale*

Soon after his return to Amsterdam, Gerhard visited his friend Frans Meijer.

"Great to see you again so soon!" Frans exclaimed as he shook Gerhard's hand and clapped an arm around his shoulder. "But I didn't expect to see you for quite a while. I thought you were out in the country, in hiding."

"I was, and it gave me time to think. After about a week of trying to relax and going for walks in the forest, I couldn't stand it anymore. It's not just the boredom. I felt selfish, useless. I was just saving myself. It didn't feel right. There's work to be done here. I probably can't do much, I'm just one man, but feel I should do something."

Frans responded enthusiastically to his friend's very personal revelation. "That's good, and I'm sure you can. I'm part of a small group that's just been formed. We're busy forging ID cards to help people go into hiding, and I'm sure your talents can be put to good use. I'll talk to the chief straight away and if he approves – and I'm pretty sure he'll welcome you with open arms – I'll introduce you to him as soon as possible. I think you'll be a great asset."

Frans spoke to his leader, warmly recommending his friend, mentioning not only his photographic skills, but also his decision to defy the authorities and go into hiding. He considered that this combination made him a very suitable person to join the Resistance.

Soon afterwards, Frans introduced Gerhard to Gerrit van der Veen, the founder of the PBC (*Persoonsbewijzencentrale*, the Personal Identification Centre).

34

Gerrit van der Veen

Amsterdam, 1941

Had anyone told Gerrit van der Veen in his youth that he would one day head a Resistance group fighting against a murderous dictatorship, he would no doubt have laughed.

He was a skilful artist and sculptor who had developed his talents as a young adult. Now in his late thirties, he had completed a commission to make a large sculpture, intended for public display, just prior to the invasion. A socially minded man, he was active in a society that brought artists together to promote their common interests and support cultural development in the wider community.

Soon after the occupation, the Nazis required all cultural activities to conform to their directives. The occupiers founded the *Nederlandsche Kultuurkamer* to give effect to this policy. Artists were ordered to join this Chamber of Culture, sign the *Ariërverklaring* declaring their Aryan ancestry and agree to obey the Chamber's directives.

Gerrit refused. Instead, he and a small group of like-minded colleagues formed an underground organisation, *De Vrije Kunstenaar* (The Free Artist). They published a newsletter calling for resistance against the occupation. The group's members understood perfectly well that this could prove dangerous, and that they would need to take steps to avoid being arrested.

Gerrit was a leader, a motivator, a creative thinker. He gathered

like-minded people together and encouraged them to work coopera-
tively. He knew that if people were to go underground and resist Nazi
oppression, they would need false identities, hiding places, possibly
even escape routes out of the country. Forged ID cards were going to
be needed. Forming the PBC was the first practical outcome of his
intention to resist. From just a loose collection of people in 1941, by
1942 it had developed into a well-organised operation.

Gerhard's friend Frans Meijer was a key member. In the early
days of the Resistance, Frans lived at Herengracht 554. Some of his
associates who knew his address were captured by the Gestapo, so he
decided it would be safer if he were to move. He rented an office at
Amsteldijk 37 and his home also became the headquarters of the PBC.

—⚏—

Even its early days, in 1941, Gerrit van der Veen was aware that the
potential scope of the PBC's operations was unlimited. More personnel would be needed to run an effective operation. He had primed
his small team to be on the lookout for capable people who could be
encouraged to join the group. Frans Meijer was therefore following
his leader's instructions when he suggested to Gerhard that he could
be useful to the PBC.

Gerrit himself possessed a formidable armoury of leadership
skills: intelligence, creativity, humane values, an organised mind and
emotional commitment to the task at hand. He also possessed that
essential attribute of good leaders: the ability to enthuse others to
work together for a common cause. His previous years of work as a
sculptor had also taught him the importance of meticulous planning
if a complex task was to be completed successfully. He drew upon
this capacity in his entirely unexpected new role as the leader of a
Resistance group. Opposing the Nazi regime was a deadly, dangerous
exercise and it was therefore crucial to ensure that every member of
his team was completely trustworthy, reliable and careful. The PBC
needed more workers, but only those with the right attributes. His
job as leader required him to be selective.

Frans Meijer arranged to meet Gerhard in the Café Eijlders in central Amsterdam, whose proprietor was sympathetic to the Resistance. It was situated in a laneway close to one of the city's main intersections. A quiet back room was available for meetings that were best kept out of the public eye. Gerrit was already waiting there. Frans introduced his friend and then left the two men together while he returned to his own work.

Even though Gerrit trusted Frans' judgement, Gerrit went through his usual routine. He asked some innocuous questions about Gerhard's personal history, and Gerhard responded with a succinct summary of his German-Jewish background, his two years as a child with Dutch foster-parents, his interest in photography and his decision (and that of his entire family) to flee Nazi oppression before the war.

"Frans told me that you were in hiding out in the country, but now you're back in Amsterdam," Gerrit asserted. "Why didn't you stay there? Surely it's safer for you there than here in Amsterdam?"

"I was there for almost two weeks, and the boredom was driving me mad. But more importantly, I felt guilty. I know I'm just one person and I'm not going to be able to save the world, but we have to oppose these Nazi bastards and I want to help."

(*Good response, thought Gerrit, no delusions of grandeur, no superhero complex, just someone willing to contribute.*)

"Frans told me you're a photographer. Tell me about your work in that area."

"I worked in Berlin for a few years in fashion photography, did an advanced course at a college there, and acquired a collection of various cameras and equipment. I can develop and print my own pictures and make enlargements. I met Marius Meijboom already in Berlin, and soon after I arrived in the Netherlands he gave me a job."

(*Impressive, Gerrit noted. He knew Marius Meijboom personally, and of course was aware of his reputation as a foremost commercial photographer. He wouldn't have offered this guy a job unless he was top-grade.*)

"That's excellent, we need a good photographer here. One of our main activities is making forged ID cards. What's your experience in that department?" (*Gerrit already knew that Gerhard had no experience at all; he was more interested in the style of his response to this probing question than the content.*)

"Forging documents? I have never done that. But I expect you have others in your group who can show me what to do. I'm willing to learn. I've been taking pictures ever since I was a teenager, and along the way, I've always tried to improve my technique and learn to do new things."

(*Perfect, thought Gerrit. Modest, no attempt at pretension, self-aggrandisement. I think we have a real team player here.*)

He concluded the interview with some small talk, told Gerhard that he would be warmly welcomed as a member of the PBC and arranged for him to visit the PBC's secret headquarters to meet some of the others in the group.

—⁂—

Through such recruits, the PBC over the course of a year became a larger and more efficient group. In turn, the PBC became linked to a much larger operation that became known as the *Verzet* (Resistance). The *Verzet* was not a single, coordinated organisation – there were sound reasons for keeping its many cells separate – but it managed to attract support from tens of thousands of people. The *Verzet* attracted people with various skills and interests. Some, like those in the PBC, made forged documents. Others arranged hiding places for people in danger. Numerous landlords provided accommodation to people in hiding. A few armed men engaged in guerrilla warfare. One group smuggled people out of the country. CS-6 was a largely Communist group that carried out sabotage and assassinated Gestapo officers and Dutch collaborators. And later in the war, a small group of leaders – Gerrit was one of them – was in contact with Allied headquarters in London to help coordinate military actions.

35

Gerhard in the PBC

Amsterdam, 1941–42

At first, Gerhard was hesitant about joining the PBC full-time. He was still finding occasional work as a freelancer, and offered to participate part-time. Later, as Nazi abuses of human rights grew and the demands on the PBC increased, he eventually devoted all his time to the Resistance. Fortunately, there were some wealthy anti-Nazi business leaders who were willing to finance the work. There was even a rumour – no one knew if it was actually true – that some *Verzet* people employed in the Nazi-controlled bank were embezzling large sums and diverting them to the Resistance.

Gerhard initially worked with a small group of people, contributing his talents as a photographer to the team and learning about their specific skills. His major task was to help create false ID cards for people who needed them: at first, other members of the Resistance and political opponents of the regime and later Jews who wanted to go into hiding.

Photographing someone who needed the forged ID was obviously essential but numerous other capabilities were required as well. Gerrit van der Veen's skill in attracting support from diverse people with specific competencies and connections was crucial.

Citizens would be found who would hand over their genuine ID cards to the PBC, and then report to a police station that they had lost their card. A particular policeman at one station was sympathetic to the Resistance and would authorise the issue of a replacement. The "lost" card would then be altered by the PBC team.

The photograph pasted to the ID had to be removed without damaging the card itself. Henk van der Tweel was a brilliant physics student with a penchant for technological design, who built equipment used in this process. Peter Roelofs was a science graduate in chemistry who devised a method for slowly dissolving the glue without damaging the card. The card was mounted in Henk's apparatus. A different chemical technique was used to remove the red ink-stamped J on an ID card. Another alteration involved replacing the fingerprint of the original owner with that of the new owner. Other details were left unchanged: the new owner would adopt the name of the previous one.

Prior to the war, Frits Boverhuis was the supervisor in a printing firm. He threw himself into supporting the work of the PBC. The group also had access to another printer, Frans Duwaer, who specialised in producing high quality forged documents.

Otto Treumann was a highly skilled commercial artist who made precise copies of Nazi logos. Frans Duwaer then used these to manufacture plates for printing counterfeit Gestapo letterheads. Otto's artistic skills also extended to forging signatures. His remarkable hand-eye coordination allowed to him to look at the signature of a top Nazi official and with a rapid flourish of the pen make an excellent copy of it.

The PBC also compiled a vast collection of Gestapo rubber stamps. One was needed for overstamping the corners of freshly mounted photographs on the altered ID. Some rubber stamps were forged copies. Some effort was saved later when a *Verzet* sympathiser was found who worked in the factory that made the genuine versions. He would make an extra copy and pass it on to the PBC.

Over time, the PBC grew in productivity, partly through attracting more personnel, and partly through obtaining better access to essential raw materials. One man devised a method of making the fake watermark paper needed to make counterfeit IDs, by gluing two sheets of paper together. Another was able to secure a batch of the genuine paper from the Van Gelder and Sons company, a leading Dutch papermaker. ("Secure" is a polite expression for sneaking it out of the factory while no one was looking.)

Much later, Gerhard's photographic skills would be employed in another *Verzet* activity. He joined the Hidden Camera group of photographers – Marius Meijboom was a prominent member – who surreptitiously captured images of Nazi officers and Dutch collaborators. The CS-6 group would make use of the photos in hunting these people in order to assassinate them.

Gerhard Badrian at work in the PBC office in the Amsteldijk.

The photographic group had another mission as well: to create a comprehensive collection of images to record Nazi actions during the war. Great care had to be taken, of course, not to be observed taking these pictures. Miniature cameras were used, often hidden behind clothing or mounted inside a briefcase. Gerhard cooperated with the group by being one of the people who developed the film and printed the images. He had access to the darkroom in Marius Meijboom's studio.

Gerhard wasn't involved in sabotage and assassination. He met one of CS-6's operatives one evening, a young woman, who told him that killing people wasn't her preferred occupation either. But she added, "We don't really have much choice. We have to stop the Nazis and their collaborators somehow, and we can hardly arrest them and put them in jail." Gerhard saw her point and didn't raise any objections. The only shooting he did was with his camera, he told her.

Members of the PBC cheered one evening after the news reached them that a cinema holding a film evening for the entertainment of the Gestapo had been bombed. Maybe the bombing had been carried out by CS-6, maybe not. They didn't know, they weren't told, and they didn't ask. But they cheered.

—⁂—

A man who is in hiding, an *illegaal,* living in the midst of a brutal fascist regime motivated simultaneously by aggressive imperialism and murderous antisemitism, is hardly likely to describe himself as happy. And yet, once he joined the PBC and became deeply involved in its work, Gerhard felt happier than he had been for a long time.

If not joy, then at least he felt satisfaction in being able to participate in a project that potentially saved lives. The feelings of boredom and uselessness that he had expressed to Cokkie in Groningen quickly dissipated. He gained pleasure from being able to work with others who shared his humane values and demonstrated the same commitment to producing high quality work that he valued in his former work as a commercial photographer. And there was camaraderie, the enjoyment of being with men and women who could do serious work and still find a little time for sharing a joke, a story, a friendly smile. His friend Frans smoothed the path by introducing him to the others, and whenever a new face appeared at a PBC meeting, Gerritt van der Veen always ensured that the newcomer was introduced personally to Gerhard.

It did not take Gerhard long to discover the range of skills that made Gerritt so effective in his role as head of the PBC. He was more than just a generator of creative ideas, more than just a skilled organiser who could delegate tasks to the right people. He was a true leader in the fullest sense of the word, a man who brought people together, enthused them, valued them, helped them to continually learn and improve.

Gerhard was soon invited to participate in small group meetings that were tasked with solving particular problems. "We are running short of genuine ID cards that we can alter. Does anyone have some thoughts about how we can get some more?" he might ask. He would praise creative contributions to the discussion. Gerhard never heard him ridicule unusual responses. No one ever left a meeting feeling diminished.

If a complex project required detailed logistical planning, Gerritt avoided adopting the persona of a dictatorial managing director ordering underlings to carry out specific tasks. He would instead turn to the group and invite them to contribute ideas. "How do you think we should organise this? Who do you think would be the best person to do that job? Do you think we might need some advice about how to handle this?" And he would allow some time for reflection, not expecting instant solutions.

Gerhard had a few years of experience at working with competent people, at the commercial photography business in Berlin and later at Marius Meijboom's studio in Amsterdam, but he had never encountered anyone whose range of competencies was as broad as Gerritt's. The involvement in the PBC triggered some unusual thoughts in Gerhard's mind, which he naturally kept to himself. "I'm doing volunteer work that won't earn me any money. There'll be no public acclaim for becoming a successful forger of ID cards. There'll be great danger if I'm found out. And yet I'm happy."

36

The Trio

Groningen, 1941–42

Cokkie Dirksen's guesthouse near Groningen, and her willingness to hide people, was known to others in the *Verzet*. As Nazi oppression grew, one Resistance group thought that perhaps the place could play a greater part in the work of saving people.

Cokkie was a quiet, unobtrusive woman in her mid-thirties. She had strong opinions about many things, but was not the sort of woman who aired them loudly or forced them on other people. She'd been raised in the Dutch Reformed Church and had a deep personal faith. She didn't know too many Jews personally, but she was well versed in the stories of the Old Testament, and respected Judaism as the religion of Jesus and as the foundation of Christianity.

Among her strong opinions was her detestation of Nazism. She was shocked when the Wehrmacht invaded. She was disgusted at the mistreatment of the Jews. She felt almost powerless to do much about it.

Almost powerless, but not entirely. She and her husband Augustus ran the small guesthouse together. It was an hour's drive from Amsterdam, near a rural village in a wooded area, close to a plantation of mainly Scots pines. The property consisted of an old two-storey house with ten bedrooms, and a collection of small cabins scattered around the forest, some of them barely visible from the main house. Augustus had inherited the property from his parents, who had died before the war. One day, not long after Gerhard's short stay, she was visited by three men who called themselves the Trio. They gave their names as Dirk, Felix and Egbert, but she was sharp enough to recognise that these probably weren't their real names, and sensible enough not to ask too many questions. Cokkie kept a deadpan expression. She was quite good at masking her emotions when it mattered.

Dirk spoke for the group. He'd been asking around, and he knew that Cokkie was a good-hearted woman who didn't like what was happening in the country. He expanded on this theme, mentioning various events. "I don't know if you've heard this," Dirk told Cokkie, "but fifteen members of a Resistance group and three Communist strike leaders were executed in Amsterdam last week. And Jewish business owners have had to hand over the running of their business to a so-called supervisor."

Cokkie had heard vague stories, but no verifiable details. Accurate news about what was actually happening was hard to get. She knew that the newspapers were all controlled by the Nazis. Then, gently, a little at a time, Dirk got to the point. Occasionally, Dirk said, some people were in great danger and they had to get away and hide for a while. A few might even have to leave the Netherlands. Could Cokkie and her husband perhaps look after them for a little while? Only, of course, until more permanent arrangements could be made. Some would have false ID papers and could be registered in the guesthouse as visitors on holiday. Others would remain unlisted. Better to keep them out of sight in one of the cabins. Some of the visitors could afford to pay, others could not. The Trio could provide some assistance, but not much. Ration coupons would be supplied for visitors who didn't have their own. (Dirk saw no need to explain that the ration coupons were impressive forgeries.)

Cokkie talked about the proposal with her husband that evening. "I'm frightened to do this," she told Augustus, who nodded sympathetically and responded that he felt the same way. "We've done a bit of this sort of thing already, but obviously there's a need to do much more. We mightn't be able to help much, but I do believe that we should do what we can. I can't stand by while innocent people are suffering and then do nothing about it. My conscience wouldn't allow it. Perhaps we can help save a few people. We have to try."

Augustus noted his wife's determined face and recognised yet again the strength of character of this woman. What she was saying was entirely consistent with her attitudes and expressions, but this was the first time in ten years of marriage that they had ever been put to such a test. "Yes, my love," he responded, "of course you're right. We have to do this. We can't say no." Neither needed to spell out the possible consequences. If the Nazis were prepared to execute people for simply protesting, what would they do to people who actively opposed them?

They agreed to support the Trio's work. When they next met, Dirk was appreciative. There were many ordinary Dutch citizens like Cokkie and Augustus, he thought to himself, just not enough of them. Most people just wanted to be invisible and stay out of trouble. He understood this. He also knew that the Nazis understood this and in fact depended on it.

It took some time for this phase of the Resistance operation to work smoothly. People wanting to hide had to learn of the Trio's existence. False IDs had to be prepared. Courier systems for bringing people had to be organised. Another courier system was needed for delivering documents.

"We work together with a man named Bernhard," Dirk told the couple on a later visit. "Sometimes he will be the person who gets in touch with you." He passed across a photograph, with just the name Bernhard written on the back. "Keep this somewhere safe."

She glanced at the photo and suppressed a smile. She recognised the face. Bernhard was one of the several cover names of Gerhard Badrian.

37

Anne-Marie Deij

Amsterdam, 1942

Anne-Marie Deij first came into Gerhard's life at a PBC meeting in Amsterdam, soon after he'd begun to be involved, part-time, in the van der Veen group. She made an instant impression on him. In her late twenties, she was strikingly beautiful, poised and well-dressed, despite the wartime privations. Later, when she spoke during the meeting, she captivated him again with her quiet, yet authoritative voice, her keen intelligence. Like Gerhard, she spoke Dutch with a strong German accent. This was someone, he quickly decided, he would like to get to know.

Anne-Marie was the liaison person from the *Verzet* group in Den Haag. She was employed in the public records section of the town hall, a job that gave her ready access to much useful information. Although by tradition, Amsterdam was the nation's capital, The Hague was actually the national government centre. The Dutch government, now in exile, had sat there before the war. The current so-called civil administration now had its headquarters there.

Anne-Marie Deij.

At work, Anne-Marie would surreptitiously remove identity records of Resistance members from the files when the PBC requested them so that they could forge false IDs for them. Appropriately altered replacements would then be returned to the files. Forged IDs were never sent to Amsterdam by post: far too risky; they were delivered personally. Anne-Marie was one of the couriers.

Numerous subterfuges were used to hide such documents in case anyone was stopped and searched by a suspicious Gestapo officer. Briefcases were made with false bottoms. Skilled tailors made coats with hidden linings. For the later local deliveries of forged ID cards to recipients within the Amsterdam area, one young mother put her baby in a pram that was fitted underneath with a thin tray that concealed a document compartment. Anne-Marie, however, never experienced any difficulties. She was a German citizen, non-Jewish, employed by the civil administration, carrying perfectly legitimate ID.

Over the course of a few meetings, Gerhard made an impression on her, too. She appreciated his quiet, gentle manner. He didn't speak often, but when he did, in his simple German-flavoured Dutch, it was to make a thoughtful contribution. He displayed no egotism, no bombastic pretence that he knew exactly what to do in every possible situation. Occasionally their eyes met across the table and they smiled shyly at each other.

After one afternoon meeting, Gerhard quietly enquired when her return train was leaving. "In about two hours," she replied, and he responded by inviting her to join him for a light meal in a nearby café, one of his favourite haunts. Happy to have the opportunity to get to know him, she accepted without hesitation. This was the first of several such post-meeting rendezvous.

The social chit-chat quickly led to more serious conversations. She asked him why he was in the Netherlands, and Gerhard outlined the story of his immediate family circle. He was similarly interested in why she had migrated. Why would a German non-Jew want to come here? Simple question, complicated answer.

A pattern of talk evolved unlike any other she had experienced in recent times. Anne-Marie rarely spoke with strangers about her personal life, but in Gerhard she found someone who was a good listener and sympathetic, someone who was non-judgemental, a man who refused to launch into offering unsought advice about what she ought to do. There was something about this man's manner that invited trust.

"I'm married, but I've separated from my husband," she began. "But I've gone back to using my maiden name. My husband and I are both German, from Essen. Simon and I were married in 1933. He's Jewish, I'm not. Simon quickly realised, long before others in his circle, that things would go very badly for the Jews, and the wisest action was to get out of the country as quickly as possible. He didn't have to work very hard at convincing me. I couldn't stand the Nazis either. We came here because this was a decent tolerant country. We didn't have much money and so coming here was a simple and cheap option. We thought we could make a fresh start here. We'd only been married a year.

"We did make a fresh start. We both found work. I got a job in the lingerie section of a large department store in The Hague and within a year the boss promoted me and put me in charge of the younger salesgirls. [I'm not surprised, Gerhard thought to himself.]

"Then came the invasion. It wasn't too bad at first; the Nazis tried to wear a gentle face and pretended to be kind to the Dutch. But soon they started behaving just like they did in Germany. My boss had a Jewish mother, so they took over his business and put an NSB man in charge of it. The new boss sacked people like me who refused to join the NSB. Simon was furious, went to the store and gave the NSB man a tongue-lashing, threatening to thrash him. Probably not a wise move.

"I had to find another job. Well, my German background is spotless. I'm a certified *Reichsdeutsche* – ha! What do you think of that? – and that got me a job in the civil administration. I had second thoughts many times about working in that environment but some friends who are now in the Resistance convinced me I could be of use in there by taking on the town hall job. Not long afterwards, an SS officer arrested Simon and called him a troublemaker. They already knew from his ID record that he's Jewish and threw him into jail. He's still in prison now, been there for months."

Gerhard looked at her with concern. "Do you hear from him? Does he have a definite jail sentence?"

"I really don't know much. He's allowed to send me a postcard every couple of weeks, and he says he's okay. He says he's not being badly treated but there's no mention of when he'll be released. He's not in the Resistance, or a trade union leader, and he hasn't committed any crime. But he's Jewish, and God knows what the Nazis have in store for him. I'm reasonably hopeful, though, that he'll be safe as long as we stay married."

Gerhard was puzzled about that last statement. He knew from his *Verzet* contacts that Dutch Jews who had converted to Christianity prior to 1941 were exempt from the Nazi anti-Jewish laws and mentioned this fact to Anne-Marie. He wondered whether a soft approach was also being used for mixed marriages.

"Yes, it's similar. But there's another complication," Anne-Marie added. "Long before all this happened, Simon and I had begun to drift apart. Our marriage wasn't working out, for either of us. And that's raised a new problem. A *Verzet* colleague of mine in The Hague has a friend who's a senior man in the Dutch Reformed Church. He tells me that the Nazis are treading very carefully with them and the Catholics as well. They're pretending to be nice because they are worried about massive church opposition. The Nazis are behaving differently here. In Germany, for example, the Nazis are pure racists and they track people if they have even one Jewish grandparent. Here they're leaving baptised Jews alone. Also, quite a few Dutch Christians are married to Jews. So far, the Gestapo don't seem to be taking much interest in mixed marriages either."

Gerhard had heard similar stories. He wasn't sure what to make of them. Was this a permanent policy difference, or just a temporary local ploy? But he didn't voice this thought. "You said this was causing you a problem. Do you want to talk about that?"

"Yes. I'm in a terrible bind. I'm not in love with Simon anymore, but we're still friends and I care about what's happening to him. Usually if a couple break up they get a divorce and if they're lucky they find new partners. But perhaps Simon will be safe as long as he's married. He's a decent man and I'm not going to do anything that might harm him. I've made a firm decision. I'm not going to divorce him until the war's over."

Tears began to well up in her eyes as she told Gerhard this story. He reached out across the small table in the café, placed his left hand on her shoulder and gently touched her face with the tips of the fingers of his right hand. This is a woman in a thousand, he thought to himself, I've never met anyone like her before. This is someone I could spend my life with. And she responded wordlessly to his touch by placing a hand over his right, left it there for several seconds and smiled despite her tears. This man understands me, she realised. This man cares. Each looked at the other with tenderness and compassion. In that moment, with that wordless act, a bond was formed. Each of them knew, at that instant, where this was leading.

On a sudden impulse he told her that with some of the information she'd brought, it would take him and his colleagues a couple days to make new ID cards for the people who needed them. One batch was for a small group of people who were hiding out in the country. "I'm going to deliver them personally. I thought I might do that next weekend then have a short break and stay in the area overnight. Would you like to come with me?"

Anne-Marie was a woman who knew her own mind and could respond decisively. "Yes," she said with a warm smile, "yes, that would be lovely."

Gerhard sent a card to Cokkie Dirksen in Groningen to book a double room in her guesthouse. He signed it Bernhard, the cover name he used for such ID delivery operations.

38

Rachel de Vries

Amsterdam and Groningen, January 1942

Sturmbannführer Ludwig Schlosser was in a good mood. The portly middle-aged major was sitting in his office in the Euterpestraat headquarters of the Gestapo, and he called across to his junior colleagues. "Come and have a coffee with me, and I mean a real coffee, not the usual shit they serve in the mess." His two underlings, *Untersturmführer* Carl Fischer and a young NCO *Unterscharführer* Bruno Boehme, weren't accustomed to seeing Schlosser in a jovial mood, and they dropped what they were doing.

"Good news today from up top," Schlosser announced. "They've arrested Frans Goedhart! We got him on the beach at Scheveningen, as he was about to escape to England." Fischer recognised the name of the political activist who'd been publishing underground material opposing the Nazi civil government. Finally the *Sicherheitsdienst* (security service of the NSDAP) had tracked him down.

Boehme hadn't heard of Goedhart, as he was new to the unit, but he was keen to learn more. "What'll happen to him?" he asked, as he sipped the first decent coffee he'd had in weeks.

Schlosser told him. "He'll be put on trial of course for his crimes – we're a civilised society after all – but there's plenty of evidence and he'll be found guilty. His shitty little newsletter is clearly designed to undermine the orderly civil government of this country."

"And then what?"

"Abbeförderung, natürlich." The senior officer smirked as he rolled his lips around the unusual German word, connoting dispatching and removal, a neat euphemism for execution. Schlosser expected that Goedhart would stew in the high security prison on the Weteringschans for a few weeks prior to his trial. This would give some of the rougher elements of the SS an opportunity to squeeze some information out of him about his collaborators. After the trial, he would be taken to the beach sands on the North Sea at Overveen and shot.

But that wasn't Schlosser's department. His group were detectives, gatherers of useful information about the enemies of the Reich, and the coffee break was merely his pleasant way to get his little team working together on a new task. He had a small job for them.

"Fischer! I want you to collect all the information you can about Goedhart's associates. And Boehme! We know that Goedhart had been in hiding before he was captured, but I want you look up where he used to live. It might give us some clues about the people he's connected with. Have something on my desk by this time tomorrow."

Boehme was new to this sort of work, but he was bright and keen to succeed. Like many of the young recruits to the Gestapo, he was a well-educated young man. He'd grown up in a Protestant home and considered himself a Christian, although he wasn't all that keen on going to church and singing hymns and listening to sermons. He had a higher calling now. He'd watched some films of Hitler giving speeches and was faintly amused by some of the *Führer's* theatrical posturings, but he basically agreed that Hitler had the right idea and wanted to restore Germany to its proper place in the world as the powerhouse of Europe. He'd been a bit puzzled in the early days about the direction the *Führer* was taking, but his professors in his undergraduate years in law school had convinced him of the need for a strong guiding light to lead the German nation to its glorious future. "Politics takes precedence over the law" was one of the guiding principles of the law school's educational approach. Germany had gone through difficult times, Boehme knew, and a strong man was needed at the helm to lead the country.

But there was no time to think about all that now. He had a job to do, and he knew how to do it. Fischer had trained him well after the young NCO had first arrived at Euterpestraat. The town records were wonderfully organised for tackling this sort of work. House cards listed the names of everyone living at a particular address, and individual *persoonskaarten* listed the names of their family members. Jews could be identified quickly by their added middle names, "Israel" and "Sara". And if someone moved from one town to another, a copy of the outdated card would be sent to the town hall of the new location. The central Population Register stored the comprehensive collection of everyone in the Netherlands. Boehme marvelled at being able to work in an occupied country where the civil service was so capable, well-organised and cooperative.

He got to work promptly, and it didn't take him long. Goedhart's current address obviously wasn't in the town records, but Boehme discovered a 1938 address in Bronckhorststraat on an old PK (*persoonskarte*). The house card for that address listed him as a boarder. The head of the household at the time was Jaques de Vries. But the old man had died in 1941 and the PK card showed that the widow, Rachel Sara de Vries-Brandon, was still living there. Boehme wrote down all the details, and a note was on Schlosser's desk that afternoon.

"Good work," the *Sturmbannführer* told Boehme. "So, now I have another job for you. Go and pay a visit to this de Vries woman tomorrow morning before you come to work. Be polite, don't frighten her or arrest her or anything like that. We're civilised people, remember. Just tell her that you'd like her to come and visit you here at headquarters in the afternoon, as we have a little problem and we need her assistance. Don't give her any hint at all as to what this is about. If she asks, just tell her you don't know, you're just passing on a message. No need to tell her that she'll be arrested if she fails to turn up. I'm sure she knows that already."

Schlosser then handed Fischer the task of looking at both the

Goedhart and de Vries files to see if there were any connections. The old woman was Jewish, of course, as the added name of Sara on her PK card attested. But the Gestapo wasn't interested in that at the moment; the priority was hunting active enemies of the Reich. Capturing Jews was not on the immediate agenda.

Fischer checked the Goedhart file. He knew most of it already. Middle-aged journalist, worked in Belgium for a while. Dismissed in 1931 for participating in a printers' strike. Came back to the Netherlands. Joined the Communist Party and edited its paper. Sacked for criticising the Soviet dictatorship. But very little about his current dirty work, producing anti-Nazi newsletters. A couple of his colleagues are mentioned. Nothing about any de Vries woman.

As for the woman, there wasn't much in the file. Promoted women's rights before the war. Her home was the address for an organisation calling for an insurance scheme for women who were ill. Probably a socialist. Might even be a Communist. Nothing suspicious in recent years.

And when Schlosser and Fischer interviewed the old woman when she turned up as ordered the next day, trembling with fear, she was subjected to a barrage of questions. She answered them truthfully, for in fact she knew nothing about her former boarder's current activities. When Schlosser suddenly asked her, "When you see him next, will you tell him that we'd like to talk to him?" she answered without hesitation, "Of course, but I haven't seen him since my husband's funeral last year and I don't expect to see him in the near future." The two men quickly realised that she had no idea that Goedhart had been captured. They let her go home. She was, of course, mightily relieved that the pair didn't interrogate her about the whereabouts of her foster-son.

Back home in Bronckhorststraat, she quickly sent a message to Gerhard about the day's events. He was shocked. Although Rachel had said that the interview at Euterpestraat had gone well, and that at no stage had the Gestapo asked her any questions about him, he thought that one interview by the Gestapo was one too many, and was concerned that his foster-mother might be in danger.

He immediately contacted the Trio and asked them to arrange for Rachel and her sister to go into hiding at Cokkie Dirksen's guesthouse.

Cokkie was happy to oblige, welcomed the sisters, and kept them in the guesthouse for a few weeks. The guesthouse and its hidden cabins were primarily intended for short-term stays. Those requiring extended hiding were moved to the homes of trusted families that belonged to her church.

Cokkie never found out whether the sisters were ever actively sought by the Gestapo. All that mattered to her was that people entrusted to her care were kept safe. This she did, with a high rate of success. The sisters survived the war.

39

The Jewish quarter

Amsterdam, 1942

The Nazi decrees against the Jews in the Netherlands were becoming increasingly harsh. Gerhard knew via reports from his *Verzet* colleagues that Jews in other occupied countries had been crowded into ghettos – walled-off sections of major cities – and death rates from malnutrition and disease were staggeringly high.

Seyss-Inquart had ordered the creation of a ghetto in central Amsterdam, but the geography of the city with its network of interconnecting canals didn't lend itself to that kind of construction. In any case, the good burghers of Amsterdam expressed loud opposition to the idea. Gerhard was never sure whether some were motivated by their opposition to Nazi ideology, and others by a desire not to have too many Jews living amongst them and spoiling the neighbourhood. Perhaps a mixture of both.

His friend Frans told him what the Nazis were doing instead. "They've created an area in the city centre and people from other towns and outlying areas are being removed and crowded into a few blocks in the centre of town, many families into a single apartment," he said. "But the funny thing is, there are no walls or fences being built, just a few signs erected around the perimeter, announcing *Juden Viertel!* I've heard people in the street cracking jokes about this Jewish quarter. They're calling it an optical ghetto."

Gerhard smiled, but he knew that it was no joke. Whatever the

Nazis did, there was always a reason behind it. His parents were among the thousands affected. Hermann and Frieda had been given a few days' notice to close up their apartment in Bussum and pack a few suitcases of clothing and personal belongings. They'd had to transfer their financial assets to a newly established branch of the Lippmann-Rosenthal bank (LIRO). They would then be given the address of their new home in central Amsterdam and after closing up, had to leave the keys to their Bussum apartment for safekeeping at the local police station.

What Gerhard couldn't know, although he had his suspicions, was that this set of Nazi policies had a dual purpose. He knew nothing of the highly secret meeting of Nazi leaders in a lakeside mansion in the Berlin suburb of Wannsee earlier that year, at which the heads of various Nazi departments were informed about the implementation of the *Endlösung der Judenfrage*, the Final Solution to the Jewish Question. Concentrating Jews into a central location would make it easier to deport them en masse for extermination.

He had also never heard of the name of one of those departments, the *Devisenschutzkommando* (DSK), whose task it was, not to kill Jews, but to strip them of their assets before they were killed. The term *Devisenschutz* means Foreign Exchange Protection, another example of the Nazis' masterful ability to disguise its true objectives with clever euphemisms.

So Gerhard would not have known, although he would not have been surprised to learn, that soon after the keys to the Bussum apartment had been safely deposited at the local police station, a polite gang of junior representatives of the DSK would arrive (with proper authorised documentation, naturally) to relieve the police station of the keys, open the door without having to force entry, strip the apartment of anything of value and transfer the plunder to a central warehouse, where it would be temporarily stored until it could be sold, all proceeds going, of course, to support the heroic vision of the Thousand-Year Reich. And if the entire apartment building was owned by a Jew, so much the better. It would be subjected to *Arisierung* – Aryanisation – and sold to a worthy, devoted Aryan supporter of the regime.

40

The yellow star

April 1942

The civil administration issued its latest edict. All Jews when outdoors now had to wear a prominent yellow star, showing the word *Jood*, sewn on to their outer clothing. The cloth star had to be purchased and one ration coupon had to be handed in along with the payment.

A week after the new regulation came into effect, Gerhard met Frans Meijer in a local café. Gerhard wasn't wearing a star.

"What's behind this yellow star business?" Frans wanted to know.

"Well," Gerhard responded, "it's just another racist measure, on top of our additional middle names and the big red J on our ID cards. The *schoften* already know where everyone lives. (Gerhard liked to impress his friend by throwing in the odd Dutch term of foul abuse occasionally, just to demonstrate that he had progressed from his schoolboy Dutch.) Now the Gestapo can just pick out someone in the street and do whatever they want."

"So why aren't you wearing one?"

"Well, Frans, I did at first, but then I thought about it for a few days. I'm very suspicious about where this is all heading. Could be the start of some even greater repression. Whatever it is, I've decided I'm not going to obey the rotten bastards. They can beat up anyone they want, anytime they like, yellow star or no yellow star, and nobody can do anything about it. So I've decided to take the risk. Anyway,

I'm already an *illegaal* – I haven't registered my address since I went into hiding. So I'm already a very naughty boy. What can they do about it if they can't find me?"

As they left the café and ambled along the footpath they noticed a pair of Gestapo officers walking towards them, but on the opposite side of the narrow street. Frans would have just ignored them but Gerhard astonished his friend by giving the pair a vigorous cheery wave as they passed by. By the time the officers were out of sight, Frans realised that the SS men would have had no idea that Gerhard was Jewish. Whatever the term "Aryan" meant, Gerhard was just as Aryan as they were. Frans knew why the Nazis had implemented the yellow star nonsense. Despite all the cartoon propaganda depicting Jews as ugly, hook-nosed characters, in reality Jews looked no different from other Dutchmen or Germans.

The episode also sparked a fresh thought in Frans' mind. It showed a side of Gerhard's personality that he'd never seen before. The man was a natural actor.

41

Cor Verbiest

Amsterdam, 1942

Commissioner Hendrik Voordewind wandered out of his office at Police Headquarters and headed for the bathroom at the end of the corridor. The floor of the building was fairly empty; most of his men were out on active duty. One of his staff, a young detective named Cor Verbiest, was in his office and the door was open.

Voordewind poked his head in the door and gave a short, sharp directive to the policeman. "Verbiest," he ordered, in a firm voice that was clearly a command, "come and see me in my office at the end of the shift, but make sure no one sees you and don't tell anyone that we're meeting." And with that, the commissioner extracted his head from the doorway and resumed his trip to the bathroom.

Detective Verbiest was puzzled, slightly concerned – had he done something to offend his chief? – but naturally he obeyed orders and knocked on the Commissioner's door at the end of the day.

Voordewind invited him in and closed the door. "This won't take long," he said. "I just wanted to invite you to have a drink with me tonight at a little club I belong to. Here's the address." He passed him a slip of paper. "Arrive sharp at 8 o'clock and ask the doorman to direct you to Room 5. And don't tell a soul that we're meeting. That'll be all."

Verbiest was even more puzzled than before, and rather worried. What was on the chief's mind? He had a couple of hours of free time before the meeting. He had no real home to go to – his marriage to Johanna had broken up and he lived alone in a tiny apartment – so he wandered for a while along the Prinsengracht and headed for a favourite place, the Café Eijlders, to escape the cold night air, have a bite to eat and catch up on the daily news, or at least the German-censored version of it.

At 8 pm, he arrived at the club – an unobtrusive ground floor entrance on the Herengracht – and the doorman pointed him in the direction of Room 5.

Voordewind was there, alone. The room was dimly lit and sparsely furnished. "Welcome, Cor. I invited you for a drink." (Why was the chief being informal and friendly, Verbiest wondered.) The Commissioner opened a cold bottle of beer and poured two glasses. "You're no doubt wondering what this is all about. Well, I'll get straight to the point. I've been watching you for quite a while. One of your recent jobs was to visit electrical stores and repair shops to collect radio sets, following the Gestapo order that private citizens were no longer permitted to own radios. Well, you did that as ordered, but I found from the copies of the receipts that reach my desk that your return rate was below that of the other men."

"I can explain that …" Verbiest tried to interject.

"Quiet, I'm not interested … I began to think that you might be harbouring some thoughts about being less cooperative with our Nazi masters than you're supposed to be, so I had you followed and investigated by a couple of cops on my staff that I know I can trust …"

Verbiest began to shiver.

"… and I discovered that some of your contacts were in cells of the *Verzet* …"

And then Verbiest's sharp detective mind cut in and he suddenly became aware of why he was here for a drink and hadn't already been arrested and possibly executed.

"… and I wanted to tell you that's okay, because I can't stand these Nazi bastards either. The Resistance has my support."

Verbiest breathed a sigh of relief. Voordewind went on to explain what he wanted Verbiest to do. "Two things. One is that there is a local group headed by a man named Gerrit van der Veen. You probably know that already, if you're as good at this sort of activity as I think you are. One of the group is a German Jew named Gerhard Badrian. I've met him. Capable man. You're to be my liaison with him. I'll pass on what I know that might be relevant to Gerrit's group, and you'll get from them what they're up to. And secondly, you'll probably be asked to participate in some *Verzet* operations as a result. Maybe even during working hours. That's okay. I'll cover for you. I'll list you in the records as out in the field doing an investigation. But don't tell me anything that I really don't need to know, because I really don't want to know … I see you haven't touched your drink! Drink up, I'll get us another bottle."

42

Tanny Tromperts

Amsterdam, March 1942

In the two years following his removal from the Frank family home, Horst experienced yet another long period of unsettled existence. Where he slept overnight and where he would spend the day would constantly change. Amid this continual disruption, there was a short window of time early in 1942 when he enjoyed a brief period of happiness. Horst made a new friend.

In the early years after she immigrated, one of the places where Erna worked was in the home of the de Groot family in Amsterdam. She was the cook, one of three women employed there. She had briefly lived with the family in the early days, but now she was employed as a daily.

A younger woman, Cornelia Tromperts, employed as a maid by the de Groots, had a little sister, Tanny, a couple of years younger than Horst. The Tromperts family lived near the de Groots; one day Cornelia, after gaining the approval of her parents, asked Erna whether she would like to bring Horst to her home. The two children could keep each other company during the day. Cornelia's mother would look after them. Erna was delighted with this offer.

The children played together happily and a firm friendship developed. Tanny had a nickname for him: she called him Horschi. Someone took a photograph of him, wearing a cheerful smile, and Erna wrote the date on the back of the photo together with his nickname and his age in a mixture of German and Dutch. Cornelia mounted it in the family photograph album.

A few weeks later, Horschi disappeared from Tanny's life. She was saddened by the sudden loss of her friend. "Where's Horschi?" she asked her sister plaintively. "I don't know," Cornelia replied. "I think he had to go and live somewhere else, but I don't know where he's gone."

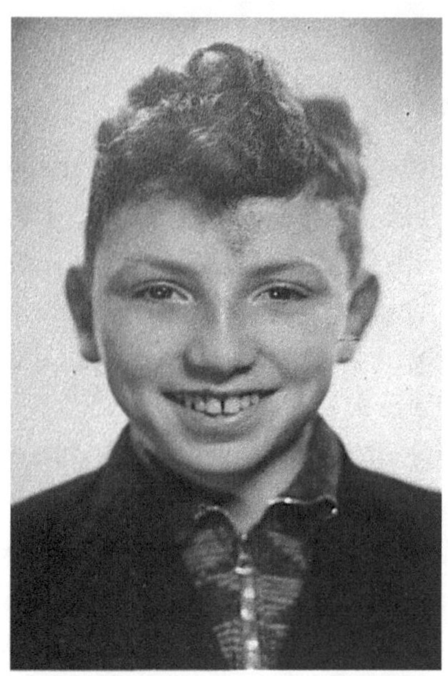

Horst Kerpen ("Horschi"),
eleven years old, March 1942.

43

The Jewish orphanage

Amsterdam, June–July 1942

Eventually, *Het Kindercomité* found what it hoped would be a better, more settled solution, although it meant an orphanage again, not a foster-home.

Horst was accepted as a resident at the *Joodsche Weeshuis* in Amsterdam. It was an ancient institution, having been founded more than two centuries earlier by an association of German Jewish settlers. Its location and building, however, were of much later vintage. In the nineteenth century, the original premises were too small to meet the growing needs of the community, and a larger building on another site, facing the Amstelgracht, was completed in 1865. The three-storey brick construction facing the canal had rows of arched Gothic windows resembling those in a synagogue (or church). An arch above the ground-floor entrance carried the name of the building in Dutch. Underneath the central window on the top floor, an inscription proclaimed the institution's Hebrew name, *M'gadlei Y'tomim*, The Raising of Orphans.

Horst, previously living in Hilversum, was admitted to the orphanage in June 1942. A month later the Board confirmed his acceptance as a permanent resident after the Committee for German Children had agreed to pay for his board and lodgings.

It was an extremely dangerous time. A few months had elapsed since the Wannsee conference. Reinhard Heydrich and his successor

Adolf Eichmann had been hard at work, all over occupied Europe, preparing to turn the *Endlösung* vision into reality. It was an ambitious vision. A new Europe would arise, once and for all without any Jews. A glorious Thousand-Year Reich would then restore Germany to its proper place as the permanent leader of Europe.

Implementing the vision would require massive, complex planning. Extermination sites would need to be constructed to facilitate the rapid murder of millions. Trains would be needed to transport them there. Hundreds of men would have to be trained to carry out the killing. Complete secrecy would be needed so that non-Jewish majorities would be unaware of what was happening to their Jewish populations. And the victims themselves would need to be deceived about what was actually intended for them.

And who would pay for the phenomenal costs of running such a mass-murder operation? In a nation already spending a fortune on ships, aircraft, tanks, weapons, bombs and the wages of the millions of personnel needed to use them effectively? Here the Nazis demonstrated the highest levels of economic wizardry in the history of mankind. Why, the victims would pay for their own demise! All of them had already been declared Enemies of the Reich. Part of their punishment for this crime included the confiscation of all their assets.

In the middle of 1942, the plan began to be implemented in the Netherlands. It coincided with the period that Horst was living in the Jewish orphanage.

44

Horst becomes an *illegaal*

November 1942

Whenever she could, Erna would visit Horst in the orphanage, bring him little gifts or a small cake that she had baked for him. She spent time with him, read him a story, asked him about what he had been doing, and told him about her work and how much she missed not seeing him.

One day, in mid-November, she arrived with a large, rather shabby canvas bag. This was unusual. Horst noticed.

"What's in the bag?" he wanted to know.

Erna showed him. The bag was empty. Horst gave her a puzzled look.

"My darling boy, I don't want you to ask too many questions right now, I just want you to be very quiet and think about your clothes and anything else you have here that you want to keep. Then we will pack everything into the bag. We're leaving here. We won't be coming back."

"But why, *Mutti?* Why?"

Erna deliberately avoided giving a detailed explanation. She had no wish to frighten her son. She kept the explanation very simple. "*Onkel* Gerhard has told me that this is not a safe place anymore, and said we should move."

"Move where, *Mutti?* Where are we going?"

"We will be leaving here in five minutes and going for a walk to meet *Onkel*. He will take us to a house where you will be looked after. Please, no more questions. Just pack the bag. Quickly. Then we're going."

The Minutes of the orphanage board's December meeting record that on 18 November, Horst *niet teruggekeerd van wandeling met zijn moeder:* he did not return after going out walking with his mother. During that period, several other children quietly left the orphanage in a similar way.

Commissioner Voordewind had been alerted to the introduction of a new Nazi policy when he was contacted by *Sturmbannführer* Willy Lages and ordered to provide a contingent of uniformed police to assist in a little spot of crowd control. "The situation in the Jewish quarter is quite unsatisfactory, Commissioner," was Lages' opening line. (Well, you bastard, thought Voordewind, you ought to know, you're the one who put them there.) "We've decided on a different approach," Lages continued. "We're going to move these people into the barracks at Westerbork, not all at once of course, and eventually resettle them somewhere else, somewhere more suitable. We'll be using the Schouwburg as an initial processing centre for a few hundred people at a time. I need you to supply daily teams of Grüne Polizei to control the arrivals at the theatre and supervise the transport of people from there to the central railway station prior to their ongoing travel to Westerbork. All understood?"

Voordewind did as instructed, but he also called in Detective Verbiest to inform him of this latest news. "There's something big going on, Cor, and I don't know exactly what it is, but whatever it is, I doubt that the SS intentions are motivated by any form of kindness. Pass the information on to Badrian so that he can alert his *Verzet* colleagues."

Cor contacted Gerhard, who pondered what the new policy might mean. Westerbork had been running as a quite civilised refugee camp, even after the occupation, but it would be impossible to house all of the Jews in the Netherlands there. Lages himself had mentioned something about resettlement elsewhere. But what did that mean? Gerhard and his colleagues had not heard of any plans to build new camps anywhere in the country. That would be a massive and expensive operation. He didn't like the sound of it at all. His foster-mother and her sister were hidden at Cokkie Dirksen's. Perhaps it was time to think about making similar arrangements for his parents, sister and nephew. It wouldn't be easy. The demand for hiding places was growing rapidly, and finding new places of refuge was becoming more and more difficult.

He thought some more about Horst, in the orphanage. What were the Nazis planning to do to the children? If the Nazis were rounding up Jews, an orphanage containing a hundred children could be swept up in a single raid. Gerhard knew there was an orphanage at Westerbork, but it consisted of a single barracks hut. It simply couldn't cater for a hundred children. And there were other Jewish orphanages in the region. No one had the resources to hide hundreds of children.

He had no answer to his own ponderings. But one thing he knew from his own experience at hiding: contact with the Nazi apparatus should be avoided at all costs. He acted on that immediately. "I think the Nazis might be planning something terrible," he told Erna. "Go to the orphanage tomorrow morning, take a bag with you, tell Horst to take whatever of his belongings he can and put them in the bag, and just tell someone at the orphanage that you are going out for a walk with him. And don't go back. In the meantime, I'll work on finding a place where you can take him, I'll meet you at the canal bridge closest to the orphanage at 11 o'clock and then I'll take the two of you to a safe house where Horst can stay."

Voordewind's instincts were sound, as were Cor's and Gerhard's. What Lages was doing was implementing the *Endlösung* program. A few weeks later, on 15 February 1943, the Nazis rounded up everyone in the orphanage and delivered them to Westerbork. A hundred children and three of the orphanage staff were then deported to their deaths in Sobibor. Horst, however, was safe. His admission to the orphanage had been registered. But now that he had left without registering his new address, he became, like Onkel Gerhard, an *illegaal.*

45

The pace accelerates

Juden Viertel, late 1942–early 1943

The pace of the Nazi round-ups had accelerated and was now a steady stream, as if the trains delivering Jews to Westerbork and deporting them out of there were running to a regular timetable.

Westerbork's administration had been changing over a period of months. Constructed on open fields in the countryside an hour's travel from Amsterdam, long before the Nazi invasion, even before the attack on Poland in 1939, Westerbork had been founded as a refugee camp for the thousands of Jews, mostly German, who had fled their homeland for the safety of the Netherlands.

Gerhard recalled a much earlier conversation he'd had with Frans Meijer. "You know," Frans had told him, "it's very odd, but the Nazis have been almost civilised in the way they're treating the refugees. The Westerbork camp is no luxury hotel, of course, but when it was set up by the government before the war as a refugee camp, it had dormitories for the adults, even with rooms for families to stay together, a separate orphanage, a hospital, a large dining hall with reasonable food supplies, even a room set up as a synagogue. What's odd about it is that after the Nazis invaded, they didn't change anything. The civil servants who ran the joint were kept on the staff. It wasn't a prison camp. People inside could have friends visit them. Quite out of character."

That was then. Now everything was changing. Frans told Gerhard the latest developments. "*Kommandant* Gemmeker is now in charge of running the camp. He's left the top civil servant, Adrian van As, in his job to organise the food supplies and look after the day-to-day administration, but there's no question that Gemmeker is the real boss of the place. The *Grüne Polizei* are on duty at the gates and check every vehicle coming in. They're turning it into a prison."

And that wasn't all. Gerhard already knew from messages from his parents in the *Jüden Viertel* that something unusual was going on. The Nazis had been arresting opponents of the regime since the early days, but now they were rounding up large numbers of ordinary people at a time. He told Frans what he had seen and heard. "You know that large theatre, the Hollandsche Schouwburg? [Frans nodded; he'd been past the impressive building close to the centre of town many times.] Well, I was pleasantly surprised when the Nazis took over the building a couple of years ago. They renamed it the *Joodsche Schouwburg* and allowed the community to hold meetings, plays and concerts there. Now that's stopped," Gerhard continued. "No more public events. The place has been turned into a temporary holding centre. A truck picks up a load of arrested people and drops them off at the Schouwburg. But they don't seem to stay there long."

"That's right," Frans chimed in. "And I know what happens to them. My contacts tell me that they're taken by tram, with a Green Police guard on board, to the central railway station, and from there a train takes them to Westerbork. And that's not all. There seems to be a regular timetable, because a large train with many carriages now leaves the camp every Tuesday. Westerbork seems to have been turned into a transit camp, and the people are being sent somewhere else."

"Do you know where?" Gerhard asked.

"No. Nobody seems to know exactly. My informant at Westerbork tells me that the night before they leave, the people are told that the camp is getting too crowded and so they'll be going to a new camp somewhere else. I know it isn't in this country. There aren't any other large camps here. I get reports that the trains are heading east."

Everything that Gerhard had learnt over the preceding ten years from his experience of Nazism – the oppression he'd witnessed in Berlin, the numerous concentration camps in which political prisoners were incarcerated in Germany, the destruction of synagogues and Jewish property on *Kristallnacht,* the execution of Resistance leaders here in Amsterdam – led him to be deeply suspicious about what Hitler and his loathsome cronies had in mind. His hatred for these murderous tyrants and the locals who collaborated with them was unbounded.

He'd gone underground, without registering his whereabouts with the authorities. He'd refused to wear the yellow star with the word *Jood* on his outer clothing. He had a false ID. He'd managed to keep his foster-mother and her sister out of harm's way.

He told Frans of his plan. He would contact the Trio and ask the group, as a matter of urgency, to hide his parents at Cokkie Dirksen's guesthouse. He would prepare false IDs for Hermann and Frieda. When that was all arranged, he would contact his parents, instruct them to pack a suitcase each with their most important belongings, then he would pick them up in his car and drive them to Cokkie's. Frans agreed with this plan. "You might need some help to move all their stuff into your car quickly," he said. "I'll come along to help you." We're close friends, Frans thought to himself, that's what friends are for.

46

Capture

Amsterdam, late February 1943

Gerhard had sent his parents a message telling them to be ready at precisely 10 am. He parked his car a block away from the address in the Jewish quarter, then he and Frans walked the short distance towards his parents' apartment building. From 100 metres away, they saw Hermann standing at the open doorway, suitcase in hand.

And they watched in horror as two SS officers arrived at the door and arrested Hermann together with Frieda, who had been standing behind her husband in the hallway, and took them both away.

—⁓—

Hermann and Frieda were profoundly shocked at the sight of the two SS officers at their front door.

"Holen Sie sich im Auto, Sie beide!" barked the older of the two men, as he pointed at the van in the street and ordered the elderly couple to get inside.

"Wohin gehen wir?" Hermann enquired. He was distraught and trembling, almost whispering. But his tone was respectful as he asked where they were going.

"Sie sind beide ins Theater eingeladen," replied the SS man. He was more courteous than before, and his statement was partly true but there was also an edge of cruel mockery in the voice. Hermann

understood perfectly well that SS men issue orders, not polite social invitations to the theatre.

The drive from the *Juden Viertel* to the *Schouwburg* took only a few minutes. Hermann and Frieda were confronted by a chaotic scene. Gestapo cars and trucks were delivering hundreds of people to the street outside the theatre building. Dutch policemen in their green uniforms were attempting to manage the turmoil in the street. The theatre frontage was at the footpath. There was no courtyard to hold the crush of people. The narrow entrance doors – there were only three of them – could not cope with the flood of humanity being forced to enter.

To add to the disorder, someone was leading a line of children out of the building in the opposite direction, heading for a crèche directly across the street. A tram was making slow progress along the street. The young woman in charge of the children was having great difficulty in keeping them together and ensuring their safety as they made their way around the slowly moving tram. A couple of young men, looking like hikers carting heavy packs on their backs, were struggling to make their way through the crowd and away from the tram.

As if all this wasn't enough, a large and stylish Gestapo vehicle whose driver blasted the horn frequently to encourage people to get out of the way, edged its way to the pavement in order to deliver his important passenger. Hermann noticed the very senior SS officer who emerged from the vehicle after the driver had parked and quickly opened the door for his chief to emerge from the car. Hermann could tell from the resplendent and spotless uniform that this was a man of high rank, but their paths had never crossed before and he couldn't know that it was *Hauptsturmführer* Ferdinand aus der Fünten, the head of the Centre for Jewish Emigration in Amsterdam.

But Hermann did recognise the man standing on the footpath waiting to meet the Nazi. It was Walter Süskind, a leading member of the Amsterdam Jewish Council. Hermann caught only a glimpse of the two men, and what he saw surprised him. He might have expected signs of aggression by the Nazi and frightened submissiveness from the Jew, but this wasn't the case at all. It was almost like friends meeting each other. Hermann had neither the time nor the energy to reflect on this observation, but his initial reaction was one of displeasure.

The crowd finally managed to enter the theatre building. In the foyer, a junior SS officer demanded to see Hermann and Frieda's ID cards and checked off their names on the typewritten list that lay on the table.

This done, they were directed to enter the theatre. Hermann and Frieda knew the building; they had been here on rare occasions. Before the war, they would occasionally catch the train from Bussum to Amsterdam to visit friends. Sometimes they would stay in the city, go out for dinner, then attend a concert at the theatre. In the early days of the occupation, they were still able to do so, much to their surprise, but now this beautiful building seemed to have an uglier purpose.

Joodsche Schouwburg had been turned into a central assembly point and processing centre. Slowly, over a period of months, the tens of thousands who inhabited the *Juden Viertel* were being removed, a few hundred people at a time.

An SS officer stood on the stage of the theatre and told the crowd the purpose of their visit there.

"Welcome to the *Schouwburg*," he announced. "We don't want to keep you here long. We know that you have been living in very crowded conditions in the Jewish quarter and this is not very satisfactory, so we have decided to send you to a much larger place where most of your community are now living, in the Westerbork camp. You will be taken by tram to the Central Railway Station, and from there we have arranged for a train to take you to Westerbork."

He went on to explain about food arrangements, toilets, and a yard at the back of the theatre where they could get fresh air and exercise. And then, almost as an afterthought, "Perhaps some of your friends and family don't know about these new arrangements. We will be distributing postcards to you so that, if you wish, you can write a brief message to them, and we will post them for you. You can collect a card from the desk in the foyer."

Hermann availed himself of this opportunity, and wrote a card to his son. He did not of course address it to Mr Gerhard Badrian as his son had long disappeared from the official records and had a fake ID with one of his cover names. He quickly wrote a brief message telling of his safe arrival at the *Schouwburg* and adding the comment: "They haven't served the coffee yet." He was sure that Gerhard would understand.

47

After his parents' arrest

Two days later

Gerhard met Frans again and talked about his feelings after the shocking event they had witnessed at the *Schouwburg*. "You know," he reminisced, "I realised years ago that the Nazi regime in Germany was going to be bad, but I was optimistic that my family and I would be able to get away. That's why we all came here.

"Even after 1940, I thought we could handle it. Sure, the Nazis were dictators, but the country wasn't a war zone for long and we weren't going to be killed by bombs. Amsterdam wasn't going to be a battlefield. But now I'm not so sure anymore. One thing I know. I'm not going to give in to these monsters. Maybe I'll survive, maybe not. But whatever happens, I'm going to go down fighting."

This was the defining moment when Gerhard decided to tell Gerrit van der Veen that he was now prepared to devote all his efforts to the work of the *Verzet*. Previously he was motivated by a simple desire to help others who were engaged in a worthwhile cause. Now he was driven by more than altruism. Now it was personal, a desire for revenge: calm, cold revenge, not impetuous bravado. Now he would devote his entire life to the cause.

Dismayed and distraught, Gerhard already knew, while he watched his parents being captured, where they would be taken. The *Schouwburg* location was confirmed when, two days after the arrest, he received a postcard from his father. The careful man had of course not addressed the card to his real name and address, nor had he written "To my dear son" in the greeting line. Hermann was well aware that the Gestapo would read each outgoing postcard, looking for clues about the location of people like Gerhard. He knew full well that his captors' handing out blank postcards together with words of encouragement to tell their loved ones that they were okay was not motivated by any humane feelings. Hermann had sent the card to a false name at a safe contact address, and it had been hand-delivered to Gerhard that morning.

The postcard also made no mention of Erna or Horst. Where were they? Had they been arrested? Of course his clever father would have realised that any specific mention of them would tell Gestapo intelligence that they were still free.

Gerhard read and reread the card and pondered the line: "They haven't served the coffee yet". Hermann had used the German word *Kaffeebohne*, coffee beans. Few people had enjoyed real coffee in the past two years. The plain meaning was that Hermann was employing sardonic humour, even at this stressful time, to indicate that the level of service at the *Schouwburg* was not quite up to the standard of a quality hotel.

But another interpretation was possible.

48

Saving children

Several small Resistance groups were active in helping children to survive. Gerhard knew that various schemes were in operation, without knowing the details of who was involved or the methods they employed.

One such scheme was operating under the very noses of the Nazis at the *Schouwburg*. The head of this operation was Walter Süskind, the very man seen warmly welcoming Fünten at the theatre. Süskind was the manager of the theatre. He was a German Jewish immigrant who served as a member of the Amsterdam Jewish Council. He was part of the liaison group between the Council and the Nazi authorities.

The Council was the Dutch version of the *Judenrat* that the Nazis created in every country they occupied. Its role was to assist the authorities in managing the Jewish community. The Council was coerced into cooperation by the implied threat that the treatment of the community would be much worse if they failed to cooperate. But a widespread view within the community was to regard the members of the Council as collaborators.

Süskind's apparently friendly manner towards Fünten was seen as evidence that he was a collaborator.

He wasn't.

Süskind was part of a small circle of people actively engaged in saving children. Felix Halverstad, another member of the Council based at the theatre, was part of the circle. A crèche was located across the road from the theatre. Children arriving at the theatre were taken across the road and were placed in the crèche. A teacher training college was two houses away from the crèche. The director of the crèche, Henriëtte Pimental, and the head of the college, Johan van Hulst, were part of the scheme.

Effective operation of the scheme involved several components. One was to lull the Nazis into the belief that the theatre management was cooperating enthusiastically with them. Süskind would ply the Nazi officers on duty with liquor and give them cigars. A small brothel was organised on the top floor of the building to keep a few of the officers entertained. Every officer keeping himself occupied upstairs was one less to observe what was actually happening at ground level.

Various tactics were used to remove the children. Parents agreeing to the scheme would not register their children on arrival at the theatre. A passing tram might shield a helper with a child from the view of the guards. Tiny children might be removed in a backpack. Deliberate miscounting of larger children in the crèche would be employed while two of them were removed via a back garden and taken to the college.

A network of helpers was required to escort the children to safety. One known helper was Piet Meerburg, a law student who founded the Amsterdam Student Group. He cooperated with other student groups to arrange hiding places for children in Utrecht and other provincial towns. About 140 children were saved this way from the crèche (and 200 more from other places).

Halverstad was a key figure in the rescue process. Simply deceiving the Nazi officers at the theatre was not enough: more had to be done to make the scheme work. Halverstad had contacts working in Fünten's Central Office for Jewish Emigration and was able to cover the tracks of the Süskind scheme by arranging for the removal or falsification of registration cards held there.

One rare SS lieutenant, horrified by the immorality of the deportation of children, actually cooperated with Süskind and Halverstad in the scheme.

Members of the *Verzet* would keep in touch with the foster-families who were hiding Jewish children. Coded messages were used. "Tea packets" were pale children who would be taken to the Friesland region. "Coffee packets" were darker children of more Mediterranean appearance who would be less noticeable in Limburg.

Although Gerhard could not be certain, perhaps the *Kaffeebohne* reference signified that Horst had not been captured, or (even better) that he had been spirited away to safety. Gerhard knew that such things were indeed possible.

In between the many demands on his time for his work in the PBC, he set out to discover what had happened to his nephew. He was equally concerned about his sister Erna. He was unable to contact her. She wasn't taken to the *Schouwburg*. She wasn't in Westerbork. Where was she?

49

Heading east

Westerbork Transit Camp, 9 March 1943

Obersturmbannführer Albert Konrad Gemmeker was a happy man, and why wouldn't he be? He'd been appointed to his new position as the *Kommandant* of the Westerbork *Durchgangslager* transit camp only a few months before, and he was enjoying the work. He ran the very complicated operation with clockwork precision. Fresh arrivals were delivered daily by train from Amsterdam, and his underlings processed them all efficiently. Exactly a week earlier, on 2 March, he had instituted the daily *Meldezettel* (registration form). A roll call was held every evening, when the day's arrivals and deaths in the camp hospital were recorded. On Tuesday evenings, the numbers who departed by train were also recorded. Next morning, the *Meldezettel* that told him the precise numbers was placed on his desk.

Several aspects of his life contributed to his expansive mood. He lived on the perimeter of the Westerbork grounds in a spacious, beautifully furnished two-storey mansion with an attic. He shared this home with his mistress, Elisabeth Helena Hassel-Müllender, a charming and attractive companion, and they regularly had good times together. He was on excellent social terms with *Haupsturmbannführer* Ferdinand Hugo aus der Fünten. Gemmeker recalled with delight the lavish banquet that his chief had arranged at Westerbork just before Christmas to celebrate his new position as the head of the transit camp.

The hospital clinic at Westerbork had been established in a barracks long before his arrival, but Gemmeker was proud of the way he had kept it running properly, even in these more difficult times. It was properly staffed: quite a few of the Westerbork inhabitants were doctors and nurses. He'd insisted to his superiors that it was important that his guests – he never referred to them as prisoners, or inmates – should be kept as comfortable as possible while in his care. Ferdinand had put in a good word and convinced his chief Willy Lages, the head of the *Sicherheitsdienst* (SD) in Amsterdam, that this was a sensible policy. Gemmeker liked to project an image of himself as a humane man, and expressed his view to his superiors that the clinic should be properly equipped. Lages, for his part, could not have cared less whether a Jew died of disease or gassing, but if it helped Gemmeker run an orderly camp, good luck to him. After the shambles at the camp caused by the incompetence of the two previous camp commandants, Gemmeker's smooth efficiency was a welcome change. If the medicine cost a bit more, well, that was immaterial; the money to pay for the camp was coming out of confiscated Jewish assets anyway.

Gemmeker's schedule on Tuesdays, and today was a Tuesday, included supervising the loading of passengers on to the trains that left Westerbork. He liked to get away from his desk and engage in this task personally. Here he could demonstrate his humanity to his guests in public. Occasionally, someone would approach him and tell him that a relative was too ill to travel on the train. Without hesitation, he would direct the sick relative to report to the clinic for treatment. He marvelled in the power he had to make such decisions, on the spot, without having to consult anyone else. He would then order one of his staff to select someone else to take up the vacant seat. Meeting the weekly Tuesday target was the only requirement.

He took great pride, too, in his extraordinary achievement in running the whole system so well. Each Wednesday morning, the *Meldezettel* would tell him how many of his guests had departed the previous day. He added the day's numbers to a running total which he recorded in a little notebook, and a smile crossed his face when he discovered that the previous week, the total had passed 50,000. A great milestone. He was doing important work.

To reach his current senior post in the SS, he had to demonstrate to his superiors that he shared the *Führer's* view that Jews were *Untermenschen*, inferior to Aryans, and parasites on the superior German society. Gemmeker had no trouble convincing them of this, as this was what he genuinely believed. But he saw no point in acting out these beliefs to the prisoners in the camp. His job was to move them out as fast as they came in, and he had reached the conclusion that the job could be done more efficiently with less trouble to himself and his underlings if he kept his real beliefs to himself and maintained a consistent outer mask of apparent decency. The Netherlands was now part of the Greater German Reich and his job was to clean it out. He was just the man to do it. He was going to do a better job than the two idiots previously in charge. The first lasted two months, the second only six weeks. This was no place for incompetent organisers or cruel drunkards.

He adopted a jolly tone, even laughing as he watched his guests climb aboard the train, cheerfully wishing them a safe journey and a happy future. Occasionally, someone would ask, "Where are we going?" and he would reply, with a smile, that they were going to a brand-new camp that had been set up especially for them in the east, where they would have the opportunities for work and new experiences. The reference to work was, admittedly, a falsehood, but the rest of it was perfectly true.

Hermann and Frieda Badrian had been informed the previous night that they would be leaving Westerbork by train next morning. They should pack all their belongings and make sure that their suitcases were properly labelled so that in case of a mix-up somewhere along the journey their belongings could be returned to them safely.

After breakfast, a contingent of *Grüne Polizei* shepherded the milling throng to the assembly area next to the waiting train. Hermann and Frieda, among the older group, married without children, were directed to the passenger carriages at the front. A few of the Dutch police hopped on board as the carriages began to fill.

As they shuffled forwards, Hermann observed Gemmeker at a distance. He seemed to be laughing. His body language was quite different from that of the SS ruffians who had "welcomed" them to the *Schouwburg* two weeks earlier. What an *Arschloch*, he thought to himself. One of Hermann's friends had told him that a week earlier, he had watched from a distance as Gemmeker had seen a young lad walking too close to the perimeter fence, which was against the rules. Gemmeker had pulled out his pistol and shot the boy dead.

No time to reflect on that now. They boarded the train. It was an ordinary passenger train; the carriages had rows of seats and windows and the travellers could stand up and move about. The same train had been used the previous week for its first trip to its current destination. But this second trip would also be its last: for all subsequent transports, Eichmann's controllers in Berlin decided that cattle cars would be used instead.

After half an hour, the train was fully loaded. The engine driver gave a blast on the horn, the locomotive slowly gathered speed and pulled away. The train passed through the open gateway at the perimeter fence and two Dutch police standing there on duty then closed and locked the gate.

Everyone was anxious, listless, confused. There was little talk. No one seemed to have much energy. Hours passed, and still more hours. Occasionally the train stopped. In the afternoon, one of the policemen opened the carriage door and passed baskets of food and drink to the passengers. Everyone had been reasonably well-fed at Westerbork, and these provisions were not too bad. Spirits lifted slightly as a result.

Hermann and Frieda didn't talk much either. They spent most of the time aimlessly looking out of the grubby carriage window, or were lost in their own worried thoughts about the immediate future. Frieda broke the silence at one point and quietly asked her husband the burning question that was on his mind, too: "Where are we going? What is going to happen to us and our family?"

Hermann turned to his wife and put his hand gently on her shoulder. They had already gone through difficult times together in the last few years. They'd experienced the growing oppression of the Jews in Germany. Their daughter's marriage had failed and the couple had divorced. Gerhard had emigrated to Brazil to see if he could make a life there for himself, and perhaps for them too, but that hadn't worked out. They'd left Beuthen five years earlier for what they thought was the safety of the Netherlands, and look how that had turned out. And now they were penniless, owning nothing beyond the contents of their suitcases and a few hundred guilders deposited in the LIRO bank. It had been two weeks since they had last seen their daughter and their little grandson, both hidden by a family who were friends of the Resistance. They had no idea whether they were still safe and the worry consumed both of them.

Hermann had always tried to speak honestly with his wife. He wouldn't pretend to knowledge that he didn't have, and he never attempted to promote a false sense of security. "I really don't know," he responded. "We know that Hitler wanted to force the Jews out of Germany, and thousands and thousands of our community left before the war. Gerhard told me that the Nazi plan is to do the same thing here. They want to eventually make the country into a purely Aryan state, all tall, blue-eyed and blond Germans."

"Just like brown-eyed, brown-haired Hitler," Frieda muttered. She hadn't lost her capacity for irony.

"Yes, and that means sending all the Dutch Jews and refugees like us somewhere else. But I really don't know where we're going. We were only in Westerbork for a few days, but other refugees in the camp who'd been there for a long time told me that life there wasn't too bad, and it didn't change much even after the Nazis took over the running of the camp. But now they just want all of us out. Perhaps they've been building large camps for the refugees in a non-Aryan country. But, my love, I really don't know."

Frieda accepted this. She loved her husband for the way he

responded to her worries with considered thought and honesty. Although they had faced many challenges together, they were still tough and resilient. Whatever the Nazis had planned for them, they would get through this next phase of their lives too.

Evening became night. The passengers dozed fitfully in their uncomfortable seats. Early next morning, the train stopped again at a small station. Hermann noticed a military truck parked next to a waiting room; he saw the contingent of Green Police walking towards it and getting on board. Perhaps, Hermann thought, their shift was over and, relieved, they would return to Westerbork.

He was right. But the relief shift weren't Dutch police. The replacements were SS men. What was going on?

The sun was rising and the train was heading towards it. Yes, they were indeed heading east. A second long day followed, and a second night. When would this journey ever end? The train passed though no major towns – just endless countryside, forests, grasslands and the occasional tiny farm house. Someone saw a sign from the moving train and told the others that he thought they were travelling through Poland. They had, in fact, travelled across the entire breadth of it, and when the train eventually came to stop, they were a mere five kilometres from Ukraine.

In the morning of the third day, the locomotive ground to a halt at a small station. A dilapidated little building displayed a single sign with the station's name. No one had ever heard of the place.

They had arrived at Sobibor.

50

Sobibor

Sobibor extermination camp, occupied Poland, March 1943

The train pulled to a stop next to a long platform. A large clock displayed the time, but it was a fake: the hands never moved. A large sign displayed a timetable listing arrival times and departures to various destinations. That too was a fake: the train returned empty to wherever Eichmann's team decided it was next needed. There were no other destinations; Sobibor was the end of the line.

This railway station was unlike any other the passengers had ever experienced. The new arrivals faced a welcoming committee of armed SS officers, some holding large dogs on a leash, and other guards. A string of baggage carts awaited them on the platform. The carriage doors were flung open and the passengers heard the SS men shouting *Raus! Raus! Put your baggage in the carts! You will be given a ticket to collect your baggage later! Men move towards the front of the train! Women stay behind!*

One old man in Hermann and Frieda's carriage, Fritz, who had been doubled up with pain, could not walk. Hermann spoke to one of the SS men about it, politely. "Yes, I understand," replied the SS man. "We have a wheelchair here and a nurse will accompany him to the hospital. Now, you and your woman, move!"

Tired and fearful, the procession began walking along a long straight path. Later, a side-path was sign-posted *"Klinik"*. At the rear of the shuffling mass of men, a woman dressed as a nurse accompanied old Fritz. A *Sonderkommando,* one of the prisoners (usually Jewish) whose lives might be spared for as long as they could do useful work, pushed him along in a rusty metal wheelchair. Ten minutes later, he arrived at the "clinic", a small building surrounded by a high fence. Fritz was wheeled inside. He was met by an SS officer who introduced himself as the camp doctor, and asked him what was wrong.

"I have this terrible pain in my stomach and I can hardly walk."

"Take your shoes and clothes off, lie down on the bed here and let me look at you."

Fritz did as he was ordered.

"Yes," said the SS "doctor". I see what's wrong and I'm going to give you an injection to take away the pain."

He did precisely that. The lethal injection took only a minute to work. Two *sonderkommandos* were called from the adjoining room, they removed Fritz's body and threw it into a large pit some distance from the "clinic".

In the meantime, the passengers had placed their baggage in the carts. They formed into a column and the men had begun to move forwards. Hermann looked around to try to understand what sort of a place this was. There were fences and trees that obscured the view. There was no sign of any large camp with numerous barracks, nothing resembling Westerbork. To the left of the platform was a collection of neat but plain one-storey buildings, with a more attractive building in the middle. Naturally no one knew what they were, but they were the living quarters of the camp commandant, the SS officers and the Ukrainian guards. No time to look, though, as the men were immediately prodded forwards and the path took a sudden sharp turn to the left. They entered a long straight building that led into a closed courtyard, with some shelters on two sides.

They were welcomed to the camp by a tall, graceful man, *Oberscharführer* Hermann Michel, the second-in-command of the camp. He wore a white coat, as he enjoyed masquerading as a doctor, although he had trained only as a nurse. Nevertheless, he had gained considerable relevant experience for his current posting, having previously worked in the euthanasia program in Germany, killing the incapacitated and the mentally defective.

Michel stood on a table so that everyone could see and hear him. He had a pleasant voice, and spoke to the assembled group of men calmly and politely. His associates nicknamed him "The Preacher".

"You are going to be sent to work in the Ukraine," he informed them. "But first, I have to tell you that unfortunately there are diseases spreading in this area. To prevent future outbreaks, our medical staff require all the new visitors to enter a Bath House and be showered with a disinfectant. So please undress and put your clothes together with any valuables in a neat bundle on the tables in the shelter behind me. An officer will then lead you to the Bath House. Afterwards you will be able to retrieve your clothing, get dressed and collect your baggage for the next part of your journey."

The naked men were then directed to the exit. Anyone seen wearing a watch or clutching jewellery was reminded that they could not take it into the Bath House. "Put it on the table near the exit. A guard will remain here to look after it for you."

Close to the exit, a narrow-gauge railway track ran parallel to another path. The path curved around to the right. It was called the *Himmelstrasse*, the Road to Heaven, but many of the SS nicknamed it the Snake Path because of its shape. None of the naked men ever knew either of those names. A minute later, the column reached a fork in the path. The men were directed to the left fork.

The women, waiting on the platform, began to move forward towards the front of the train. Ruth, an attractive young woman who had travelled in the front carriage, had stayed near Frieda. A well-built SS officer, Karl Ludwig, came up towards them, pointed at Ruth and ordered in a sharp voice, *Komm mit mier!* Ruth, too tired and dispirited to argue, followed orders and he led her to a side-path off the platform. Frieda knew that the girl had done nothing to disobey orders since alighting from the train, but was too lost in her own thoughts to intervene. She never saw Ruth again.

The women followed the men's routine, about half an hour later. Michel repeated his welcome speech about the Bath House and disinfectants and clothing and jewellery. And then he mentioned undressing. Undressing!! Frieda's mind was a confused mass of emotions. *Am I meant to undress in front of these men? What disgusting animals they are!* Nothing like this had ever happened to any of them before. Many of the women, even more profoundly shocked and frightened than they were before, began to weep.

And then, at the start of Snake Path, they were directed to the right fork and entered another long straight building where they suffered yet another indignity. They were told that because of the Bath House procedures, their hair was to be cut off. Two teenage boy *Sonderkommandos* ran amongst the naked women and sheared off their hair. Who were these boys, Frieda wondered, who were dashing about amongst the women cutting off hair? They were obviously expert at their job, but they didn't look too happy doing it.

The men were now well ahead of the women. After the fork, both sides of the Snake Path were enclosed by a 2.5 metre high fence made of barbed wire braided with pine branches. The men could see nothing. The few who could think about their situation at all were puzzled. At Westerbork, there had been 50 barracks to house the inhabitants. Yet at no stage since their arrival at Sobibor had they seen anything resembling dormitories. Where were they going to sleep tonight? But very few of the men had such thoughts.

Others along the walk detected a strange smell that pervaded the entire area. They couldn't identify its source or its composition ... burnt rotten meat? Smoke? Diesel fumes? But most of the men were too preoccupied with other concerns to notice.

At the end of the Snake Path, they reached The Tube, a dark tunnel that led straight to the Bath House. An SS man led them through it. A small team of Ukrainian guards followed to prod any stragglers along. When they reached the Bath House, the SS officer stood aside as the men entered. One of the guards then slammed the door shut and barred it.

Erich Bauer from Berlin, a 40-year-old World War I veteran and a dedicated Nazi, officially employed as a driver, was waiting nearby. He had a specific additional task to perform at the Bath House. Outside the building, a tank engine was mounted with its exhaust pipe passing through the wall into the chamber. It was Bauer's responsibility to turn the motor on and leave it running for ten minutes.

Inside the dimly lit room, the naked men were shivering with cold and fear. Within minutes, streams of exhaust gas began to fill the room. They began to gasp for breath. Some of the men soon realised that they were being suffocated. A few tried to mouth the words of the daily prayer which a devout Jew is supposed to recite if he knows that death is near. *Shema Yisroel, Adonai Eloheinu, Adonai Echod*, Hear, O Israel, the Lord our God, the Lord is One.

Carbon monoxide is a slow poison and it takes a few minutes to do its work. The men began to choke and scream and fall in a contorted mass of tangled bodies. Hermann's last thoughts as he lay dying were of his beloved Frieda and their children, Erna and Gerhard.

His special task done, Bauer switched off the motor.

51

The population register

Amsterdam, spring 1943

Most of the PBC's work was unobtrusive, engaging in activities that were entirely out of the public eye. Forgery was a quiet, secretive occupation, carried out in hidden rooms. The forgeries were good: if an SS officer were to stop an individual in the street at random to carry out a cursory check, the counterfeit would pass muster.

There was, however, a potential flaw in the system. If a suspicious character was stopped in the street and arrested, their credentials would be checked. The complete set of population records was stored in the *Bevolkingsregister*, a building in the Plantage Kerklaan, around the corner from the *Schouwburg*. If someone was carrying an ID that didn't match the details in the register, or if no such person existed in the records at all, the holder would be in serious trouble.

Gerrit van der Veen and his leadership team were aware of the problem. Gerhard was present at a meeting where they discussed a possible solution. One bright spark – literally a bright spark – suggested an imaginative solution. "Blow the place up! Destroy it! If there aren't any original records, the bastards won't be able to check anyone's ID!"

After the laughter in response to this fanciful suggestion died down, Gerrit smiled and said, "You know, that's not such a bad idea." The forgery group, a gentle group of men and women with a range of technical skills, had no experience of turning such a mad idea into reality, but these were not the only people in the *Verzet*. Gerrit also had links to CS-6, men (and occasionally, women) of action, who were not averse to violence.

What was most relevant, however, was that CS-6 had access to explosives. Gerrit quickly put his organised mind to work to plan an operation. The forgers wouldn't be needed for this operation. Neither would the assassins of CS-6. Gerrit had no moral qualms about killing evil men, but he would not countenance the murder of civilian officials who were just doing their required jobs.

Planning took a few weeks. It would be a night-time operation. CS-6 would provide the bombs. Gerrit began to assemble a team of men in the Resistance, 27 of them. A few would be dressed as Gestapo officers who would approach the guards on duty at the building and put them out of action. Gerrit contacted an Amsterdam tailor, Sjoerd Bakker, and asked him to make four Gestapo uniforms. For a night-time operation, they didn't have to be perfect, just near enough. The impersonators would have pistols to threaten the guards, but the guards would be temporarily disabled by injecting them with anaesthetic. For that part of the operation, Gerrit included some medical students in the team. The sleeping guards would be carried to a public park not far from the building so that they would not be harmed by debris from the exploding building.

Gerrit's planning for the attack, though mostly thorough, wasn't faultless. One originally planned date, 22 March, coincided with full moon. Not a good idea, he realised belatedly, and postponed the operation for a few days. On the new date, the wicks for the bombs had been left behind, so the operation started late as a result. Gerrit called his girlfriend Guusje Rübsaam to bring the wicks to the building by bicycle.

Gerrit instructed his colleague Gerben Wagenaar to contact his friends in the city's Fire Department. The *Verzet* knew that most of the firefighters were sympathetic to the Resistance. The brigade would of course have to respond to the alarm. They would do their job with complete attention to professional detail. The fire trucks would drive fast to the scene, but not too fast, to give the flames a bit more time to destroy the building. The men would carefully assess the scene before deciding to pour water on the flames. But first, smash the windows of the building! (To allow extra air in to keep the fire burning.) And afterwards, when the flames were extinguished, pour huge quantities of water on any surviving documents.

Despite everyone's best efforts, the operation was not very successful. The explosives were not powerful enough to blast open every steel storage cabinet, the fire not hot enough to demolish the building. Only a small proportion of the cards was destroyed. The action disrupted the Gestapo's procedures, but did not result in a knockout blow.

The Gestapo leadership was understandably livid. Security chief Willy Lages, after dealing with his immediate burst of rage, organised a special operations group of officers who spent weeks on a hunt for those responsible. Twelve members of the *Verzet* were rounded up, arrested and given the standard rapid trial. On 1 July, they were executed. Gerrit van der Veen and others went into hiding and were safe.

Gerhard was naturally disappointed with the results of the operation.

Arson attack at the National Population Register.

Weeks later, he was angry and grief-stricken when he learnt that half the team had been executed. He didn't know these brave men personally; it was standard practice to keep cells of *Verzet* members separate as much as possible. The Gestapo were known to use torture on captured prisoners in an attempt to extract the names of their colleagues. The less anyone knew, the safer it was for everyone else.

His emotions weren't long-lasting. This was wartime and there was important work to do, every day. Emotions had to be suppressed. Gerhard had his own personal feelings to deal with, having witnessed his parents being arrested by the Gestapo. He never heard from them again, and feared the worst. The whereabouts of his sister and nephew were, at the time, also unknown.

Gerhard also thought about the fact that the entire Dutch army, admittedly totally ill-prepared for the Wehrmacht onslaught, had surrendered in four days. The twelve brave men whose lives had been snuffed out were among the all-too-few who were upholding the honour of the Netherlands. They were soldiers, real soldiers, but unlike prisoners in a war between honourable armies, they were murdered instead of being sent to a POW camp. The thought made him determined that he would act in ways that would honour their memory.

52

Otto Treumann

After observing for several weeks that Gerhard was highly skilled and efficient in his work as a member of the team producing altered ID cards, Gerrit decided that it was time for his colleague to expand his range of skills.

"I'd like you to visit Otto Treumann at his studio. You've met him here once or twice, but as you know he doesn't work here. He has his own collection of specialist equipment. He also prefers to work quietly and undisturbed. I've asked him to teach you the art of producing fake Nazi documents."

Gerhard needed no explanation of why Otto should have an assistant. The demands on the PBC were growing in volume and complexity. Even if they weren't, there was the ever-present danger that Resistance members could be discovered and arrested. Every well-run organisation needed a contingency plan to deal with emergencies.

"That's fine with me, chief," Gerhard responded. "Where does he work?" Otto, following standard protocol strictly enforced by Gerrit, never told any of his PBC colleagues his cover name or his address. Otto had a false ID, pretending to be a German businessman running a commercial agency in Amsterdam. Gerrit kept no written list of the addresses and false IDs of any of the PBC personnel at PBC headquarters. He encouraged everyone to use nicknames at work. If the Gestapo captured someone and tortured him to extract information, the unfortunate victim could eventually state, truthfully, that his closest colleague was called Long John. Since the victim didn't know that Long John's real name was Hans van Gogh, the information would be of no use to the Gestapo. (In any case, Hans also had a fake ID.) Gerhard had several different nicknames – Albert, Bernhard and others – that he employed in different roles.

Next day, Gerhard visited Otto, whose studio was twenty minutes' walk from the PBC office. Gerhard also observed standard procedures to ensure that he wasn't being followed. It was a pleasant sunny afternoon, and he sometimes wished he could have just been a tourist in peace-time and enjoy the unique streetscapes of Amsterdam with its distinctive and picturesque houses overlooking the canals and bridges of the central city. He would have enjoyed photographing these scenes. His path took him along the north bank of the Amstel, across the river via the attractive Blauwbrug and then a few blocks westward along the Herengracht.

He knew this area well, as Marius Meijboom's business was in the neighbourhood. He'd once asked Marius why the bridge was called the Blue Bridge when it wasn't blue at all. Marius knew a little of the history of the area and explained the current large and impressive bridge replaced a small wooden one built in the seventeenth century. The original had been painted blue.

Gerhard's meeting with Otto was the first of several over the following weeks. They shared a common background: both were German Jews in hiding. Gerhard enjoyed these meetings, as he was able to have an intelligent conversation in fluent German with this educated younger man. They were both experts, in different ways, in the visual arts. Otto was an artist with a special interest in graphic design. His speciality before the war was to design logos for commercial companies. Both of them understood, without having to articulate it, the value of creativity and precise work.

Otto explained two major components of the work he was doing for the PBC. One was to compile a comprehensive collection of significant civic documents and logos. The other was to make precise counterfeit copies. Some were quite simple: a form authorising someone to own a bicycle, but one had to ensure the right type-font and forge the correct signature of the issuing official.

Over the course of a few meetings, Otto briefed Gerhard about the complex process of document forgery. He explained that others were also involved in the process: expert printers had to make plates based on his artwork. He showed Gerhard various samples of paper used in some of the more important documents and explained how to get in touch with the printers.

Otto, like Gerhard, was a humble man, but occasionally he delighted in showing off his skills "Look at this," he said to Gerhard. It was the signature of a high-ranking Nazi official. Then, picking up a pen and dipping it into a bottle of ink, he faithfully reproduced the Gestapo officer's signature with swift sweep of the pen. Gerhard was impressed. He didn't think he could do that himself, but he was willing to try. "Don't analyse it, don't copy it in bits," was Otto's advice. "Look at it intently, fix the image in your mind, and try writing it in a single continuous movement of the pen. As if you were signing your own name. And practise!"

53

The death of Erna

June 1943

Gerhard's initial attempts to find out what had happened to Erna and Horst proved fruitless. Enquiries through *Verzet* contacts who placed hidden children in safe houses, usually in outlying towns and rural areas, failed to find any trace of the boy. Gerhard knew that Horst had not been captured together with his grandparents as he himself had witnessed their arrest. It was possible that Horst had been captured somewhere else and then taken to the *Schouwburg*, but there was no evidence of that either.

It took many weeks for the facts to come to light, and for Erna, the outcome was tragic. She had been arrested at around the same time as her parents, but had not been taken to the *Schouwburg*. As a younger woman who might be of some temporary economic benefit to the regime, Erna was sent to Vught, where the Nazis had recently constructed a slave labour camp to imprison gypsies, homosexuals, political opponents and Jews. Some prisoners were forced to carry out hard physical labour. Erna was employed along with other women in a section that assembled radios and torches for the Philips company. Prisoners doing useful work were given slightly better rations.

The living conditions were appalling. Food was scarce, sleeping arrangements nightmarish, toilets foul. Many died of starvation or disease. For Jewish prisoners like Erna, Vught was merely a *Durchgangslager*, a temporary transit camp on the way to Westerbork and deportation. After three months in Vught, Erna was placed on a train late on 7 June and arrived early next morning, a Tuesday, at Westerbork. That was the day that trains departed each week for the extermination camps. After an uncomfortable overnight journey from Vught, she was hustled out of one train and shoved onto another that was about to depart.

Two days later, she arrived at Sobibor and followed exactly the same path to the Bath House that her mother had trodden three months earlier.

Gerhard's face turned ashen when he finally learnt what had happened to his sister. By now, despite the best efforts of the Nazis to suppress all information about the fate of deportees from Westerbork, members of the Resistance were well aware that deportation meant a train trip to death.

54

Horst in Westerbork

But where was his nephew? What had happened to Horst?

Westerbork was now a prison, but not a high security prison. People were reasonably well fed, there was no maltreatment of the longer term inhabitants, and except for the weekly departure of a large number of temporary residents, it continued to operate as a peaceful place for the remaining residents. The Dutch public servant, van As, continued to administer the camp, under the watchful eye of *Kommandant* Gemmeker.

Van As was such a competent administrator that Gemmeker kept him on after the Nazis took over control of the camp. Van As and his wife were unfailingly cooperative and deferential to Gemmeker, who had no idea that the Dutch civil servant was linked to the Resistance and did everything possible to save people, by insisting that they were doing vital work in the camp. The couple also helped people to escape.

A Jewish couple, Yehoshua and Hennie Birnbaum, had run the orphanage in Barrack 35 ever since it was established in pre-war days. Security was not tight. Messages could be sent to and from people inside. Children in the orphanage could even receive visitors.

Gerhard was able to connect with the Birnbaums, and this yielded the only good news about his nephew after three months of horror. Horst (who called himself Hans) was in the orphanage; he had been there since 8 June. Two transports of children from Vught had arrived that day and were immediately put on a departing train, but Horst was not. Hennie Birnbaum didn't know whether the boy had been in Vught or had come from somewhere else.

Gerhard, now fully aware of the Nazis' unlimited capacity for brutality, even towards children, wisely decided that Horst should be rescued from Westerbork as quickly as possible, and set to work on a plan. He would pretend to be a middle-ranking plainclothes senior investigator in the *Sicherheitsdienst*, not too senior – the Gestapo wouldn't be sending top brass to Westerbork just to remove a child – but senior enough to be able to order other people around without being challenged. He would pretend to be *Kriminaldirektor* Westerman, a rank something like a chief inspector, and prepared appropriate documentation to back up that story. He hadn't done anything like this before, but he thought that he could carry this off. He began to think like a playwright and worked on a script. The storyline would be that Horst should not have been admitted to Westerbork at all. It was all a terrible mistake. Some junior officers of the SD had captured a non-Jewish boy. The boy's parents were actually Franciscus and Maria Kerpen, a German couple, members of the Evangelic Church, living in Amsterdam. Sadly the father, a German businessman, had died recently. His widow, a loyal *Reichsdeutsche*, was not merely distraught, but rightly furious at the Gestapo for arresting her son. It was Westerman's task to rectify this plainly unsatisfactory situation.

Gerhard then prepared a small collection of counterfeit documents to support this story. After printing a fake German birth certificate issued by a provincial *Standesamt* in 1930, he rubbed a mixture of damp tea-leaves, grease and dirt on to the paper and folded it numerous times to give it an aged, well-used appearance.

In case of complications, he also constructed a fall-back story. Yes it was clearly the fault of his underlings at the SD, but surely the officials at Westerbork had a responsibility, too. Good thing, admittedly, that the boy hadn't been put on a departing train, but why was he even being held in the camp in the first place? Didn't anyone check? However, he wasn't here to make trouble, it was just his job to clean up this embarrassing mess as quickly as possible and return the boy to his mother. If everyone kept quiet about the whole business, he promised there would be no repercussions. He would see to it himself.

Gerhard put the plan into action. His contact was a truck driver who could deliver messages into the camp. A note to Hennie Birnbaum asked her to inform Horst that his uncle was coming to visit him, very soon. However, she was not to mention this to anyone. Horst was to be told about the impending visit but he also must not talk about it at all. When his uncle arrived in the orphanage, Horst was to pretend that he was a complete stranger. No signs of recognition, no greeting, no smiles, nothing. Just ignore him. Just do what he tells you.

The *Kriminaldirektor* parked his green Opel car carrying Wehrmacht numberplates outside the Westerbork gate, showed his SD pass to the Dutch policeman on duty, walked to the office of the administrator van As, who was entirely cordial and cooperative, even to the point of accompanying him as he visited the SS duty officer to repeat the story. Van As helped by sounding apologetic, agreeing that such a mistake should never have happened and thanked Westerman for his understanding. The SS officer showed little interest and knew better than to engage in unnecessary discussion with a senior SD man. *Befehl ist Befehl*, Orders are orders, had been drummed into him ever since he joined the service, and orders from a senior officer are to obeyed without question. He signed a voucher authorising the Kerpen boy to leave the camp.

Westerman was promptly accompanied to Barrack 35 and introduced to Hennie Birnbaum, whom he had never met before. He explained that he was here to take Horst Kerpen out of the orphanage. "This is Horst Kerpen," she said, "but he likes to be called Hans." The boy looked at his uncle in stony silence. "It's all right, boy, nothing to worry about, just behave yourself, you're coming with me." His tone was serious, but not aggressive, the voice of a competent professional just doing his job.

The two walked together in silence to the exit gate. Gerhard showed his SD ID and the boy's exit voucher. They boarded Gerhard's car and drove off.

And while the Westerbork records note Horst's admission to the camp on 8 June 1943, there is no record anywhere that he actually left the camp later that month. A few weeks after the event, van As surreptitiously visited the records room and removed the documents relating to his exit.

55

Peter Roelofs

PBC office, August 1943

Peter Roelofs normally dropped in to the PBC office regularly to assist with the production of forged documents and to be assigned other tasks by Gerrit. One day, he failed to turn up to a scheduled meeting, and all subsequent attempts to locate him were unsuccessful.

Gerrit called his leadership team together and directed each of them to find out what might have happened. "Gerhard, I want you to get in touch with your police contact and see if you can get any useful information from him." After briefing each of the others in the team, he ordered them to report back daily.

It took Gerhard two days to get a message to Cor Verbiest, and another few days for the detective to discover what had happened to Peter.

"Peter was arrested by the Gestapo two weeks ago," Gerhard informed Gerrit. "My police contact doesn't know what he's been accused of, but it can't be a major crime, otherwise he'd be in the big prison on the Weteringschans. He's being held in a cell in the South Amsterdam police station."

Another leadership meeting was called. "Any thoughts about what we might do?" Gerrit enquired of the team.

One member of the team suggested a guerrilla operation: call in CS-6, attack the police station in force and break him out of there.

"That might work," Gerhard commented, smiling – the others all recognised that this approach might have devastating consequences – "but I've had some thoughts about a rather different approach." He outlined what he had in mind, explained it would take him few days to plan it in detail. "I'll need one assistant, Long John here will do quite nicely for what I have in mind."

Gerrit was impressed and gave his blessing. No one could be sure that the plan would work, but most agreed it was worth a try.

56

SS Officer Werner

South Amsterdam, Thursday, 18 August 1943

The sun was still shining brightly on this summer evening as *Unterstürmführer* Werner, accompanied by a junior SS officer, parked his Opel car outside the small local police station in South Amsterdam and strode confidently inside. At the front desk, Werner, wearing an immaculate Gestapo uniform, introduced himself to the police captain, showed his ID card and announced, in a voice that brooked no argument, "You're holding a prisoner Roelofs here in custody. We're here to take this animal to headquarters in The Hague for further questioning. Here's the authorisation."

The police captain knew about Petrus Roelofs. He'd been arrested by the Gestapo a month earlier. The captain, not a Nazi, just a Dutch civilian doing his job, was aware that Roelofs wasn't a common criminal. As he'd been brought in by the Gestapo he assumed that Roelofs was in the *Verzet*. In the police station records, the duty officer at the time of the arrest had noted the Gestapo advice: "Be careful with this man – he'll do everything to try to escape." Well, the station had certainly done its job. He was still here, safely in custody, a month later.

The captain glanced at the Übernahmeschein document that Werner handed over. He'd seen similar documents on previous occasions. Signed by *Brigadeführer* Hanns Albin Rauter, the highest-ranking SS policeman in the Netherlands, it authorised the handover and appeared entirely in order.

The captain instructed a junior colleague to bring Roelofs from the cells. Roelofs saw the two Gestapo men in the foyer of the police station and stared at them with a sullen expression.

Werner approached him angrily and slapped him across the face. "*Schmutziges Schwein, kommst du mit uns an die Zentrale.*" The police captain winced as he observed this episode. While occasionally some prisoners deservedly had to be dealt with roughly, he disapproved of unnecessary violence, especially as Roelofs had done nothing to provoke this treatment. But he said nothing. He knew better than to argue with a senior Gestapo man, especially a brute like Werner. He watched silently as the two forced Roelofs out the door and bundled him into the back of their car.

The captain returned to his desk and duly wrote in the register:

> 18.40 hr. The prisoner W.P. Roelofs, waiting to be taken to the headquarters in The Hague, was collected by *Unterstürmführer* Werner and taken from this police station.

The car drove off, not to The Hague, but to a safe house in another Amsterdam suburb. The three men broke into joyous laughter at the way the whole episode had gone. Peter noticed that despite the joy of the occasion, Gerhard's hands were trembling as he steered the car, but made no comment. "My God," he thought to himself, "the man's probably shit-scared and he still managed to carry this off perfectly."

Later, at the safe house, they celebrated with a glass of beer. "Sorry I had to slap you, Peter," said Gerhard apologetically. "I hope I didn't hit you too hard. And well done for keeping a straight face when you first saw me at the desk."

"Quite okay," Peter replied as he downed his beer. He hadn't had a decent drink for a month. "But where did you get hold of the Gestapo uniforms? Yours is a first-rate piece of tailoring."

Long John, Gerhard's colleague Hans van Gogh, chipped in. "That's my department. My own uniform isn't perfect, but it's good enough for me to pass as a junior SS officer. I know a good tailor who has made a few of these that we use on various occasions. But Gerhard's is a real work of art, because it's genuine! We have a dry-cleaner who works with us. He does lots of business with the Gestapo. Today's Thursday. When a senior SS man brings his uniform in on a Wednesday evening to be cleaned, he's told it will be ready first thing Friday morning. It was actually cleaned straight away last night and I picked it up for today's little event. I'm taking it back to him right now and he'll clean it again so that it will be in perfect condition for his loyal customer tomorrow morning."

Peter had naturally not seen the Übernahmeschein document that was an even more important part in the ruse. Gerhard took quiet pleasure in the success of his handiwork. He'd compiled it himself, making use of one of the PBC's growing collection of Gestapo rubber stamps. The final touch was his forgery of Hanns Albin Rauter's signature. Gerhard's colleague Otto Treumann would probably have done a better job, but there wasn't time to get the paperwork to him. Gerhard was, however, satisfied with his own effort.

57

Gerhard at home

After the day's successful charade, Gerhard parked his car in a closed garage and removed the false numberplates. The two men then walked to PBC's headquarters wearing long coats to cover their Gestapo uniforms prior to changing back into ordinary clothes. Long John then took Gerhard's slightly sweaty uniform back to the drycleaner's.

Gerhard then headed home. The Nazi monster became a quite different man as he set out.

At a local florist, he would buy a flower to present to Anne-Marie with a kiss, signifying that all went well. They would celebrate the day's successful outcome with a glass of wine over dinner, but quite deliberately they would talk about many things totally unconnected to the war. The unspoken rule was that this was relaxation time, not a military debriefing session.

One of their pastimes after dinner was to read German poetry aloud to each other. They both appreciated the works of the German writer, Rainer Maria Rilke, especially his love of poetry. This was their way of building a peaceful cocoon around themselves, to focus on each other and shut out the horrors of the outside world.

For that evening's reading, Gerhard selected one of Anne-Marie's favourite poems, Rilke's *Slumber Song*.

> Some day, if I should ever lose you
> will you be able to go to sleep

without me softly whispering above you
like night air stirring in the linden tree?
Without my waking her and watching
and saying words as tender as eyelids
that come to rest weightlessly upon your breast,
upon your sleeping limbs, upon your lips?
Without my touching you and leaving you
alone with what is yours, like a summer garden
that is overflowing with masses
of Melissa and star anise?

And then they would slowly and gently undress each other and for a long and unmeasured time immerse themselves in each other before drifting off to sleep.

58

Groothand rescue

Amsterdam, autumn 1943

Gerrit patted Gerhard warmly on the back when he heard the good news of the Roelofs rescue. The episode differed dramatically from the routine daily work of the PBC. Forging IDs to protect people was important and satisfying work, but saving a colleague from the jaws of the Gestapo was something to get really excited about. "I remember you telling me about the *Köpenick* story from your boy-hood days," he told Gerhard, "and now it seems we have a real live modern version in our team. Great job!"

Gerrit had watched with enormous satisfaction the development of this man. Gerhard had always displayed considerable competence. He was normally a quiet, gentle man who worked unobtrusively in the background. Gerrit admitted to himself that he would never have predicted that in the space of a year, Gerhard would be able to adopt the persona of a brutal Gestapo officer. He had a unique combination of attributes that made him a rare acquisition to the PBC – the right age, build, German language – but now he was displaying something completely unexpected, a natural talent to act convincingly without ever having studied acting. The man seemed to be driven by a newly-found inner source of energy. Perhaps, thought Gerrit, burning inner rage at the loss of his parents had triggered something in Gerhard's brain.

Another opportunity arose soon afterwards to act again with a different script, different stage setting, different bit players but the same star performer. Johanna Groothand, who called herself Bob, had been arrested by the Gestapo. An important member of the *Verzet*, she arranged safe houses for people who needed protection: Jews, Resistance members and political opponents of the Nazis.

Like Peter Roelofs, the SS had imprisoned her in the cells of a suburban police station, a different one from the earlier Roelofs incarceration. Bob, like Peter, wasn't top-level Resistance. Had she been, she would have been held in the Weteringschans.

Gerhard had obtained some useful intelligence that generated a variation in the script. Cor Verbiest had told him that the station's police captain was a *Verzet* sympathiser. When the date for the rescue operation was set, the captain passed on a message to Bob: at a specified time in the early afternoon, Bob was to feign appendicitis and scream out in agony, clutching her stomach. The captain would call an ambulance and order a junior policeman to accompany her to the Wilhelmina *Gasthuis*, the city's major hospital.

59

Wilhelmina *Gasthuis*

Later that day

An hour later a senior *Sicherheitsdienst* officer accompanied by a junior colleague marched into the hospital entrance, presented his ID at the front desk and demanded to be taken immediately to see Bob Groothand. A nurse led them up the stairs to the ward where a uniformed policeman was seated next to a patient's bed.

Politieagent Hoedemaker was startled by the sudden unexpected appearance of the two men. The more senior man was properly turned out in the grey uniform of the SD, a neat cap with the Gestapo emblem firmly fixed on his head and a shiny black leather holster on his belt. "This is prisoner Groothand?" he demanded imperiously.

"Yes."

"What's she doing here?"

"She has appendicitis. She's going to have an operation."

"Oh, that's what you think, do you? Well, she's not. She's coming with us," he said as he handed the policeman a document. Hoedemaker was unfamiliar with situations like this but he wasn't about to argue. He glanced at the document. On the letterhead of the *Befehlshaber* of the SD in The Hague, it authorised *Sturmsscharführer* Bernhard Scharf to collect prisoners and bring them to headquarters. A photograph of the SD officer, overprinted with the rubber stamp of the Gestapo, was affixed to the bottom of the letter.

Without waiting for Hoedemaker to finish his inspection of the document, the SD man turned angrily to the patient in the bed. "*Schmutzige Schlampe!* Appendicitis? Nonsense! You're faking it!" [True!] Bob probably had a limited knowledge of German obscenities and was unaware that she'd been called a filthy slut. In any case, she showed no reaction, but stared at him with a cold expression.

The SD man held out his hand to retrieve the authorisation document, passed it to his junior accomplice and yanked Bob out of bed. The modern-day captain from *Köpenick* and his partner proceeded to frogmarch Bob, still wearing her white hospital gown, out of the ward, down the steps to the main entrance, pushed her into the car inconsiderately parked in the semi-circular driveway in a spot strictly reserved for medical staff and drove off.

But not towards The Hague. Bob, with her nightgown now covered with a rug, began to laugh when they were some distance from the hospital. "You know," she told Gerhard as his partner Ko den Hartogh sat beside her in the back seat, "at first I didn't recognise you, you both look so different in those uniforms. I was actually terrified for a while. But of course I knew that something else was going on."

They drove her back to her home in the Herengracht, which was still safe; she hadn't been arrested there. Soon she would be back in action in the *Verzet*. First, however, she would need a fresh set of clothes. The outfit she had worn that morning was hanging in a cupboard in the hospital. She didn't plan to go back to collect it.

60

The Groothand house

Amsterdam, July 1943–April 1944

After rescuing Horst from Westerbork, Gerhard did everything possible to keep his nephew safe. It wasn't easy: safe houses in Amsterdam were difficult to obtain and maintain. The Gestapo was continually looking for hidden Jews.

NSB members and Dutch collaborators were also always on the lookout for signs of hidden Jews. Some of the hunters were infused with the antisemitic ideology of the Nazis. Others, less driven by personal hatred of Jews, were keen to show their loyalty to the new masters running the country. Still others saw an economic opportunity. Earning 7.50 guilders for every Jew they uncovered, a quarter of a worker's monthly wage, was simply good business in these difficult times.

By the end of 1943 most of the Jewish population had already been deported, so finding the remnant still in hiding was challenging. The keener bounty hunters were still at work, looking for unfamiliar faces in a neighbourhood, reporting apartments being visited by unusual numbers of strangers.

Despite the difficulties, Horst remained successfully hidden. Two women, friends of the *Verzet*, hid the boy in their homes for a few weeks. Other solutions were less than ideal: short day-time stays in the offices of *Verzet* members, and even at one stage a brief stay in Frans Meijer's business office in the Amsteldijk, the PBC's headquarters. Sometimes Horst had to hide in a cupboard if there was an unexpected knock on the door.

The long-term solution was to find a safe house out in the quiet countryside, like the guesthouse out in the forest. Bob Groothand organised that sort of thing. People awaiting more permanent placement were housed temporarily in the Groothand sisters' apartment on the Herengracht.

The arrangement worked well.

Until it didn't.

61

Groningen

1942–44

Gerhard made several visits to the Groningen guesthouse during the war. There was always a good reason. Gerhard would be the courier who brought false IDs and counterfeit ration cards produced by the PBC. However, there were some side benefits. He could visit his foster-mother and her sister. He could also enjoy a much-needed short break in the country. For a few hours, he could just get away from it all.

Occasionally, Anne-Marie accompanied him. Groningen would always be associated in their minds with the memories of that unforgettable first night they spent there together. They called that time together their *Hochzeitsreise*, their honeymoon trip.

Cokkie and the Trio took care of increasing numbers of *illegaals* as the war dragged on. The group obtained seven additional houses in the neighbourhood to shelter and feed those in hiding. A local doctor provided medical care. Friendly farmers would occasionally donate some produce.

Money was needed to run this operation. Guests who could afford it paid their own way. The Trio had some funds available to assist. Cokkie was active in her local church, and secret collections would be made after services on Sunday mornings. She carefully avoided making any public announcements. One never knew whether or not the occasional stranger in the congregation might be an informant.

Cokkie relied on individuals whom she trusted to slip her an envelope when no one else was looking.

The Nazis never discovered the existence of the Trio. Altogether, 90 people were hidden under the Trio's care for various lengths of time during the war, of whom 72 survived.

62

Razzia

Amsterdam, March 1944

One early spring evening Gerhard was working in Marius Meijboom's studio on the Herengracht. He was expecting a visitor. The coded knock on the door confirmed the arrival of his friend and colleague, Dudok van Heel. His friends called him Jack.

"Come in, Jack, I've been expecting you. What have you got for me?"

Dudok took off his rucksack, took out a folded woollen pullover and undid the hidden compartment underneath containing his precious tiny Leica camera. It wasn't wise these days to walk around the streets of Amsterdam with a camera hanging around your neck. This wasn't a tourist city anymore. Someone might want to know what he was photographing and why.

Dudok was a member of the Hidden Camera group. The group kept busy documenting the actions and war crimes of the Nazi occupiers and their Dutch collaborators. Frequently, their cameras would be literally hidden inside a box with a hole, or concealed behind clothing. It wasn't quite the done thing to walk up to an SS man beating a man in the street and enquire whether he'd mind having his picture taken.

Gerhard's access to Marius' studio and darkroom allowed him to help by developing the pictures. Dudok told Gerhard that he didn't have to hide his camera earlier that day. "This morning I visited my in-laws in South Amsterdam," he explained. "I think you know their apartment, on the corner of Euterpestraat and Albrecht Durerstraat. I happened to be looking out the corner window, grabbed my camera and took a shot that I think you should see."

Gerhard picked up the camera, rewound the 35 mm film back into the cassette, took it to the darkroom, switched on the weak red light, then developed the film and hung it up to dry. He hadn't seen Dudok for a while, and the pair spent part of the evening in small talk as well as sharing information about more important events.

When the film was dry, Dudok identified the image that particularly interested him. Gerhard put the spool of film into the enlarger, wound the reel to find the chosen image and made a large print of it. He enjoyed this aspect of the work. It was quiet, relaxing. He could concentrate his mind entirely on what had to be done and forget about everything else while he was engaged in the task at hand.

The two men studied the image intensely. It was a very calm scene. No traffic. About 25 men and women were walking on the street. A quite separate, much smaller group of pedestrians – two men, two women and a boy were strolling sedately on the footpath behind, and well away from, the larger group.

"Give me a magnifying glass, Gerhard." One was found in a drawer in the studio, and the two men studied the image with great care. Dudok spoke first. "You can just see that the man on the left of the large group in the middle is a soldier and he has a gun. The other small group are just ordinary pedestrians, ambling along, taking no notice of what's happening in the street. What do you make of it?"

Gerhard didn't take long to respond. He knew the South Amsterdam area. "It's a *razzia*." (The Dutch had incorporated the Italian word for raid, round-up, mass arrest into their vocabulary.) "It's obvious where they're going. Gestapo headquarters is just two blocks away. Officially, the Nazis have declared the Netherlands *Judenrein*, free of Jews. This group is probably a collection of hidden Jews who've been discovered, perhaps betrayed by their neighbours.

They won't be processed at the *Schouwburg*, they'll go straight to Westerbork and from there on the next train to Poland."

Neither had to spell out to the other what would happen next.

Amsterdam street scene, 1944.

63

National Printing Works

Amsterdam, April 1944

Even though the productivity of the PBC had improved steadily since the group's inception, demand still exceeded supply. The stolen consignment of genuine watermarked paper used in making IDs helped, but the group required more.

Frits Boverhuis proposed a brilliant but challenging idea to his colleagues. The blank forms used to make genuine IDs were produced at the National Printing Works in The Hague. "The *Algemeene Landsdrukkerij* must hold a large stock of the watermarked paper. Why don't we just go in there and steal some?"

"Nice thought," Gerrit responded with a smile. His former career as a sculptor demanded creative thought as well as technical skill. He recognised this combination in others and he especially valued the contributions of those in his team who could think laterally. His colleagues knew that their chief was never one to quickly reject an idea on the grounds that it was outlandish, even crazy. "But I don't think we can just break in one night and steal the paper. I'm sure that it won't be lying around in boxes at the front entrance. The stocks are probably held in a very secure vault. How could we get around that?"

Gerhard chimed in with his contribution. By now he'd had several months experience of masquerading occasionally as a Gestapo officer. "I think we can do it without breaking in or busting into the vault. I'll go in as an SS officer, and Cor Verbiest can accompany me and show his detective badge. I'll work out a story that will force the director to open up the vault, and we'll take it from there. I know it sounds mad, but I really think we could manage it."

The group responded positively and spent some time discussing the details. A key component was the timing. Just before noon on a Saturday morning was considered ideal. Government offices then closed for the remainder of the weekend, most of the staff would go home, and they would have to deal with only a small number of key administration staff and guards prior to the building being locked up. It would take a few days to assemble the team, and then they were ready to go.

64

The raid in The Hague

The Hague, Saturday morning, 29 April 1944

The PBC group swung into action. Gerhard, in Gestapo uniform, drove from Amsterdam to The Hague, accompanied by Frans Meijer, in plain clothes but wearing an NSB badge. In the trunk of the car lay a bag containing 18 pistols. No violence was expected, but it was always sensible to be prepared. Events could turn out badly and they might have to shoot their way out to escape. The other team members arrived individually by train, made their way to a rendezvous to pick up a pistol, and then went to the neighbourhood of the printing works.

Frans and Gerhard arrived in The Hague much earlier than noon and sat in a deli to enjoy a light lunch. This happened to coincide with an Allied bombing raid on the city. Numerous bombs exploded in the neighbourhood, but the deli and the Printing Works were unaffected. At one point, however, Frans thought that he had eaten his last roll.

A few minutes before noon, everyone was in place. A group of five approached the building, led by *Hauptmann* Dietrich, resplendent in his Gestapo uniform. He was accompanied by Gerrit, Long John (Hans van Gogh) and Cor Verbiest, all in plain clothes. Frans Meijer chatted up the guard at the entrance, telling him that he needn't worry, this was just a routine police investigation. The remaining members of the contingent wandered around the neighbourhood, all keeping within sight of the building in case of trouble.

Gerhard entered the building with his colleagues and headed straight for the director's office. Cor showed the director his detective's badge. Gerhard got straight to the point. "You and your organisation have been engaging in some serious malpractice and you've been getting away with it for far too long." The director, not unexpectedly, began to protest, but Gerhard ignored this and told him to shut up. "We'll soon see. Just open up your vault. We want to inspect your stock of supplies and your accounting records from the past two years."

The director knew he had nothing to fear from such an inspection. He was a faithful and honest civil servant and had done nothing wrong during his administration. He wisely kept his thoughts about the Gestapo and its methods to himself and did as he was instructed. He opened up the vault, then pointed to the shelf containing the printing work's accounts and the packed boxes of various types of documents.

"Okay," Gerhard responded. "Take the director back to his office." Long John obeyed orders; he knew what to do. He took the now frightened director and tied him up with his hands behind his back. The raiding team readied themselves to carry out the booty. They found exactly what they wanted: five boxes, four reams to a box – a wonderful haul of 10,000 blank ID forms.

Gerhard looked in on the director as the team was about to leave. "You've got nothing to worry about. We're really not interested in your accounts, which I'm sure are in perfect order. We're just taking away your stock of blank ID cards." Gerhard stopped playing the role of a Gestapo officer and spoke to the director in a perfectly friendly tone. The director realised that he wasn't dealing with the Gestapo at all.

"I'm sorry about this," said Gerhard, "but you obviously will have to report it to the authorities, so we have to keep you tied up and put a gag in your mouth to stop you calling for help immediately."

"No, no, please don't do that!" The director was fearful again.

"There's no one around and I'll be tied up here until Monday morning. My wife will be terribly anxious and wonder what's happened to me if I don't come home this afternoon."

Gerhard thought about this for a moment, and quickly realised that the director was right. The Resistance was not in the business of tormenting innocent people. He put the gag away and untied the director's wrists. "All right," he said, "You'll go out the front door with us, behave normally and tell the guard that everything's okay. We'll take you with us for half an hour and drop you off somewhere, and then you can call the police and tell them whatever you like. And don't worry, we're not going to hurt you." As the other raiders carried out the boxes past the guard, Gerhard gave the man a happy smile and told him that they had to make some urgent deliveries.

They led the director to the Opel, set off for Amsterdam and released him in Leiden.

65

Raid in the Herengracht

Amsterdam, 30 April 1944

The *Sicherheitsdienst* had been compiling information about the Groothand sisters, Johanna (Bob), Maria and Rika, for some time. They had already arrested Bob once, and the head of the SD, Willy Lages, had exploded in fury when he learnt of her escape from the Wilhelmina hospital the previous year.

As tiny pieces of evidence began to mount up, the Nazis started to suspect the sisters of running a safe house. A building at Herengracht 522, a six-storey, brown-brick apartment block overlooking the canal that gave the street its name, was thought to be the site.

Hauptsturmführer Franz Tesch was good at his job. He'd been promoted to this rank after only five years in the service. He muttered to himself about the absurdity of the announcements made by his chiefs upstairs in the larger offices of Gestapo headquarters that the country was now Judenrein. If all the Jews have been cleaned out, he thought to himself – opinions like this, he knew, should not be voiced either up or down the chain of command – then why the hell are my men still going out on raids and finding dozens of these creatures? However, he approved wholeheartedly of rooting out the Resistance and their Dutch hangers-on who refused to obey clearly stated laws. They didn't deserve to be treated as proper Aryans. They had to be caught and dealt with. Thorns in the side had to be plucked out and discarded before they caused more pain.

Tesch assembled his men, briefed them about the residential area and the people to be arrested. He arranged for three carloads of officers to raid the Herengracht building and called for a closed truck to take away the prisoners. He asked his superior to contact police headquarters. A contingent of Dutch police should be placed around the block in case there were unknown escape routes. Anyone running away or acting suspiciously should be arrested.

Commissioner Voordewind received the request and acted promptly. He also informed Detective Verbiest that an SD operation was about to commence in the Herengracht.

Tesch told his men that he would personally take command of the operation and would decide on the spot where the prisoners would be taken. Resistance people such as the Groothands would be taken to Euterpestraat for questioning. Quite intense questioning, actually. He was good at that too, and took pleasure in extracting useful information from uncooperative people. Low-level captives, Jews and others, would be distributed to various police stations and dealt with the following day.

The operation was launched in the early evening. The men entered the building, knocked on doors. Some were opened, revealing a frightened householder and his family but no one else. Unanswered knocks resulted in the use of a battering ram, but revealed an empty apartment. After fifteen minutes of methodical searching, however, the operational objective was achieved. One apartment contained three rooms full of people, mostly women, a few men, and two boys. One of them was a thirteen-year-old, Horst Kerpen.

Rika Groothand was arrested. But Bob Groothand wasn't there. Although she had been back in action in the *Verzet* for many months after her rescue from the Wilhelmina hospital, Tesch didn't know – nobody in the Gestapo knew – that she was in fact already in custody. She had been arrested again in an earlier operation but was carrying a false (but perfectly forged) ID card.

One of the women caught in the *razzia* was Riete Gompertz, who was carrying false ID in the name of Rita Horvat. She was a young artist of mixed Jewish/Christian background and a member of the PBC. She had arrived at the Herengracht only half an hour before the raid.

She didn't see the boys again that night, as the captives were distributed to various police stations, but they were reunited at Amsterdam's main prison the next day. She noticed them and took an interest in their welfare, as far as that was possible.

66

Weteringschans

Amsterdam, Monday, 1 May 1944, morning

Cor Verbiest relayed the Herengracht news to Gerhard, who contacted Gerrit van der Veen. The detective had heard from sympathetic colleagues that the captives had been distributed to various suburban police stations overnight, but had been collected by Gestapo officers in the morning. A few had been taken to Euterpestraat for further questioning, while most had been transported straight away to the House of Detention, the high security prison on the Weteringschans. Cor thought that the Nazis had woken up to the various tricks that the *Verzet* had played to free Resistance members from captivity in police stations, and had tightened up their procedures as a result.

Cor thought that the Gestapo would have no reason to take a thirteen-year-old kid who was hidden in a safe house to headquarters for questioning, and assumed that Horst was now imprisoned in the Weteringschans. Gerhard agreed with this assessment. He met with Gerrit van der Veen to talk about what might be done.

Gerhard was deeply concerned about his nephew. Twice before, he had intervened to protect him, once by telling his sister to pull him out of the Jewish orphanage, and once by walking him out of Westerbork. Since then, Horst had been successfully hidden in temporary places, but the long-term solution hadn't been found in time. The Herengracht house was never intended as a long-term hideaway: it was just a halfway house on the way to somewhere more permanent.

His concern for Horst's safety hinged upon one crucial unknown. The boy was obviously not a member of the Resistance, and even if he had been, junior members of the Resistance were at most imprisoned, not executed. Children of his age didn't require ID cards and he wasn't pretending to be some else. Yes, he called himself Hans Kerpen rather than Horst, but that wasn't a capital offence. Gerhard had rescued him in Westerbork the previous year by "proving" a case of mistaken identity, that Horst was really the son of Christian parents. Immediately after that, he thought he might be able to protect him by giving him a document to carry, proving that Hans (a quite different boy) had been baptised in the Dutch Reformed Church prior to 1941. The document was easy to forge: ordinary paper, typescript and printing, with a forged signature. It would be very difficult to check as the boy's father, the real Hans, had never come to the Netherlands and his mother, Erna, was dead.

If this Protestant identity held up, Horst was likely to survive, but if the Gestapo ever discovered that it was a forgery and that Horst was really Jewish, then the boy was in great danger.

What to do now? He could hardly propose that Gerrit should mount a full-scale assault on the prison just to free his nephew. But he didn't need to. There had already been plans in place for months to storm the prison with the aim of releasing high-level members of the *Verzet* held there.

All the earlier plans had failed to materialise. One operation, almost ready to run, was abandoned when the PBC chief received intelligence that the Gestapo had possibly found out about the operation and were prepared to counter it.

Gerrit was naturally desperate to save his fellow members, as was Gerhard. Germany was losing the war and the Gestapo was becoming increasingly savage, if that were possible, frequently executing opponents within days of capture. Rescuing Gerhard's nephew was hardly at the front of the leader's mind, but if that could be achieved as well, it would be a bonus.

The plan had been worked out in detail. It was like a well-oiled machine, all the parts in place, fully fuelled, ready to go. All it needed was an operator to turn on the ignition.

The artistic sculptor turned Resistance leader was a man of decisive action, and a man of few words. "We go," he said to Gerhard. "Tonight."

67

Failure

House of Detention, Weteringschans, 1 May 1944, night

The *Huis van Bewaring* was a formidable fortress on the edge of one of Amsterdam's numerous watercourses. The nineteenth-century building was intended as a secure prison, but not for its current purpose of brutal suppression of innocent people and political opponents. The objective of the Dutch government during the previous century was certainly to incarcerate convicted criminals, but with the intention of rehabilitating them, not punishing them further.

The prison was built of solid stone. Climbing up into the building or breaching the walls were out of the question. A more devious plan was required.

The *Verzet* had borrowed a large van, belonging to a biscuit manufacturer. The green tarpaulin covering the frame over the goods tray carried the name of the company. It was reversed, so that only the plain green of the canvas was showing. It now resembled a Wehrmacht vehicle. Not perfect, but good enough at night.

Gerhard, dressed in an SS uniform, would head the incursion, part of a team of 28 men. A few of them would be armed Resistance members, dressed in German uniforms. Others, including a rag-tag bunch of tough-looking ruffians who had taken part in previous operations and were not averse to violent action if necessary, were to pretend to be newly arrested criminals being delivered to the prison.

A few of the group had arrived in their cars, which were parked in scattered locations some distance from the prison. Others came, individually, by tram. They then joined the team at the designated assembly point.

The prison guard on night duty at the large gate at the roadway entrance to the prison was known to be sympathetic to the Resistance. In any case, he was not required to do anything that would suggest he was cooperating. Gerhard would show him an authorisation document and order him to open the gate to let the new batch of prisoners inside. Architects' drawings of the layout of the prison had been obtained and rough pencil copies made and distributed to the team. It was known that once inside, the raiders would have easy access to the cells areas. Information obtained from previous inmates, low-level criminals who had served their sentences and had been released, had provided useful detail of where different classes of prisoners were housed. One area was for "enemies of the Reich", i.e. members of the Resistance; another had been designated as the Jewish section.

Gerhard did not know where Horst's cell was located. It could be anywhere: a special children's section? Together with the Herengracht captives taken the previous day? Or, if his Jewish origins had been exposed, in the Jewish section? In any case, the prime objective of the operation was to free the *Verzet* leaders. If all went well, and there was time, he would search for Horst.

The plan of action was simple. Rush past the administration area near the entrance to the prison, burst into the section containing the cells, point their guns at the guards and disable them, kill them only if necessary, force them to hand over the keys, release selected prisoners and race back out of the prison.

The operation failed. The team entered the prison as planned, and rushed to the cells. After that, chaos erupted. There was more surveillance than anticipated. German shepherd dogs were guarding the area, trained to be obedient to their masters but vicious to strangers. Advance intelligence had informed Gerrit about this obstacle, but he thought that it could be dealt with. In any case, the objective was so important that all risks had to be taken.

When one of the dogs began to growl and race towards the team, a *Verzet* member shot it dead. The shot alerted the other guards and the alarm was sounded. The team retreated quickly. Gerrit, who had been leading the team , was now at the rear of the pack. Two shots fired by a distant guard hit him in the back and he collapsed, unable to walk. Gerhard picked up his leader, hoisted him over his shoulder, struggled with him to the nearest *Verzet* car, and directed his colleague to take both of them to the nearest safe house, Henk van der Tweel's home on the Lijnbaansgracht. Gerhard then carried his severely wounded leader to the door. Almost out of breath, in his heavily German-accented Dutch, he told Henk, "Raid failed. Man wounded."

The PBC leader's active service was at an end. Although not mortally wounded, he was incapacitated. A *Verzet* doctor was called in, but nothing could be done to restore him to health. Strong pain-killers helped a bit, but the damage was inoperable. PBC colleagues visited Henk van der Tweel's home in the days following the failed raid. From his bed, Gerrit asked Gerhard, Frits Boverhuis and Frans Meijer to take over the leadership of the PBC.

The top brass at Euterpestraat were shocked at the audacity of the attempt to breach the prison and ordered their best investigators to find the leader of this troublesome Resistance group. It took them less than two weeks. Gerrit Van der Veen was arrested on 12 May and taken to headquarters for questioning, but, despite torture over the next four weeks, he steadily refused to reveal anything about his colleagues. On 10 June a "court" presided over by a Nazi judge found him guilty of treason against the state.

To prevent any attempts by *Verzet* colleagues to free him, he was taken on the same day to the beach sands facing the North Sea at Overveen, along with a group of other captured *Verzet* members. He asked two of his colleagues to hold him upright so that he could look directly into the faces of his enemies before he was shot. His PBC colleague, the printer Frans Duwaer, captured two days earlier, was executed at the same time.

The bodies were thrown into a previously dug mass grave and covered with sand.

68

The prisoner dispatch committee

Gestapo headquarters, Euterpestraat, Friday, 5 May 1944

Hauptsturmführer Viktor Lippert sat in his office at Euterpestraat with two junior colleagues for a meeting of his committee. The committee met as needed, but usually weekly. The frequency of meetings was determined by the number of new prisoners to be processed and dispatched.

The relatively young captain had been put in charge of this new committee by Willy Lages. Months earlier, the chief had become increasingly furious at the actions of *Verzet* members masquerading as Gestapo officers, releasing prisoners from suburban police stations and other places. Lages introduced several policy changes. One of them was not to hold prisoners in police stations for any length of time. "A day or two," he ordered, "and then pick them up and bring them to the Weteringschans. That won't give their Resistance scoundrel colleagues enough time to find out where they are." The unsuccessful raid a few days earlier had aroused his fury – the brazen behaviour of these *Verzet* criminals! – but at least it did vindicate his new policy. Not a single prisoner had escaped.

Changes in policy frequently lead to new consequences. The high-security prison was already rather crowded, and there weren't enough cells to house an unlimited number of new captives. What was needed was an efficient dispatch system, to move prisoners out at the same rate as they came in. Lages himself would decide what to do with top-level criminals. Any leader of a Resistance movement would be dealt with as in the past: kept in the jail for further questioning, under torture if necessary, then given a perfunctory trial and taken out and shot.

Most of the new prisoners each week were not at this level of criminality. All that was required was a dispatch procedure with a competent officer to assess each prisoner's record. Lippert was bright and capable, and Lages put him in charge. Serious criminals could continue to be held in the Weteringschans, or sent to a concentration camp or labour camp in Germany. Full Jews would, as in the past, be classified P (Priority), transported to Westerbork and deported to Auschwitz. Low-level criminality would receive an S (*strafgeval*) classification: punishment for criminal activity, which meant internment at Westerbork. Lages trusted Lippert to make the right decisions and invariably approved the committee's recommendations.

Lippert inspected the week's list. Several had come from the Tesch round-up at the Groothand safe house, but there were additional prisoners from smaller Gestapo operations.

"I think our work this morning is rather straightforward," Lippert told his men. "I can't see any top-level enemies on this list, but when we catch the men who planned Monday's raid that will be a different story." His colleagues nodded and smiled at the prospect.

"This Groothand woman who's been hiding numerous people at her home, that's a serious crime. Recommend her transfer to Ravensbrück? All right?" His junior colleagues hardly ever bothered to say anything. Lippert, they thought, was smart and made the right decisions.

Lippert then directed the committee's attention to the others captured at the Herengracht house. "Three full Jews here, according to their PK cards. Send to Westerbork, P classification?"

Among the remainder was the young woman named Rita Horvat. "*Mischling* ("half-Jew"), worked as a courier for the Resistance. Westerbork? S-classification?" The others agreed. (Rita Horvat wasn't her real name, she had false ID, and although her father was baptised as a Christian as a young man, his parents were Jewish, as was Rita's mother. Rita was therefore, according to Nazi law, a full Jew, and a candidate for deportation. But neither Lages nor Lippert knew that.)

Lippert commented on the unusual case of the two young boys. "No idea why they were in the house. No evidence that they're Jews. Parents weren't in the safe house. Maybe they are orphans and someone in the Resistance was looking after them. Well, they're not guilty of anything. We don't have to classify them as either P or S. Recommend placement in the orphanage at Westerbork, no punishment. Agreed?" Lippert liked to think of himself as a civilised man. He saw himself as an efficient civil servant, simply doing a job in accordance with established Nazi law.

They wrapped up the meeting quickly and the three of them headed for the staff canteen for some second-rate coffee and rather stale cake. Lippert then wrote his report of the meeting and passed it on to Lages' office.

Transport arrangements were someone else's responsibility. Most of the prisoners assessed by Lippert's committee were destined for Westerbork. The numbers were small. Trains were hardly needed for this trip any more. Prison vans were used instead. The next van was scheduled for the following week.

And so, on Tuesday 9 May, early in the morning, twenty of the Weteringschans inmates were peremptorily ordered out of their cells, led by armed guards to a waiting van and driven out of the city and through the countryside to Westerbork.

Rita Horvat sat close to the two young boys on board. The guards didn't seem to object to the prisoners talking to each other. She introduced herself, giving her (false ID) name as Rita and asked them for their names. Although they responded to this, they were clearly apprehensive and withdrawn. She tried to cheer them up a little by telling them that she had noticed them in the prison and saw that they were unhappy, but thought they had been very brave. She avoided asking them any personal questions but told them that she was an artist who liked to paint pictures of gardens and people and buildings. The boys were unresponsive. She was careful not to reveal too much about herself to other people, and was therefore not surprised to find others who acted in exactly the same way. Even children.

After two hours, the van arrived at Westerbork. Of all the passengers, Horst was the only one who had been there before. He still had memories of the weeks he had spent in the transit camp the previous year, especially of the day his uncle, pretending to be someone else, had taken him out. He remembered the young lady in charge of the orphanage – although he'd forgotten Hennie Birnbaum's name – telling him that he was to pretend that he didn't know his uncle, and just do whatever his uncle told him to. He didn't mention any of this to Rita or to anyone else. Horst had learnt to distrust people he didn't know, even if they seemed friendly.

Once again Horst was placed in the orphanage in Barack 35. He didn't recognise the older woman now in charge. The young woman who had cared for the children the previous year wasn't there anymore. Good, he thought, the fewer people who know I've been here before, the better. The thirteen-year-old boy had developed survival skills not usually needed in a normal world. But this was not a normal world.

69

The *Meldezettel*

Westerbork Durchgangslager, Wednesday, 7 June 1944

VERWALTUNG
STATISTISCHES BÜRO   DB 6

MELDEZETTEL Nr. 464
7. Juni 1944

	N.L.	A.L.
Lagerbestand 5. Juni 1944	2529	558

Zugänge:	N.L.	A.L.		
Transport	89			
Geburten	-		89	-
			2618	558
Abgänge:				
Transport	-			
Todesfälle	-			
Entlassungen	-			
Vermisste	1		1	-

Lagerbestand 6. Juni 1944	2617	558
Gesamt		-- 3175 --

Vermisste :

Korpon ,   Hans   19.10.30   stls.,prot.,gek. 9.5.44 aus
Bussum, Möklenburglaan 23 a

The *Meldezettel*.

It was an ordinary quiet Wednesday, like any other Wednesday at the transit camp, in fact like most days of the week, ever since the regular weekly Tuesday train departures had stopped. No need for them anymore, *Kommandant* Gemmeker mused, the country had been declared *Judenrein*. Not a single Jew left in all of the Netherlands! He chuckled quietly to himself, not at the wonder of this achievement, but because he knew perfectly well that this was big-noting *Pferdescheisse* put out by the top dogs in the Euterpestraat. Of course there were Jews still in the country, and he was still sending the occasional trainload out to the east. Some of these *Untermenschen* had miraculously avoided the round-ups and the arrests and the deportations, hidden away in all sorts of places, with the help of Dutch people who didn't know where their true loyalties ought to lie. But the bounty payment for turning in a Jew was still attractive, and the SD men were still on the job, ferreting out the last of these evasive people. His bosses just didn't want to admit that the claim of *Judenrein* wasn't actually true. He wondered if the chiefs had actually informed Berlin that they were turning up newly discovered Jews almost every day. Not my problem, Gemmeker thought, my job is to run the camp, as smoothly as ever. If others want to spread horseshit, that's their problem.

It was a bright sunny day, not much to do. He was at peace with the world.

Until he saw the daily *Meldezettel* on his desk.

The top lines were completely in order. Meldezettel No. 464 informed him that on 5 June there were 2529 Dutch and 558 Other prisoners in the camp. Yesterday 89 new prisoners, all Dutch, had been brought in, bringing the total of Dutch to 2618.

No transports out, no one died.

But then he exploded with fury as his eye reached the bottom of the page.

Vermisste: What? One person's gone missing? An escapee? Shit!

So the *Lagerbestand* was now 2617 Dutch, 558 Other, Total 3175.

And, of course, from the roll call, they know who it is!

Kerpen, Hans, born on 30 October 1930. Arrived 9 May. Stateless, Protestant, last known address Bussum, Meklenburglaan 23a.

A damned thirteen-year-old child! How the hell does a child manage to escape from my camp? (And if he'd known that this was the second time that this Kerpen boy had escaped and that he wasn't a Protestant but a 100 per cent Jew, he would have been not merely furious but apoplectic. But of course he couldn't have known that: Horst's first escape the previous year was never recorded as *vermisste*. The SS duty officer had given the boy a perfectly valid exit voucher, and as well van As had made the previous Kerpen file disappear from the camp records.)

And so, furious but not apoplectic, he shouted for two of his underlings to come at the double; he ordered them to put a team together to organise a search of the camp and make some enquiries.

Gemmeker of course couldn't have cared less about what happened to the boy. He just didn't like evidence of sloppy administration under his watch reaching HQ.

Perhaps he had not yet heard the news that on the previous day American and British troops had landed at Normandy. Had he known that and thought about its implications, he might have realised that perhaps there were more important things for him to worry about.

70

Herta Caan

Unterscharführer Alfried Flick didn't waste any time. He didn't think one person missing in a camp containing thousands was of any great importance. Although the lowly corporal was unaware of the Allied landings, he had heard on the grapevine that the Wehrmacht was gradually being crushed by the Soviets, and here was Gemmeker getting enraged over one shitty little kid missing from the camp? But not for him to reason why. He was entirely aware that if his chief was in a rage, then the matter had better be dealt with, or else. Gemmeker was definitely not a man to be crossed.

Flick headed straight for the records room in the administration office, marching straight past the chief public servant, van As, without giving him so much as a good morning greeting. He never understood why the administration of the camp had been left in the hands of a Dutchman who was not even a member of the NSB. In any case, members of the SS didn't have to be polite to the inhabitants of an occupied nation. He knew that the Dutch, officially, were being treated as if they were Aryans, but if that were really the case, why weren't all of the Dutch military incorporated into the Wehrmacht in 1940? (But he was just clever enough to keep that thought to himself.)

Flick looked up Kerpen's card in the records. Nothing much there: the kid had been in Westerbork for only a month. The corporal headed straight for the orphanage barracks. The middle-aged woman in charge confirmed that she was the one who had reported Kerpen missing, straight after last night's roll call, and had informed the administration office immediately.

"Yes, very good, you were doing your job well," Flick told her. "But do you remember the last time you saw him yesterday?"

"Actually, I do. It was early in the afternoon. He was in the corner of the barracks where the children can play inside. He was with a young woman who comes here a few times each week to read stories to some of the older children. The boy had a terrible headache, and she told me as she left the orphanage that she was taking him to the clinic."

"What was the woman's name?"

"Don't know her first name. The German children call her Fraulein Caan."

Flick thanked her and left. Immediate next stop: the clinic, to check the story. "Yes," said the nurse on duty, "I remember, a young woman came in with the Kerpen boy – I know him, I've seen him here before – he had a bad headache and I gave him two aspirin tablets in a glass of water and after a little while, they left."

"Did you see where they went?

"No, sorry, no idea."

Flick returned to the records room and extracted the Caan card. First name Herta. Arrested for helping the Resistance. Classified S. Small beer: Flick recognised the symbol for *strafgeval*, punishment, imprisonment for a minor offence. If she'd been a P for Priority, she would have been transported east on a train. (And if she'd been a really important *Verzet* member, she would not have been here at all – they would have just taken her to the beach and shot her.)

It took him a little while to track down her whereabouts in the camp.

"You're Herta Caan?"

"Yes."

"You know Hans Kerpen?"

"Yes. Why do you ask? Has something happened to him?"

"I'm asking the questions here, not you. Shut up. Did you see him yesterday?"

"Yes." (Herta knew exactly how to play this pompous idiot. She would answer his questions with no elaboration whatsoever.)

"When?"

"After lunch."

"Where?"

"In a room at the orphanage."

"What were you doing there?"

"Reading him a story."

"I'm told you left the orphanage together. Is that correct?"

"Yes."

"Why did you leave?"

"Hans had a terrible headache. I thought he should go to the clinic."

"Did you take him there?"

"Yes."

"What happened there?"

(What do think happened there, you idiot, she thought.) "They gave him some tablets and a glass of water."

"And then?"

"He swallowed the glass of water with the dissolved tablets."

Flick was becoming increasingly irritated with the woman, but couldn't understand why, because she was apparently answering his questions completely truthfully. "No! I meant afterwards." His voice now sharp.

"Sorry, I didn't understand your question. We left the clinic."

"Together?" Flick's voice was becoming more aggressive. He was getting nowhere.

"No. We parted at the clinic." Herta remained completely calm, at least on the outside.

"Where did you go?"

"Back to my barracks."

"Where did he go?" not quite shouting.

"I didn't see. He started walking off, and I headed to my barracks, in the opposite direction."

"Did he tell you where he was going?"

"No." (And, you fucking Nazi moron, thank you for not asking me the thousand-guilder question, did I know where he was going, saving me the trouble of having to lie with a straight face.)

Flick kept his report to Gemmeker brief and to the point. Kerpen was in the orphanage, was taken to the clinic by prisoner Caan. She returned to her barracks. The boy was not with her. No one had seen him after that.

71

The vegetable truck

The events of the previous day, Tuesday 6 June 1944

The vegetables for the camp were delivered in a truck driven by a Herbert Blau. Herta knew him personally: in the early wartime years they had worked together in a travel goods shop in Amsterdam.

Herbert's status as a driver was unusual. Most drivers who delivered goods were from outside the camp. They arrived with a full load, delivered their goods and left empty. Herbert, in contrast, left empty and returned full. The Blau family were inmates of Westerbork. Herbert couldn't use his unusual status to drive off and escape, because he knew perfectly well that his entire family's exemption from deportation depended on his reliable return each time with the vegetables.

But as diligent as he was in observing the rules of the camp, he also did whatever he could to help others. He was in touch with the *Verzet* and was one of the couriers who relayed messages to and from the camp. If Gerhard, one of his contacts, wanted to send a message to Herta, Herbert was the go-between.

And so, on an otherwise normal early summer's day in June, Herbert was standing next to his truck near the camp kitchen. He had just completed loading it up with empty crates and sacks, ready to drive out to the farmlands in the countryside and exchange them for a regular consignment of fresh vegetables to be delivered to the kitchen in the evening.

At 2.30 pm precisely, a teenage boy walked slowly towards the truck. Herbert was expecting him.

72

Preparing to be *Vermisste*

Earlier planning, May–June 1944

Of course Herta knew exactly where Horst was going, because his uncle Gerhard had begun planning this episode together with her ever since the boy was brought to Westerbork from the Weteringschans prison.

Van As, the Dutch camp administrator, was involved in passing coded messages from outside to the intended recipients inside. He was often able to do much more than this. It was possible to escape from Westerbork – the Kerpen escape was a classic case – and occasionally he could make checking up on missing people more difficult by removing their registration cards from the records room. He couldn't do that this time, because Gemmeker was already fully aware that a prisoner had escaped under his watch.

Gerhard and Herta had known each other for years, ever since they worked together in Marius Meijboom's studio. Later, they were colleagues in the *Verzet*. Following her capture by the Gestapo some months earlier, Gerhard had discovered through a mutual acquaintance that she was imprisoned in Westerbork.

Gerhard had been informed by Cor Verbiest that Horst had been taken to Westerbork, and this was confirmed by an exchange of messages with Herta via Herbert Blau. Gerhard had asked Herta to look after the boy. The plan to take Horst out of the camp was daring, yet relatively simple. Food supplies to the camp arrived by truck.

Some of the food suppliers and the truck owners and drivers were sympathetic to the Resistance. In the current episode, the driver was an insider. The Green Police guarding the gates gave the incoming supplies a cursory check, but seldom bothered to look at a familiar empty truck leaving the camp.

On Tuesday, 6 June, Herbert Blau's truck loaded with empty boxes and sacks would depart to pick up its regular load of vegetables at 2.30 pm. During the previous week, Herta had told Horst of his uncle's plan to rescue him. She took him for a walk around various parts of the camp, with special attention to the pathways between the orphanage, the clinic and the food delivery area. The plan would hardly be a complete surprise to Horst, as she knew the story of Gerhard's success in openly walking out of the camp with him the previous year. The same trick could hardly be used again.

In the early afternoon, Herta visited Horst in the orphanage and sat with him, read him a story and talked. He had been instructed to pretend he had a shocking headache – a bit of acting was required, but that was no problem for him at all – and Herta would take him to the clinic. If he was treated immediately, Herta would suggest that he lie down and rest quietly until he felt better. At 2.30 they would leave the clinic and Horst would walk by himself to the truck. Horst should check that there was no one there except the truck driver. A large empty crate had been arranged, Horst would get in, and Herbert would cover it with other crates and empty potato sacks.

Horst would then be delivered to a previously designated spot along Herbert's normal route, where he would be reunited with his uncle. The farmhouse of a potato grower sympathetic to the Resistance, off the main road, was a perfect location.

73

Moving headquarters

May 1944

Ever since 1942, the PBC's headquarters were located in Frans Meijer's office on the Amsteldijk. The place was owned by a German businessman who had leased it to Frans, who was a legitimate Dutch businessman. The owner naturally had no idea what was actually going on in the rented premises. Neither did the *Sicherheitsdienst.*

After the leader's arrest, it was standard procedure to move office. Even a Resistance leader with the utmost loyalty to his colleagues who would prefer death to revealing anything about his associates or their work, might crack under the combination of drugs and torture that the SD were known to employ.

Gerhard and his colleague Frits Boverhuis now formed the core of the PBC leadership group. They decided, after consulting with Frans, to move their operations immediately to Gerhard and Ann-Marie's apartment on the Vijzelstraat. Their landlord was Charly Hartog, who lived in another apartment in his own building. Charly was not a member of the *Verzet,* but was certainly supportive of its aims. He was one of a few thousand Dutch landlords who didn't care for the Nazis and were prepared to take people in to shelter them, no questions asked. Such people were among those who helped save perhaps a quarter of the Jews in the Netherlands. Despite what the Nazi top brass claimed, Amsterdam was certainly not *Judenrein.* Charly was a sociable man, on friendly terms with Gerhard (whom he knew under a cover name of Max), and would occasionally invite him up to his own apartment for drinks and a chat.

An unfortunate event occurred shortly after the move. A *Verzet* member in Gerhard's apartment was handling a pistol and it accidently discharged. No one was injured, but a bullet was fired into the ceiling. Gerhard was immediately concerned: perhaps someone had heard the shot and reported it to the authorities.

Gerhard promptly contacted Commissioner Voordewind who asked Cor Verbiest to investigate. The policeman showed his badge to the lady of the house in the top-floor apartment immediately above Gerhard's. He gave her a cover story to mask his real interest, telling her that there had been a complaint about lights being seen emanating from one of the apartments in the building. "Oh, no," the woman replied. "We know about the blackout and are very careful." She showed him around the apartment and pointed to the heavy curtain that could be pulled across to cover the window. Cor nodded appreciatively, commending her for her excellent cooperation, while all the while checking the floor for a bullet hole. There was none.

"Maybe it was the apartment downstairs?" he ventured. "No, no," the lady responded. "That's just an office and there's no one there in the evenings."

The Commissioner passed on the all-clear message. But Gerhard was not completely convinced. Quite apart from the pistol shot episode, Gerhard and Anne-Marie's Vijzelstraat apartment was quite small. In view of Gerrit van der Veen's arrest, Gerhard considered that the Amsteldijk office might no longer be secure and argued that a new venue be found, large enough to house all of the PBC's equipment. Frits Boverhuis agreed.

74

Dries Riphagen

Amsterdam, 1944

Since the entire Nazi regime comprised a sophisticated criminal organisation with finely-honed skills in the arts of mass murder and swindling, it comes as no surprise to learn that the administration was delighted to utilise the skills of clever professional crooks, provided they had the proper attitude to their work.

Bernard Andreas Riphagen, commonly called Dries, but nicknamed Al Capone by his gangster cronies, had all the right qualifications.

A handsome man in his mid-thirties, with a smooth, clean-cut face, eminently suited to his work as a con man, he'd been a seaman in his teenage years and had spent two years in the US working for Standard Oil. On returning to the Netherlands as a young adult, he quickly acquired a criminal record. Antagonism to the current social order coupled with fervent antisemitism drew him to join a Dutch Nazi group that hoped to turn the nation into a province of the German Reich.

His combination of professional skill and the right ideological outlook made him a perfect fit for employment in the *Devisenschutzkommando*. By 1944, three-quarters of the Jewish population were already dead, and so most of the DSK's asset stripping had already been achieved. Prior to their deportation from Westerbork, Jews had been required to deposit their liquid assets in the LIRO bank and park their jewellery in safety deposit boxes "for safe-keeping". Home owners were required to lock up their houses and hand in the keys to a local police station. Not long afterwards, some DSK low-life would collect the keys and strip the homes of their furniture and artworks. The houses could then be sold.

Despite the *Judenrein* claim, the Nazis were actually well aware that quite a few Jews were being rather difficult, deliberately disobedient, in fact. They were hiding, presumably holding onto assets that properly belonged to the German Reich. Stripping them of their assets was all perfectly legal, of course, since all of these recalcitrants were, by definition, enemies of the Reich.

Which is where Riphagen and his cronies came in. Their mission was simply defined: smoke these people out of their hidey-holes, and fleece them. The job came with automatic bonuses. On top of his generous salary as a middle-ranking SS man, his superiors would have no serious objection if he kept the odd banknote or a few pieces of hidden jewellery for himself. Dries would actually keep more than the occasional 20-guilder note or gold ring. His ethical standards were quite flexible. He was an equal-opportunity crook who would happily fleece Nazis as well as Jews. His masters had no way of knowing how much booty had actually been collected. On top of that haul, there was the standard bounty for every captured Jew handed over to the more brutal sections of the SS. Increased bounties were paid for capturing someone important. What happened to them after that wasn't his concern, of course. He was just doing clean economic work. A form of tax collection, really.

What a wonderful job he had, where he could use his highly trained abilities as a gangster with the full support of the government!

He didn't have to do all this by himself. He had a team of junior workers to help him.

One of them was a young woman named Betje Wery. Over a couple of beers in a hotel bar he talked about her with one of his SS colleagues. Dries offered his opinion that she was a rather hot little number. "I'd be very careful if I were you," the colleague replied. "I hear on the grapevine that she's Willy Lages' current mistress. It mightn't be too good for your health to upset our *Sturmbannführer*."

75

Betje Wery

Amsterdam, 1943

Betje Wery was born in Rotterdam. After her school years, she worked as a nurse for a few months in 1939. She proved inept, and was sacked. Soon afterwards, she was caught shoplifting and given a short jail sentence. Later she found work as a shop assistant in a shoe store.

In 1941 she married a man who was a sales representative – a drunkard and a womaniser who later became involved in foreign currency dealing without the permission of the authorities.

He was also a Catholic, and to marry him, Betje converted to Catholicism. Neither of them cared a whit about matters of religion and faith. In a normal society, the conversion and marriage would have been unremarkable events.

But given the time and the place and the circumstances, Betje's conversion was quite remarkable. She was Jewish. Her mother was Jewish and her father was not, but he had one Jewish parent. Whether she was now Catholic, or Jewish, or three-quarters Jewish, or half-Jewish all depended on whose definition one adopted. Such obsession with word meanings was entirely irrelevant in the context of a country under Nazi control. The Nazis had their own lexicon for defining who was a Jew. A "full Jew" was anyone with three or four Jewish grandparents. In the 1941 Dutch census conducted by the

Nazis, Betje was counted as one of the 136,000 full Jews who would be marked for extermination.

When the Nazis introduced the compulsory wearing of yellow stars, Betje didn't give the edict a second thought. She was Catholic, nothing to worry about. In August 1942, however, the Nazis gave her something to worry about: they arrested her after she was caught not wearing the prescribed yellow star. She was immediately sent to a prison camp at Amersfoort.

Fortunately, her husband was not completely useless. He had an influential German relative who managed to convince the authorities, if not with the power of logic then perhaps with the aid of a substantial bribe, that she was only half-Jewish. This actually worked, and poor Betje was released and granted a *Sperre*, an exemption certificate. She was promptly released from prison and was not required to wear a yellow star. Given the granting of the *Sperre*, and her marriage to a non-Jew, this would have saved her from the threat of deportation.

Life might have proceeded fairly smoothly after that, except that in 1943 both she and her husband were found to be engaging in unauthorised financial dealings and diamond trafficking. Around that time, he had a fatal car accident, leaving the poor young widow to face criminal charges.

The normal chain of events in a civilised society would have been for her to be put on trial and, if found guilty, handed a sentence of a stiff fine or a period in jail. But this was not a civilised society and Betje Wery wasn't a normal Dutch criminal.

The Gestapo looked at her record and passed the information upstairs to the highest echelons of Euterpestraat. *Sturmbannführer* Willy Lages decided that she was more than a half-Jew after all, and took a personal interest in handling her case. (Later, he took a personal interest in handling her as well.)

He directed his senior staff to keep her imprisoned for a few days and to indicate to her that because of her criminal behaviour, her

Sperre was to be revoked. She would then be taken to Westerbork, put on the next train and deported to the east. "Let her think about that for a few days," he ordered.

This was followed by the masterstroke, the making of an offer that she couldn't refuse. "Talk gently to her," was Lages' next directive. "Tell her that she can stay out of jail and go free if she'll do some work for us. Nothing messy, just fundraising work, really. I'm sure she'll agree, she's not completely stupid. This Jewish bitch could actually be a real asset. Then take her out and introduce her to Riphagen. But tell Riphagen to keep an eye on her. She'll probably be too scared to put a foot wrong, but you never know."

Riphagen and his new apprentice made an unlikely pair. Had they both been honest workers in a democratic society, they might have built a successful career as undercover agents working for a government tax office, searching for smugglers, money launderers and tax avoiders. Except that in an honest society, such civil servants' salaries are well below what Riphagen was earning by skimming seized valuables intended for the Nazi coffers.

Early in 1944, Riphagen set Wery up in a comfortable vacant apartment in Rubensstraat in South Amsterdam. The building was on the corner of Euterpestraat, diagonally opposite Gestapo headquarters. There she would host a gambling club, running roulette evenings in the apartment, and spend her days roaming around the city, chatting up wealthy-looking men in hotel bars or infiltrating private parties, and issuing invitations to join her secret club. Riphagen's instructions were quite simple. "Just be the charming hostess," he told her. "Keep your eyes open and look for men who seem to have plenty of cash to spend. Don't do anything, or say anything to them – just keep me informed."

He told her to use a consistent cover name. She should call herself Bella. If someone asked about her surname, she should add the name of her dear departed husband. She would be Bella Tuerlings.

76

Two-way cat and mouse

Vijzelstraat, Amsterdam, May 1944

Bella Tuerlings was just doing her assigned job, following Dries Riphagen's instructions to move around, meet people and look for shady characters who might have undeclared barrels of money stashed away that properly belonged to the authorities.

One of her acquaintances was Charly Hartog, who lived in an apartment in the Vijzelstraat. She had mentioned his name to Riphagen and told him that she was planning to visit him that evening. Riphagen told her to go ahead – the more people she met at random, the better.

The Vijzelstraat house was a small narrow building with a shop at street level, and two storeys of tiny apartments above. Each front apartment had a window overlooking the narrow street. The building was topped by a gable roof, with a traditional opening at attic level containing a pulley wheel to allow heavy goods to be lifted or lowered. Charly owned the building and made a modest living by renting out the shop and the other apartments. Bella didn't suspect Charly of anything; he didn't look like a man who flashed money around. But Charly had friends, and in her job, Bella never knew when she might just meet one of Charly's rich friends, invite him to her regular roulette games and pass the name on to Dries. Just doing her job.

One evening, she dropped in unannounced on Charly, who

invited her in to his apartment. He just happened to have a few people visiting at the time, but that's okay, come on in and meet them, come in for some tea and cake. Charly was a sociable man and he was pleased to welcome this rather stunning young woman and include her in his circle of friends. Bella accepted the invitation without hesitation. She was sociable, too.

One of the guests was a quite distinguished-looking German man, late thirties, balding, introduced to her as Max Albers. They talked a little, but neither of them gave away much about themselves. As the guests began to leave, Max asked her where she lived and how she was getting home. She told him she lived in south Amsterdam, and that she would walk and take a couple of tram rides.

"Look," Max said, "it's a bit late and the streets at night aren't always safe. My car's just outside and it's only a few minutes' drive. I'll take you home."

A man with a car, she thought. Who is able to afford a car these days? She accepted gratefully and graciously. Her puzzlement deepened when she saw the car, a German Opel. And she became completely confused when she saw that in a tray underneath the dashboard, Max had a pistol. This worried her. Who was this man?

She need not have been frightened. Max dropped Bella off outside her apartment, watched as she entered the building, turned the car around and drove back to the Vijzelstraat.

Bella's first thoughts were that Max was a plainclothes SS man. Had he perhaps been sent there in advance by Riphagen to keep an eye on her, check that she was doing good work?

But she wasn't sure about this. Something about Max was still puzzling as she visited Vijzelstraat a few times in the next couple of weeks on the off-chance they might meet again. On two occasions they did. Riphagen, for his part, was keeping an eye on her (following Willy Lages' directive to the letter) and had her followed. He wondered why she was going there so frequently.

Eventually, after another conversation with Max, she decided that he wasn't in the SS. So who was this German? He didn't seem to be the owner of a local business or an employee with a steady job; he didn't seem to be a wealthy criminal with money to burn. So how does a guy like this get to drive around in a car and own a pistol?

She had a thought. Maybe he's in the Resistance? Maybe he's a German Jew in hiding?

A few months with Riphagen had taught her much about the arts of the confidence trickster. Her schooling in Rotterdam hadn't taught her much of practical value, but being married to a drunken, womanising crook had given her some useful basic education, and the more sophisticated Riphagen had provided advanced professional development.

She decided on a risky course of action, with a fall-back procedure in case it went wrong.

She would tell Max that she was Jewish, and in hiding, and was desperate to get out of the country. Did he know of anyone who could help her?

And if it all went wrong, and news of it got back to Riphagen, she would assure her boss that it was nothing more than a ploy to discover who the guy really was. She was playing cat-and-mouse with both men.

The ploy worked. Max could indeed help her, provide her with some false ID and put her in touch with a group that would hide her somewhere else for a few weeks while more complex arrangements were made to take her out of the country.

And then a final touch. Who knows who suggested it? Did she suggest it to him, or did he suggest it to her? That flat in South Amsterdam. It will be vacant. Possible place for Max to move in with his girlfriend?

Bella, Betje Wery, was not actually trying to flee. She was loyal to her masters. She reported everything truthfully to Riphagen, who did his duty as a devoted Nazi criminal and informed the SD. It would have done his reputation in the Nazi hierarchy a power of good. And so the trap was laid.

77

The ending

Amsterdam, 30 June 1944

A small café in the heart of the city. Lunchtime. Five people are sitting around a table. One of the five, Gerhard Badrian, has invited the others. He's a man in his late thirties, medium height, well built, distinguished in appearance, and slightly balding despite his relatively young age. Next to him is Anne-Marie Deij, an attractive woman in her late twenties; they have been a couple for the past two years. The others are two of Gerhard's close associates, Frans Meijer and Frits Boverhuis, and another striking young woman, Bella Tuerlings, a more recent acquaintance.

Although there is not much to be cheerful about in wartime Amsterdam, the group is in good spirits. The Germans are heading for defeat. The Russians are pushing steadily towards eastern Germany and the Americans and Canadians are advancing through parts of the Netherlands. But the main reason for the happy frame of mind is that Gerhard and Anne-Marie have been looking for a new place to live, as their existing apartment is no longer suitable. Their new-found friend Bella has offered them hers. She says she won't be needing it any more, as she's about to flee the country with false papers. Straight after lunch, they intend to inspect Bella's apartment.

It's time to go. Gerhard pays the bill. Frans excuses himself, saying he has to leave. Bella flashes a warm smile. "Oh, come along, you should see my apartment too!"

"Thanks, but no," Frans replies, "I'm off to get a haircut, and anyway, Gerhard's car's too small to fit the five of us comfortably."

The four of them drive the short distance to South Amsterdam, to an apartment block on the corner of Rubensstraat and Euterpestraat. A large, dark-grey building diagonally opposite the brown-brick apartment block was once a girls' secondary school before the occupation, but no longer serves that purpose.

Euterpestraat, South Amsterdam

The building on the right, a girls' secondary school before the war, was requisitioned by the Nazis and served as the Amsterdam headquarters of the Gestapo. The cross-street in the foreground is Rubensstraat. Betje Wery's apartment was diagonally opposite the Gestapo building.

Gerhard parks the car, a German-made Opel. It's not too hard to find a spot. Traffic is light in wartime Amsterdam. Few people can afford a car or the petrol to run one. The four of them emerge. Bella leads the group up a flight of steps to the first floor, and invites them all in.

The apartment isn't empty. There are men inside: SS – *Schutzstaffel* – the Nazis' surveillance and terror organisation. Within seconds, Gerhard sums up the situation. It's an ambush. He pulls out his pistol and shoots one of the men, who falls, critically injured. Anne-Marie and Frits are arrested. Gerhard is quick. He runs out of the apartment and leaps down the stairs to the street. But as quick as he is, the SS has planned this operation. Other SS men are covering the street. One of them shoots Gerhard dead as he reaches the footpath.

This is a major triumph for the SS. Berlin is quickly informed of the successful elimination of one of the leaders of the *Verzet*, the Dutch Resistance, in Amsterdam.

A van comes by to take the body away. It's 30 June 1944. This was the day that Gerhard Badrian died.

Aftermath

78

End of a life, not of a story

No man is an island,
Entire of itself,
Every man is a piece of the continent,
A part of the main.
If a clod be washed away by the sea,
Europe is the less.
As well as if a promontory were
As well as if a manor of thy friend's
Or of thine own were:
Any man's death diminishes me,
Because I am involved in mankind,
And therefore never send to know for whom the bell tolls;
It tolls for thee.

– **John Donne,** from *Devotions upon Emergent Occasions* (1624)

A man lies dead on an Amsterdam street. That is the end of his existence. Unmarried, without descendants, that is the point where a leaf representing the intersections of the family trees of his parents, grandparents and his countless ancestors falls from the tree.

But the end of his existence is not the end of his story. His life and his death had consequences. Some occurred within hours, others only after days, months, years, decades. No man is an island, wrote the Elizabethan poet John Donne. The metaphorical island of Donne's poem refers to a person's physical existence and his relationships to other people. The island might also be considered as an island in time, allowing us to relate the man's existence to events in his society that occurred later, sometimes much later.

This is the story of the aftermath.

79

Immediate consequences

Rubensstraat, 30 June 1944

Frits Boverhuis and Anne-Marie Deij are arrested in Betje Wery's apartment. Frits, who together with Gerhard is the joint leader of the PBC group, is executed soon afterwards. Anne-Marie is briefly imprisoned in the Weteringschans and then deported to Ravensbrück, the women's concentration camp in Germany, 90 kilometres north of Berlin. She survives the war and returns to the Netherlands.

Frans Meijer, neatly trimmed after his haircut, notices numerous SS vehicles rushing around the neighbourhood and senses catastrophe. One of them contains Gerhard's landlord, Charly Hartog. He has been arrested. He is later found guilty of harbouring a Jewish "terrorist" and is executed.

Gerhard's body is taken in a van to the Wilhelmina *Gasthuis*, From the hospital, it is transferred to the Driehuis-Westerfeld crematorium. The ashes are placed in an urn, numbered 16001NN. The urn is taken to the Velsen police station, near Haarlem. Police Captain Spannenburg, the officer in charge, is a member of the NSB. He has thoughts about displaying the urn with a sign, proudly announcing "This is what happens to terrorists", but has second thoughts about that. He eventually decides simply to keep the urn in his office as a souvenir.

Wilhelmina *Gasthuis*, Amsterdam.

80

Two dead Nazis, one in combat, one by friendly fire

Amsterdam, July 1944

SS Officer Joseph Heinen, shot at the Rubensstraat apartment, dies of his wounds. He is probably the only person that Gerhard has ever killed.

Inspector Hermann Radke leads a raid at night of an apartment building suspected of being the office of the PBC. Gestapo officers living in the building become aware of a disturbance, unaware that it is a Gestapo raid, and assume it is a Resistance operation. They burst into the apartment and shoot Radke dead. He is accorded a funeral service with full military honours, held in the Amsterdam concert hall.

81

The SD discover the PBC office

Amsterdam, 12 July 1944

It doesn't take long for the SD to find the PBC's resources and compile a report in which they gloat over the triumph.

```
Der seit langem als führender Terrorist bekannte, emigrierte
Jude Gerhard  B a d r i a n, der unter den Decknamen "A L-
B E R T, A l f r e d, H a n s, M a x und B e r n a r d" als
Nachfolger des kürzlich zum Tode verurteilten Gerrit van der
V e e n  in letzter Zeit die Personalausweisfälscher-Zentrale
leitete, wurde im Kampfe mit Angehörigen der Sicherheitspolizei
der Aussendienststelle Amsterdam erschossen, nachdem er den
Polizeiangestellten  H e i n e n  tödlich verwundet hatte.
Über seine festgenommenen Mitarbeiter konnte in einem Amster-
damer Geschäftsgebäude die in drei grossen Räumen unterge-
stellte Fälscher-Zentrale ermittelt und sichergestellt werden.
```

Introductory paragraph of SD report, 12 July 1944.

The opening paragraph states:

> Known for a long time as a leading terrorist, the immigrant Jew Gerhard Badrian, who used cover-names Albert, Alfred, Hans, Max, and Bernard and was a follower of Gerrit van der Veen, recently sentenced to death, who in recent times led the Personal-Identity-Counterfeiting Centre, was shot while in the company of his associates during a battle with the Aussendienststelle Amsterdam der Sicherheitspolizei (the Amsterdam Outpost of the SD), during which Police Officer Heinen was fatally wounded. After the arrest of his [Gerhard's]

associates, investigations led to three large rooms in an Amsterdam commercial building which were confirmed as the location of Counterfeit-Central.

The address is not given, but the description of three large rooms in a commercial building refers to Frans Meijer's office in the Amsteldijk. The fact that the PBC materials had been located only after the Rubensstraat ambush implies that Gerrit had not cracked under torture before they executed him in mid-June.

The report then includes an inventory of everything found there. One line refers to Wehrmacht uniforms, weapons and battle clothing (the SD were perhaps too embarrassed to include SD uniforms in the list). It then lists in astonishing detail various categories of materials, including:

- *Anfragen* (Applications requesting false IDs.)
- *Stempel* (Rubber stamps, dozens of them, in eight different sub-headings, including towns, government authorities, employment bureaus, universities, police stations. Some were individual signature rubber stamps, the most notable being that of Ferdinand aus der Fünten, the SD officer in charge of Jewish deportation.)
- *Schwarze Liste* (Black list of Dutch citizens who collaborated with the Nazis.)
- Blank personal ID forms (stolen in the National Printing Office raid).
- Seals of various kinds for stamping or embossing official documents.
- Writing paper with fake letterheads representing various government authorities.
- False police identification cards.

At the end of the long inventory, the anonymous SD author notes with some satisfaction that the authorities had taken possession of the Opel car that "the Jewish leader" had used in assaults and rescue operations. (It had been parked in a street close to the Rubensstraat apartment.) The SD officer goes on to express pride that the capture of the PBC's counterfeiting equipment and material has struck the Resistance a "savage blow, from which they would not easily recover". This is probably true.

However, in the following months, the armies of Soviet Russia from the east, and the combined Allied forces from the south and west, proceed to strike the German forces with an even more savage blow, from which they never recover at all.

82

The end of the war

The Netherlands, 4 May 1945

A harsh winter stalls the progress of the Soviets and the Western Allies in their relentless battles to bring the war to an end. Almost a year has elapsed since the Normandy landings. Eventually, the Dutch are liberated from Nazi rule. Four days later, Germany surrenders unconditionally to the Allies, bringing an end to World War II.

83

Betje Wery's Life after Rubensstraat

After the Rubensstraat episode, Betje Wery receives a generous reward of 1000 guilders for her work and hides for several weeks in various apartments. She receives regular visits from Willy Lages, perhaps to check on the welfare of his loyal underling, perhaps for other reasons.

In August 1944, following Lages' advice, she moves to Belgium, using the alias Elisabeth Stips. There she is in contact with the German occupation forces and again works for the DSK. After Brussels is liberated, she is arrested on 24 December 1944 and interned in a monastery. In August 1945, she is transferred to the *Huis van Bewaring* in Amsterdam, where she shares a cell with two other collaborators.

In May 1948 she is tried for war crimes. The prosecutor calls for the death penalty, but she is spared and given life imprisonment. Although this sentence is later confirmed, she is released in 1954.

In prison, she meets Mijndert Vonk, a convicted murderer, who had worked for the SD in Groningen. They later marry, have two children and set up a marriage agency.

Years later, in 1979, she plans a TV show about marriage, and reacts with outraged incomprehension when the program is cancelled following a public outcry when her background is revealed.

She dies in 2006.

84

A crook gets off scot-free

After the war Wery's boss, Dries Riphagen, gets away with his many crimes. He is believed to have been smuggled out of the Netherlands (some say in a coffin!) and then via Belgium and France to Madrid. In 1948 he boards a boat for Argentina, where he has high-level friends (some say Juan and Eva Peron). He dies in Switzerland in 1973. (A Dutch movie, simply titled *Riphagen*, is released in September 2016. Betje Wery and Gerhard are minor characters in the film.)

85

The Berg Foundation orphanage

Laren, 1945–48

Horst Kerpen, now aged fourteen, survives the war, the only member of his family still alive. Social welfare authorities place him in the *Bergstichting* orphanage for Jewish children in the rural town of Laren, 26 kilometres from Amsterdam. The orphanage arranges a belated bar mitzvah celebration for him and three other boys. He remains at the orphanage until early adulthood. He subsequently finds employment in low-paid jobs as a salesman or clerk.

86

The memorial plaque

Amsterdam, Saturday, 22 December 1945

The Amsterdam city authorities receive a submission from the few surviving members of the PBC and prepare a memorial plaque that describes Gerhard as a German Jew who fought and died for Dutch freedom. The plaque is mounted on the exterior wall of the apartment building in the Rubensstraat where he was killed. The Euterpestraat cross-street has already been renamed Gerrit van der Veenstraat to honour the memory of the chief of the PBC and to erase its connection with the Gestapo headquarters, now a ruin as a result of Allied bombing.

A public unveiling at the site is arranged. Members of the *Verzet* send out an *uitnodiging* (invitation) to its mailing list. Rachel de Vries-Brandon, Gerhard's foster-mother, is one of the survivors present. She expresses her deep gratitude to all those who had cooperated to place this memorial at the place "where my unfor-gettable foster-son Gerhard Badrian was shot". Horst is brought to Amsterdam for the occasion. The teenager offers a few words of thanks to those attending.

A newspaper publishes a brief report of the unveiling. A subsequent commemoration on Dutch Memorial Day when survivors in the Resistance and members of their families gather in the Rubensstraat initiates an annual tradition that continues to the present day.

Memorial plaque in Rubensstraat., Amsterdam.
"Born as a German Jew and at this place on Friday 30 June 1944 was killed in action as a fighter for the Netherlands' freedom".

87

The urn

Amsterdam, December 1947

Two years later, Horst visits Amsterdam again for a more private ceremony. Detective H.H. de Waart has discovered the numbered crematorium urn in the Velsen police station. His investigation identifies the deceased as Gerhard Badrian and reveals what happened to Gerhard's body after he was shot.

As Gerhard's closest relative, the urn is presented to Horst, but he immediately hands it to Anne-Marie Deij, who has returned to the Netherlands after liberation from the Ravensbrück concentration camp in Germany. Horst explains that Gerhard and Anne-Marie were very close, and she deserves to receive the urn. In any case, he does not have the resources to ensure that his uncle's remains would be given a proper burial. Anne-Marie accepts the urn and promises that she will look after it until a proper memorial can be arranged.

Anne-Marie's husband survives the war. They later divorce, and she remarries.

88

A radio documentary, "16001NN"

Amsterdam, 1978

Thirty years later, the number on the urn becomes the title of a two-part radio documentary on the life and death of Gerhard Badrian. The documentary is compiled from interviews with members of the *Verzet* who worked with Gerhard. Anne-Marie reminisces about the man who was the love of her life and she recites a verse of a poem by Rilke.

89

Voordewind and Willy Lages

1944–52

Late in the war, the *Sicherheitsdienst* discovers that Commissioner Voordewind is sympathetic towards the Resistance and deports him to a German concentration camp. He survives and returns to the Netherlands after the war, resuming his position (briefly) as a police commissioner. He is offered the post of chief commissioner, but declines and retires.

The career development of the SD chief Willy Lages takes precisely the opposite direction. The former *Sturmbannführer* is convicted as a war criminal and sentenced to death. Queen Juliana commutes the sentence to life imprisonment. Lages is imprisoned in the southern town of Breda. He has Ferdinand aus der Fünten and a few other top Nazis for company.

A proposal in 1952 to shorten Lages' sentence provokes a massive public protest, with thousands of people marching behind banners proclaiming *Lages moet terug in zijn cell* (Lages must return to his cell), *Levenslang is levenslang* (Lifelong is lifelong), or *Geen extra gratie voor Nazimisdadigers* (No extra pardon for Nazi criminals).

The protest is effective. Lages remains in prison.

In the meantime, the retired Commissioner authors a trilogy, *The Commissioner tells …* describing his experiences during and after the war. One episode, a nice example of role reversal, takes place in a prison cell. The former Commissioner is paying a visit to the former SD chief and they reminisce about their experiences. The conversation includes their recollections of the Rubensstraat ambush, the deaths of Gerhard Badrian and Frits Boverhuis, and Lages' happy memories of his time with Betje Wery. Just two old policemen having a yarn about old times.

90
Horst and Tanny

Amsterdam, 1954

Horst Kerpen, Trompenburgstraat 6,
Amsterdam, 30 October 1954.

Horst Kerpen reunites with the Tromperts family and is invited as a guest to Tanny Tromperts' wedding. The photograph, taken outside her home, shows a smartly dressed and quite handsome young man. It is the only known photograph of him as an adult in the Netherlands. Around this time, he is meeting with a German Jewish lawyer based in Amsterdam to discuss laying a claim for compensation from the German government. He also visits the Austrian consulate in Amsterdam. Previously rendered stateless by Nazi law, Horst has his citizenship restored. Although born in Germany, his original citizenship is defined by his father Hans' citizenship, so he is now an Austrian. Horst has never been to Austria in his life.

91

Going home (?)

The Federal Republic of Germany, 1956–93

In 1956, now aged 25, Horst goes back to Germany after a seventeen-year absence. The return of a Holocaust survivor to the country that has oppressed him and murdered his entire family would seem inexplicable. However, his choices are extremely limited. He has no close family anywhere in the world, German is his mother tongue, and he has insufficient funds to migrate anywhere else. He might have stayed in the Netherlands, but he has no reason to love that country either.

He finds employment in sales and factory work in various central German towns and marries a divorced Catholic woman who has a daughter from her first marriage. The girl is living in an orphanage, and Horst, arguably a world expert on the experience of living in orphanages, insists that she be taken out. He treats her as if she were his own daughter.

Horst and his wife then have a son of their own, Robert. During this period, Herta Caan corresponds with Horst, and visits the couple and their young son on one occasion in the 1970s.

Robert grows to adulthood, marries and the couple have three children. Horst sees all three of these grandchildren before his early death from cancer in 1993.

After his death, three more grandchildren are born, and a generation later, two great-grandchildren.

Nine living Germans in three generations owe their existence to a German Jew who died in Amsterdam while fighting for the right of people to live in freedom.

92

Ereveld Loenen

Loenen, 1947

After the war, Gerhard's close friend and *Verzet* colleague Frans Meijer, the survivor who decided to have a haircut after lunch instead of going to Rubensstraat, writes about the feats of his colleagues:

> Ordinary men and women can do exceptional things [...] Not with bravado, but despite natural fear. They just continue to carry on until it is time to act, and they may tremble for years afterwards. Despite being terrified about what they had to do, they still could bring themselves to do what unfortunately seemed to be necessary.

In 1947, the Dutch government decides to establish an *Ereveld* ("Field of Honour"), a war cemetery. It is to honour the victims of war, those who died in the Netherlands and those who had fallen abroad. It establishes the *Oorlogsgravenstichting* (War Graves Foundation). A site is selected in the town of Loenen. *Ereveld Loenen* was officially dedicated in 1949.

The flat gravestones cover the remains of soldiers, political prisoners, forced labour victims of the *Arbeitseinsatz* program, civilians and members of the Resistance.

In 1969, Anne-Marie, now remarried and known as Mrs A-M Griesheimer-Deij, receives a letter from *Ereveld Loenen* inviting her to present the urn to the cemetery. She agrees, and fulfils the

Gerhard Badrian's gravestone.

promise she made to ensure that Gerhard's remains would receive a proper burial.

The gravestone is simply inscribed G.J. Badrian, together with his dates of birth and death. Five Hebrew letters beneath his name represent the words *T'hei nishmato tzura bitzror ha'chaim*, May his soul be bound in the bond of (eternal) life.

93

Another ending

"There are moments when you can't tell a story anymore, when
you have to face an ending."

– Malcolm Angelucci, 2019

Melbourne, Australia, 1938–2019

Gerhard's cousin, Irma Badrian, moves from Beuthen to Berlin, and
then to Karlsruhe, where she meets and marries a salesman, Lothar
Gärtner. He has relatives in Australia who sponsor the couple's
emigration. They leave Germany, the only passengers aboard the
Stassfurt, a cargo boat out of Hamburg, and arrive in Melbourne
in 1938. Their son, born the following year, develops an interest in
family history, learns as a young adult that his mother had a cousin
named Gerhard Badrian. Decades later, he learns many details of his
life and death.

The son considers him as the unsung hero of his family and in
2015 he visits Gerhard's German relatives. He decides to write a
book about him.

This is the book.

Acknowledgements

The writing of this micro-history of Gerhard Badrian and his closest family members, set in the context of World War II and the Holocaust, depended on the contributions of many people.

I have benefited from the enormous help given by my Dutch colleague Frieda Voorhorst. Her energy in obtaining crucial information from various archives has been astonishing; her knowledge of relevant books, radio programs, archives and websites has been invaluable. Without her input, this book could not have been written. She has my deepest appreciation. However, I should mention that her preference would have been for a book based solely on documented facts. In making my later decision to add fictional episodes in telling Gerhard's life story in a narrative style, Frieda was not consulted and is therefore not responsible for those parts of the book that arose from my imagination.

The idea for the book arose from my previous research on my Badrian ancestry. Had I not worked on that project, I would never have learnt of Frieda Voorhorst's existence and her interest in the *Verzet* and Gerhard Badrian. Elke Kehrmann in Germany and Roger Lustig in the United States both provided crucial information that helped me elucidate my Badrian family tree. (And it was my young cousin Ryan Badrian's question about the origins of his surname that led me to Roger Lustig.) The birth, marriage and death records provided by helpful staff in the Polish archives of Bytom, Racibórz and Katowice were crucial. Finding accurate genealogical information about Horst Kerpen's grandfather Hermann Badrian, which allowed me to link his branch of the family to our common ancestors Joseph and Johanna (Handel) Badrian (my great-grandparents) was also important. Claire Gamston, a Badrian descendant living in England, made a small but absolutely vital contribution. Had I not seen (and responded to) her online search for Badrian information, I would not have been introduced to Frieda Voorhorst.

Many other people contributed to my development as a genealogical researcher and writer of family history. My wife Helen, equally enthusiastic about both fields, has always been a steady source of help, support and constructive criticism. Our older daughter Naomi Coleman also encouraged me to write this book and made numerous thoughtful editorial comments on various drafts. Our younger son Tony made several useful suggestions for improving a late version of the manuscript.

In Amsterdam, Dr Jan Verbiest, the son of the late detective Cor Verbiest, gave Frieda access to his father's files, which provided us with much useful information about Gerhard and his circle.

Others made critically important contributions that facilitated my writing about Gerhard's nephew Horst Kerpen: Guido Abuys, for providing information from the Westerbork files; Simcha von Benckendorff, whose response to my email to former Laren residents led me to Herta de Wolff (née Caan), and who subsequently provided me with further information; and to Herta herself, who (via Simcha) explained her role in rescuing Horst in 1944; Miriam Keesing, of DOKIN (*Duitse Oorlogskinderen In Nederland*: German War Children in the Netherlands), who gave me the earliest details of Horst's arrival in the Netherlands and his later time in various orphanages; my good friend and former university colleague Professor Emerita Gilah Leder, for her assistance with Dutch translation; Michiel Schwartzenberg, for providing important post-war correspondence from the Dutch Red Cross archives; Bronislawa Sarnowski of the UNESCO International Tracing Service at Bad Arolsen, Germany, for documentary evidence relating to Horst, his mother and his grandparents; Dr Gertjan Broek, of the Anne Frank House in Amsterdam, for his assistance in locating some important sources; Tanny Wessel-Tromperts, for the two stunning photographs of Horst as a boy and young man and her friend, Dirk Veenhuizen, whose research made them available; and to my new-found cousin Robert Kerpen in Germany and his sister Linda in the US, for providing photographs and personal recollections of Horst as a mature adult.

Mention should be made of the many unnamed computer technologists whose years of effort gave us the websites that are invaluable for genealogists and historians information (especially Ancestry, JRI-Poland, JewishGen and Wikipedia) Their work allowed me to obtain important text information and photographs in ways that were undreamed-of when I was a little boy and my father first showed me his handwritten and illustrated family tree, which no doubt sparked my interest in genealogy and family history.

The current version of this book is a completely rewritten version of an earlier one that began life in 2015. Titled *Gerhard Badrian: family hero*, it took two years to write. Although during my former professional life as an academic I managed over a period of three decades to produce an extensive list of publications, the present work is in a totally unrelated field. I needed some advice from people with experience in the areas of history and literature about turning my work into something that might be publishable. Professor Andrew Markus at Monash University put me in touch with his colleague and co-author Dr Margaret Taft. She suggested that I take my manuscript to a professional editor, and recommended Nadine Davidoff. Nadine is an experienced freelance editor who has previously worked for major publishing houses, and who runs writing courses at RMIT and The University of Melbourne.

Nadine read the earlier version and considered the Gerhard Badrian story to be unusual and worth telling, but suggested that I should remove much of the genealogy and the underlying research techniques and rewrite it in the form of compelling narrative. Stick to the basic facts, but tell a story. So, while the narrative in the book is governed by facts, many minor characters and scenarios have been invented to add colour and energy. (The Epilogue lists all the real people at the heart of the story.)

It was Nadine who proposed several potential publishers, with Hybrid at the top of her list. It was the first one I approached. I was naturally delighted when Louis de Vries promptly agreed to publish my book. I am particularly appreciative of the work of Anna Blay who skilfully polished the final version of my manuscript (or computer file, to use 21st century language, it was never handwritten!) Among the many joys associated with the development of this book was the pleasure of meeting some of my helpers in person. Genealogical research is not just about documents and gravestones and websites. It's about people: the people on your family tree, and the people who help you find them. In 2015, during a six-week trip around parts of Europe, my wife and I spent a week in Germany. We enjoyed meeting Elke Kehrmann for a day in Dresden, followed by a few days with the family of my new-found distant cousin Robert Kerpen. From there we travelled to the neighbouring Netherlands. In Amsterdam we met Frieda Voorhorst (and members of her delightful family). Claire Gamston (and her husband and father) came across from England especially to meet us. (Since then I have been searching for her father's Badrian roots in an attempt to repay my debt to Claire for her earlier assistance.) Dinner one evening with Simcha von Benckendorff, Herta Caan's friend, rounded off a very full few days.

Two years later, I attended my very first international genealogy conference (in Florida) where I gave an illustrated presentation of the Horst Kerpen story. I had the opportunity to meet Roger Lustig there, one of the key helpers in 2014 in my early Badrian research.

Sir Isaac Newton once acknowledged that he stood on the shoulders of giants. I make no claim to compare my modest skills with those of Sir Isaac, but I identify completely with the point that he was making. My deepest thanks go to all of those good people on whose shoulders I have stood who made this personal tribute to my unsung family hero possible.

– Paul Gardner, Melbourne, 2020

The Author

Dr Paul Gardner AM, born in Melbourne, Australia, retired from the Faculty of Education at Monash University in 2002. An active member of the local Jewish community, he was chairman of the B'nai B'rith Anti-Defamation Commission for several years and in 2016–19 served as a member of the  Board of Governors of B'nai B'rith Australia/New Zealand. a founding member of the Jewish Christian Muslim Association in 2004, in 2008 he was appointed as a Member of the Order of Australia in the Australia Day Honours List for his work in organisations combating racism and promoting interfaith relations. He is currently a member of the Victoria Police Human Research Ethics Committee.

A keen amateur genealogist, in 2017 he attended the International Association of Jewish Genealogical Societies conference in Orlando, Florida, where he presented a paper about Gerhard Badrian's nephew, Horst Kerpen. Three of his papers have since been published in *Avotaynu*, the international Jewish genealogy journal: *The Early Badrians of Oberschlesien* (in the online edition), *The Unusual Case of Emanuel Emil Badrian* and *Heinz Badrian and Elfriede Badrian: A genealogical detective story* (both in the print edition). He lives in Caulfield South, Australia.

Epilogue

1. Fact and fiction

The Unsung Family Hero contains a mixture of styles. The main characters are all real people. The Badrian family are known from my mother's recollections and from my family history research. The main members of the Resistance are drawn from documented material in books and websites, as are the leading members of the Nazis. Many other characters are fictional, introduced to tell the story in a narrative style. I don't really know what the midwife said to Gerhard's father after he was born, or what the leader of the Dutch Nazis told his cronies after returning from his secret visit to Hitler, or what Herta Caan said to the SS officer who grilled her after Horst's escape. I invented it.

Here's a list of all the real people in the book. All the other characters are fictional, although a few of them were inspired by real people who performed similar actions.

The family, their circle, friends and other innocents

Gerhard Badrian

Hermann and Frieda Badrian: née Herrnstadt: his parents

Erna Kerpen, née Badrian: Gerhard's sister

Hans Kerpen: her divorced husband

Horst Kerpen: their son

Louis and Emma Badrian: Gerhard's uncle and aunt

Irma, Rudi and Walter Badrian: three of their six children, Gerhard's cousins

Rabbi Max Kopfstein: rabbi of the Beuthen synagogue in the early twentieth century

Rabbi Dr Ludwig Golinski: his successor in the 1930s

Jaques and Rachel de Vries: Gerhard's foster-parents during the Great War

David and Marianne Frank: Horst's temporary foster-parents in Hilversum

Jo David and Jacques Frank: their sons

Cornelia Tromperts: a maid in Amsterdam

Tanny Tromperts (Tannetje Wessel-Tromperts): Cornelia's young sister, Horst's childhood friend

The Resistance

Gerrit van der Veen: head of the PBC (*Persoonsbewijzencentrale*)

Frans Duwaer: expert printer, close associate of Gerrit

Guusje Rübsaam: a girlfriend of Gerrit

Gerben Wagenaar: a colleague of Gerrit

Frans Meijer: friend and colleague of Gerhard

Henk van der Tweel, Peter Roelofs, Frits Boverhuis, Hans van Gogh, Otto Treumann, Kobus den Hartogh: colleagues of Gerhard

Anne-Marie Deij: Gerhard's lover

Frans Goedhart: founder and publisher of the Resistance newspaper *Het Parool*

Cor Verbiest: Amsterdam police detective

Dudok van Heel: a photographer

Herta Caan: photographer, colleague of Gerhard, interned in Westerbork

Johanna (Bob) Groothand: organiser of safe houses

Maria and Rika Groothand: her sisters

Supporters of the Resistance

Marius Meijboom: leading Amsterdam commercial photographer

Hendrik Voordewind: Commissioner of Police in Amsterdam

Walter Süskind and **Felix Halverstad:** members of the Amsterdam Jewish Council based at the Schouwburg theatre

Henriëtte Pimental: director of the crèche opposite the *Schouwburg*

Johan van Hulst: head of the teacher training college near the crèche

Piet Meerburg: founder of the Amsterdam Student Group

Adrianas van As: civil servant, administrator of the Westerbork refugee camp

Sjoerd Bakker: an Amsterdam tailor

Yehoshua and Hennie Birnbaum: in charge of the orphanage at Westerbork

Riete Gompertz (aka Rita Horvat): artist, Resistance supporter, in hiding

Charly Hartog: Gerhard's landlord in 1944

The Germans and their collaborators

Adolf Hitler: *Führer* of the German Reich

Joseph Goebbels: Reich Minister for Propaganda

Reinhard Heydrich: *Obergruppenführer*, in charge of the deportation and extermination program

Adolf Eichmann: head of the Central Office for Jewish Emigration in Vienna and later *Obersturmbannführer* (lieutenant colonel), in charge of deportation and extermination

General Alexander von Falkenhausen: the initial military governor of the occupied Netherlands

Arthur Seyss-Inquart: Reich Commissioner in the Netherlands

Willy Lages: head of the *Sicherheitsdienst* in Amsterdam

Ferdinand aus der Fünten: head of the Central Office for Jewish Emigration in Amsterdam

Albert Gemmeker: *Kommandant* of the Westerbork transit camp

Elisabeth Helena Hassel-Müllender: his mistress

Anton Mussert and **Cornelis van Geelkerken**: founders of the Nationaal-Socialistische Beweging in the Netherlands

Hermann Michel: *Oberscharführer*, deputy chief of the SS at Sobibor

Erich Bauer: operator of the gas chamber at Sobibor

Karl Ludwig: SS officer at Sobibor

Jacob Lentz: a Dutch civil servant

Dries Riphagen: member of the *Devisenschutzkommando*

Betje Wery, aka Bella Tuerlings: his assistant

Joseph Heinen: Gestapo officer

Hermann Radke: *Kreisrevisor* (District Inspector) in the *Reichskomissariat*

2. The story behind the story

This book is the result of four years' work, although its origins can be traced back half a century earlier. My parents Lothar and Irma Gärtner were refugees from Nazi Germany, the only passengers aboard a cargo ship that left Hamburg in 1937 and arrived in Australia, early in 1938. They promptly anglicised their surname. I was born in Melbourne the following year.

My father had brought with him a *Stammbaum*, a family tree, which he had prepared as a young man. Today it hangs in my dining room. It was drawn literally as a tree, with a trunk, branches and leaves on a single sheet of paper. It represented what he knew of his Gärtner ancestors and their descendants. Not all of the information in it was accurate, but it would take me almost 75 years to find that out. I have little doubt that my father's tree helped plant the idea that family history was interesting and important.

I went to school and university, where I met Helen, my wife-to-be. We were engaged after I graduated, in 1961. My father died later that year. After Helen and I married two years later, I decided to keep the idea of a family tree alive. I purchased a simple spiral-bound artist's sketch book. Facing pages were allocated to various branches of my father's and mother's families, and my wife's. For several decades, births, marriages and deaths were recorded in the book.

My mother Irma was born in the then German town of Beuthen, Upper Silesia, now known as Bytom in Poland. Her maiden name was Badrian. She was the daughter of Louis and Emma Badrian. She knew when her father was born and when he died. She had some knowledge of her mother's ancestry, helped no doubt by the fact that there were cousins from that side of the family who had also managed to leave Germany and migrate to Melbourne.

On her father's side, she knew very little. Her lack of detailed knowledge is perfectly understandable. Louis died young, at 45, when my mother was only ten years old. Children at that age don't seek accurate genealogical information. She knew that Louis Badrian was a specialist shoemaker. She had personal memories of a spinster aunt, Minna, of her uncle Hermann and his wife Frieda, and their two children, Erna and Gerhard, all of whom lived close by in the same town.

She had no idea of what happened to her aunt Minna, and to this day, neither do I. She did know that her uncle and aunt and the children went to the Netherlands and perished during the Holocaust, without knowing any specific details.

But she knew one more item of information. Her first cousin Erna had married and divorced. First name and surname of ex-husband: unknown. The couple had a child: gender, name and fate: unknown. I represented this as a blank box on the family tree in my sketch book. (*The blank box became a person* was the title of my Florida presentation in 2017.) The lack of knowledge was also understandable: Irma had left Beuthen as a young woman and moved to Berlin. During the Nazi period, she moved to Karlsruhe, in southern Germany where she met and married my father. They left Karlsruhe before her relatives fled from Beuthen, and lost contact.

When the age of the computer and the internet arrived, the sketch book became obsolete. Half a century would elapse before the metaphorical blank box on our family tree could be filled with details.

I learnt the details of Gerhard's death from the photograph of the memorial plaque that my Israeli cousin Arye Badrian gave me in 1985. I discovered a few more facts (several of them inaccurate) about Gerhard from the web. However, it was not until 2014, when I began my serious study of family history and genealogy, that I began to learn much more about the Badrians who fled to the Netherlands. The information that I received, with much help from many people, was assembled each year into various chapters of an annual journal. Each year, one copy was printed and bound, purely for family consumption.

In 2015 when Helen and I travelled around Europe, we spent a few days in Amsterdam, meeting some of the people who had helped me with my family history research, and visiting the spot in South Amsterdam where Gerhard was shot dead. Eventually, I realised that his biography deserved a book-length treatment. Indeed, when I told some friends about his exploits, some commented, "Steven Spielberg could make a film about him!"

I spent two years writing the book, initially titled *Gerhard Badrian: Family Hero.* It drew upon and expanded the material written up in successive chapters of the annual family journal, and grew to 150 pages of text and illustrations.

At the beginning of 2018, I sought advice about publication from a Monash University staff member with experience in the field. She offered some useful advice about how to present material to a potential publisher. Her advice included seeking a professional editor to read my manuscript. She recommended a highly experienced editor, Nadine Davidoff.

I followed the advice. A month later, Nadine gave me her opinion. Although the Gerhard story was unusual and definitely worth telling, if I wanted it to be commercially published, much of the genealogy and the historical research should be stripped out, and the material rewritten, in the form of a historical novel. To bring the story to life, I should invent fictional characters, situations, conversations, thoughts and feelings. Retain the known facts as the basis, but dramatise the story. The revision took almost a year.

The Unsung Family Hero is the result.

In the process of writing it, however, I continually faced some tension, a conflict between writing a work of history and writing a novel.

Writers of fiction don't have to explain the source of their ideas. Perhaps a scene was triggered after drinking a strong coffee at breakfast, or recalling a dream, or seeing a movie. Who cares? Nobody wants to know. A novel has to stand on its own two feet as a self-contained work of literature.

The Unsung Family Hero, however, is not a work of historical fiction. Certainly, it is peppered with scenes where characters (some of them fictional) think, speak and act in ways that are purely the product of my imagination. But the foundations of the story rest on a body of research about real people and what they did. There was no need to mention the research in the historical novel. Just tell the story, I kept reminding myself. (And when I forgot, son Tony reminded me again.)

So why the tension? Why this long epilogue? No one would begrudge an author a few pages of author's notes at the end of a novel where he explains (briefly!) the origins of the work and acknowledges the people who helped him along the way.

I could have done that, but decided against it, for three reasons.

First, in my professional career I was a science teacher and then an educational researcher for most of my life. I came to genealogical research late (and writing historical narrative even later!). I have an aversion to rote learning, for the transmission of knowledge without any appreciation of the basis for that knowledge. I remember with distaste history lessons in school where we copied down notes about people, dates and events, which then had to be memorised and reproduced on exam papers. I recall university chemistry lectures that belonged to the same genre. But I also remember being influenced in the 1960s by books on the history and philosophy of science, and works of history that set out to rebut common myths by offering alternative evidence and argument. In short, I became interested in epistemology, the question of *how do we know what we know?*

I therefore wanted to offer anyone interested at least a partial account of the research underpinning this book. What evidence is there for the core of the Gerhard Badrian story? I am not going to do the academic thing – be grateful! – and cite every reference, complete with numbered footnotes. But I did want to share with the readers a sample of the kinds of evidence that were crucial in the writing of this book.

Secondly, I wanted to express my appreciation to many people for their extraordinary help. The **Acknowledgements** section that was presented at the end of the book was brief and entirely conventional. However, I felt that a few of my helpers deserved more, partly because of the great importance of their contribution, and partly because of the unusual ways in which I learnt of their existence. So, a later section in this Epilogue, **Four particularly helpful people**, tells this story. I also wished to share with readers several remarkable and highly improbable chains of events that led me to communicate with (and in some cases, later meet with) these people. I still consider it a minor miracle that this book was ever written at all.

Thirdly, I know that a historical narrative has to stand on its own two feet without any further explanatory props to hold it up. However, there were numerous points in the story where I could have said more, but decided against it. *The Unsung Family Hero* is essentially a work of micro-history, an exploration – partly factual, partly fictional – of the lives (and deaths) of a single family, set within the context of a major historical event, World War II and the Holocaust. Obviously, I was not writing a history of World War II in the Netherlands. Nor was I writing a PhD thesis, where every statement must be based on evidence and documented in a footnote. At various points in the story, however, I wanted to explain what was fact and what was fiction, and to provide at least some of the relevant evidence. Should I include a copy of Gerhard's birth certificate in the actual story? (Answer, no.) A photograph of the house where Hermann and Frieda lived in Bussum for about four years? (No.) The map of the Sobibor extermination camp and extracts from the war crimes trial evidence of the monsters who ran that camp? (No.) There were dozens of such Nos. I reached a compromise solution, by adding an extensive section simply called Notes that provides additional commentary on some of the chapters. It is not essential reading but it does supply some explanatory background. Was there actually a Captain from Köpenick? (Yes.) Did Gerhard Badrian know the Köpenick story? (I have no idea.) Did the Bussum synagogue actually have a rabbi in 1918? (No.)

An additional explanation for this supplementary section stems from my personal relation to the subject matter. Most books about the Holocaust are written by historians or novelists who are not related to the people in their story. A smaller but still significant number are memoirs of survivors setting down their personal experiences of that terrible period. This book is neither. It's unusual, although it's not unique: Daniel Mendelssohn's *Lost* is a fabulous account of the author's personal involvement as he travelled the world to reveal the stories of several members of his extended family. His superb book wove together in a masterful way the genealogy, the history and his personal involvement in uncovering the story.

I haven't closely followed Mendelssohn's literary model, although it was a guiding influence. My book is about Gerhard, his parents, his sister and his nephew. It's not about me. My mother, my grandparents and other Badrian relatives from Beuthen get a passing mention, but they are not central characters in the book. I never knew any of the Badrian family who went to the Netherlands: all except Horst were dead before my fifth birthday. Horst and I were contemporaries, but I knew nothing of his existence until twenty years after his death in 1993. Nevertheless, the research that underpins this book was motivated by my family connection to them. My mother knew her uncle and aunt and their children personally: they lived in the same street in Beuthen. Although I have removed myself from the story of *The Unsung Family Hero*, I still wanted to convey something of my desire to find out as much as possible about my mother's first cousin. As I said in the Prologue, Gerhard is not just *an* unsung family hero: he's *my* unsung family hero.

3. Sources

The Unsung Family Hero has been written in narrative style. Many of its chapters therefore contain conversations, thoughts and feelings which I have invented. However, the biographical, genealogical and historical facts that underpin the story are all drawn from research.

Biographical accounts of people in modern times are often derived from an extensive collection of literature relating to the person: letters written to him, or by him, detailed published articles about him, and so on. In the case of Gerhard Badrian, no such collection exists. In the entire book, two sentences in a newspaper obituary for his foster-father are the sum total of what we know he wrote. His sister Erna has produced a larger oeuvre: one letter to the Dutch Ministry of Internal Affairs – asking for her young son to be moved from an orphanage and brought closer to where she works – is all we have of her words. As for her son Horst, the sole survivor of the family, we have nothing at all. In short, this a book constructed out of very thin literary fragments.

Back in the 1960s, my mother's recollections of her uncle and aunt Hermann and Frieda and their two children were of no special significance at the time. Although they were just four names among the dozens of relatives whose names she remembered, those memories were also crucial in laying a foundation for the present book.

A quarter of a century would elapse before the next critical event, when in 1985, my Israeli cousin Arye Badrian gave me a copy of a photo he had taken of the Rubensstraat plaque during a visit to Amsterdam.

But another quarter century had to pass before this significant piece of documentary evidence would trigger the detailed and intense research required to write the present book. I needed the luxury of free time that comes with retirement, the technology of computers and the internet that allows for rapid communication and access to information, and the help of numerous wonderful people in various parts of the world.

The central factual structure of the book was derived from numerous sources. I haven't listed all of them: an indication in general terms where much of the factual information was obtained should be enough.

However, there are also some stories that I consider worth telling. One of them is about how a tiny little "fact", mentioned briefly in the book was actually crucial, for without it, much of the story could not have been told at all. Several other extraordinary sequences of events were equally vital in revealing particular episodes mentioned in the book.

I have already mentioned in the Acknowledgements section of the book the key people whose contributions to my knowledge made this book possible. Another set of stories in a later section of this Epilogue is about the remarkable chains of events, with probability levels close to but obviously not equal to zero, that led me to learn of the existence of these people, nearly all of whom I had never previously met or heard of before 2014.

In the present section, I will outline the sources of information that my helpers drew upon, or in some cases I discovered for myself.

Organisations

DOKIN: Duitse Oorlogskinderen In Nederland (German War Children in the Netherlands) is an organisation that has traced victims and survivors among the German children who migrated to Holland before the war in an attempt to escape Nazi persecution. When I was eventually able to obtain a copy of Horst Kerpen's PK (identity card) from the Amsterdam City Archives, I noted that his first address was at Quarantainestraat, Rotterdam. That was the address of the Quarantine Station that had been converted into a refugee reception centre. A photo of the building on the web was credited to DOKIN. I followed that up and obtained an extensive body of information that related to Horst's life in Berlin in 1939 and his first three years in the Netherlands. http://www.dokin.nl

No.	Name	Adresse	M.No.
		BERLIN	
1	Fischbein, Margret	Berlin-Grunewald,Winklerstr.19	M 979
2	Hirschberg, Heinz Martin	Berlin-Charlottenbg.,Kantstr.59	M 982
3	Katzenstein, Rita	Berlin W. 15,Bregenzerstr. 1	M 985
4	" Steffi	" "	M 986
5	Kerpen, Horst	II.Waisenhaus der juedischen Gemeinde Pankow, Berlinerstr.120	M 987
6	Marchand, Gerda	p.Adr. Blum, Loewestrasse 16	M 998
7	" Egon	" " "	M 999
8	Plasterk, Hans-Joachim	Berlin-Steglitz,Schlosstrasse 10	M 1005
9	Plasterk, Klaus-Juergen	" "	M 1006
10	Weissenberg,Marion-Henriette	Berlin-Schoeneberg,Kaiserplatz 14	M 1023
11	" Ursula-Marie	" "	M 1024
12	Meyer, Stefan	frueher Herrlingen, jetzt: Berlin, Meinekestrasse 19	M 1002

List of *Kindertransport* arrivals from Berlin, 16 February 1939.

UNESCO International Tracing Service: Based at Bad Arolsen in Germany, this organisation maintains a major archive of documents relating to the Nazi period. It provided me with detailed information about Hermann, Frieda, Erna and Horst. Sometimes the absence of information is as telling as its presence. The German archive contains precisely one card entry for Gerhard Badrian, obtained from Dutch records. This card shows his name, his date of birth, his Bussum address, and the name and date of birth of his father, but nothing else. This provides striking evidence of Gerhard's capacity to avoid coming to the attention of the authorities until the last few weeks of his life. https://www.its-arolsen.org/en/archives/

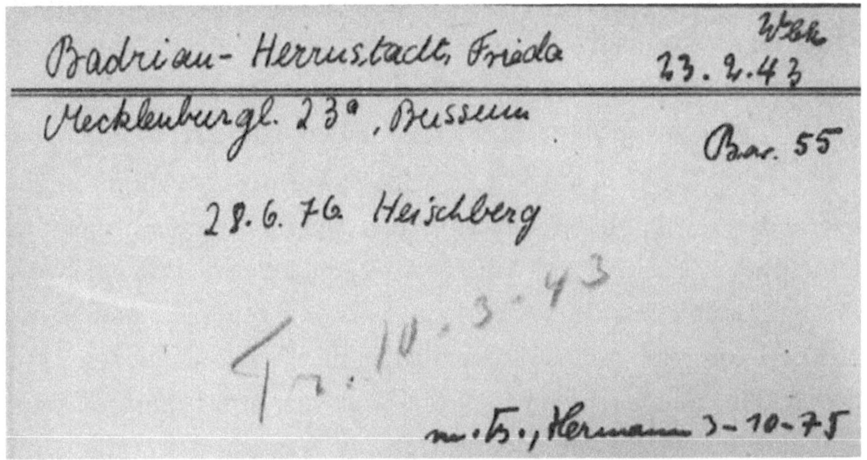

Frieda Badrian's registration card in Westerbork.

The card lists her date and place of birth, her maiden name, her husband's name and date of birth, her former address in Bussum, her admission to Westerbork (Wbk) on 23 February 1943 and her location in the camp (Barrack 55). The pencilled "Tr 10–3—43" is the date of deportation to Sobibor.

Various Dutch archives: The archives of three major organisations – the *Gemeente Stadsarchief Amsterdam* (Municipal City Archives), the *Nationaal Archief* (National Archives) and NIOD – were important sources of documents. The three now cooperate and a massive collection of images is now accessible through *Beeldbank* (Image Bank), https://beeldbank.amsterdam.nl

NIOD was originally known as RIOD (*Rijksinstituut voor Oorlogsdocumentatie*, Royal Institute for War Documentation), later changed the "Royal" to "National", and still later adopted its current name. the *NIOD Instituut voor Oorlogs-, Holocaust- en Genocidestudies*, a constituent of the Royal Netherlands Academy of Arts and Sciences. Its information-collection specialist, Harco Gijsbers, was particularly helpful in locating known images (and finding better ones) and granting permission for their reproduction.

A letter following a search of the RIOD files indicated that Horst Kerpen could not be found in the Vught files. Horst's mother Erna arrived at the Vught slave labour and transit camp on 24 February

1943 and was transported to Westerbork on 7 June 1943. Normally if a mother arrived with a child they would both be recorded, but there was no mention on her card of a child. The institute's researchers had looked for both her married and her maiden name.

Red Cross: The Dutch Red Cross files informed me about correspondence involving the lawyer (named Martin Rosenbaum) whom Horst met in the 1950s in Amsterdam. One letter mentions Horst's first admission into Westerbork in 1943 (on the same day as his mother) and refers to his rescue by his uncle, without any details of the method that Gerhard employed to extract him from the camp. The Bad Arolsen files do not mention any Westerbork event involving Horst between June 1943 and June 1944, but he must have been removed after the initial admission in order to be captured again early in 1944. My interpretation is that this is based on Horst's own testimony given to Mr Rosenbaum. Then 24 years old, he would have remembered his uncle taking him out of the camp as a twelve-year-old soon after Erna's deportation. The story told in the book of how this was done is fictional.

Westerbork: The *Herinneringscentrum Kamp Westerbork* is a memorial centre that houses an extensive collection of documents about the people who were interned there. It was the source of several vital pieces of information, especially the 7 June 1944 *Meldezettel* recording Horst Kerpen's second escape from the camp. It was from Westerbork records that I first learnt of Horst's forename, after Frieda Voorhorst discovered Erna's ex-husband's surname.

Barak 56, partly reconstructed, at Westerbork. Hermann and Frieda Badrian were housed in Barak 55 from 23 February to 10 March 1943.

The Westerbork website provides much information about the history of the camp.

Ereveld Loenen: The *Nationaal Ereveld Loenen*, the cemetery honoring victims of World War II (and later wars) maintains a searchable website describing the history of the cemetery and the people interred there. The photograph of Gerhard's memorial stone can be found at:

https://oorlogsgravenstichting.nl/persoon/5375/gerhard-joseph-badrian

The cemetery also records the names of other victims not interred at the cemetery. Hermann (Haymann), Frieda and Erna are included in this list.

Archief en Necrologie at the Oorlogs Graven Stichting (the Dutch War Graves Foundation): Its coordinator, Johan Teeuwisse, was helpful and permitted me to reproduce the photos of Gerhard with his foster parents and the gravestone at Ereveld Loenen.

Wikipedia: This was an invaluable source of background about towns, places, historical events, biographies of leading Nazis, the hierarchy of ranks in the Gestapo, and testimonies of Sobibor survivors.

United States Holocaust Memorial Museum supplied two of the images reproduced in this book. As required by their authorisation, I therefore state that "the views expressed in this book and the context in which the images are used do not necessarily reflect the views or policy of, nor imply approval, or endorsement by, the United States Holocaust Memorial Museum".

Documents

Persoonskaarten: PKs are mentioned several times in the book. These Dutch records contain a wealth of biographical information, and were important in constructing timelines of the many significant events in the lives of the Badrian family. They were obtained from local town halls and the Amsterdam City Archives, mostly by Frieda Voorhorst. Many records are now available online.

Children living with a parent would be listed on the parent's PK.

Horst Kerpen didn't live with his mother and his name appeared to be absent from the PK records. For some time during 2014, we did not know whether Erna's boy was even in the Netherlands. A later PK, up to his departure to Germany as a young adult, was in the city archive, but marked "private", and to obtain access to it, I first had to obtain documentation from Germany that Horst was no longer alive before the Amsterdam archive would release it.

Not surprisingly, Gerhard did not leave a trail of address changes for the PK records. Quite late in the research, I learnt that he had taken out a life insurance policy but had discontinued paying the premium. The insurance company sent me copies of the documentation and included a PK which told me that he worked not only as a photographer but also as a photography lecturer, and also told me when he went VOW, *Vertrokken, onbekend waarheen* (departed, destination unknown). In other words, when he went into hiding.

Erna Badrian's PK.

Gerhard's 1937 visit to Brazil is recorded on his PK, and is also mentioned in an entry about Nazi victims buried in the *Ereveld Loenen* war memorial cemetery. Brazilian immigration records covering that period are available online. A search revealed that numerous people surnamed Badrian had immigrated there before and during the war, but Gerhard's name is not amongst them.

Newspapers: Occasionally, contemporary newspaper cuttings provided valuable information, as seen in these obituaries for SS Officer Heinen and District Inspector Radke.

Death notices in the *Deutsche Zeitung in den Niederlanden*.

SS Officer Joseph Heinen was shot by Gerhard Badrian at the Rubensstraat apartment on 30 June 1944 and died from his wounds two days later. ("He fell in the war against the enemies of the Reich.") The day after his death, Kreisrevisor (District Inspector) Hermann Radke was shot dead by mistake by other members of the SS during a raid on the Vijzelstraat apartment, carried out in the hope of capturing or killing other members of the Resistance. He died by what today would be called "friendly fire" but the notice stated that Radke "gave his life in faithful fulfilment of his duty".

The term *Kreisrevisor* can be found in German usage in the eighteenth century. Kreis means a district, or county, or province. *Revisor* depends on context: it can mean auditor or examiner or inspector.

Henk van der Tweel's crucial book: As mentioned earlier, the gender, name and fate of Erna's child were all unknown when my research began.

Early in 2014, Frieda Voorhorst provided me with data about Erna and her parents, but there was no mention at that stage of any child in the pre-war and wartime records. For all we knew, the child might have died in infancy in Germany. There was nothing to show that the child was actually in the Netherlands.

Until Frieda discovered a line in a book, an autobiographical memoir by Henk van der Tweel, one of Gerhard's PBC colleagues, co-edited by two people (his daughter and another) and published posthumously: *Van hoofd en hart* [Of head and heart]: *Henk van Tweel 1915-1997*, edited by Annelies Strackeer-Kater and Marjolein van Tweel, Amsterdam, [1999].

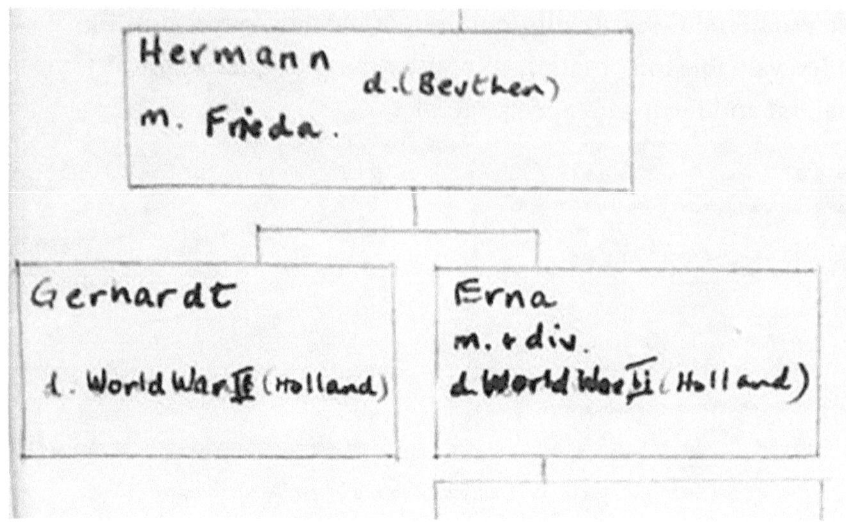

Extract from the Badrian family tree, c. 1960s.

One chapter is devoted to the work of the PBC forgers in Amsterdam. The sentence referring to Gerhard's saving of his (unnamed) nephew from Westerbork in 1944 following his capture was the very first evidence that there was a male child of Erna's alive in the Netherlands at that time. All of the later research – discovering Horst's name and his history before and after that event – arose from that single sentence.

An important radio program: Producer Bob Uschi prepared a two-part radio program, broadcast on Dutch radio in 1978, documenting the life and death of Gerhard, based on interviews with surviving *Verzet* colleagues. Frieda Voorhorst sent me a recording which my local colleague Gilah Leder translated.

A minute book: The Board of *M'gadlei Y'tomim*, the Jewish orphanage in Amsterdam, kept a minute book of its meetings. After the war, the secretary of the Board emigrated to Israel and took the Minute Book with him. Later in life, he decided that the book should properly be housed in the Amsterdam City Archive, and asked a friend of his to take it with him and deliver it in person. The book has no index and has not been digitised, but its presence in the Archive allowed Frieda Voorhorst to go through the volume, page by page, and locate the references to Horst's admission to the orphanage and his removal by his mother five months later.

4. Four particularly helpful people

*"Dans les champs de l'observation le hasard ne favorise que
les esprits préparés."*
(In the fields of observation, chance favours only the prepared mind.)

– Louis Pasteur

I have already expressed my appreciation for the contributions made by Frieda Voorhorst, Claire Gamston, Simcha von Benckendorff and Elke Kehrmann at the end of the book. I had never heard of any of these women prior to 2014. I have corresponded with them regularly ever since, and fortunately enjoyed meeting each of them, briefly, during a visit to Europe with my wife in 2015.

What I want to do here is to write about their connections to the Gerhard Badrian story, how they became involved in it and, most importantly, the improbable and distinctively different chains of events that led to my learning about the existence of each of them. Yes, genealogical and historical research requires access to documents, newspaper cuttings, books and websites, but as important as these sources are, it sometimes requires incredible good fortune as well.

This is another branch of the story behind the story, an account of how in the poker game of life, I was dealt four royal flushes in short succession. There is, I discovered, an invisible college of people out there in the world, people who, out of pure altruism, love to help others discover their family history. What are the chances of encountering four of them, each within the space of a few months?

Frieda Voorhorst

Genealogical and historical research are rational enterprises, and a prepared mind, to use Pasteur's memorable term, is certainly necessary to allow one to make sensible interpretations of observable data. No amount of rational thought, however, can account for the chain of events that in mid-2014 put me in touch with Frieda.

Frieda Voorhorst.

Frieda is a social worker. She is married but uses her maiden name, Voorhorst, in her professional work. In her spare time, she is an amateur genealogist and historian, with a special interest in the history of the Dutch Resistance in World War II.

The Netherlands, like many other nations, has an annual commemoration of the victims and heroes of war. The Dutch actually have two consecutive days, 4 and 5 May. The second day, *Bevrijdingsdag*, Liberation Day, celebrates the end of the occupation by Nazi Germany in 1945. The previous day is known as *Dodenherdenking*, Remembrance of the Dead, honoring those who fought and died. Commemoration gatherings are held at numerous sites throughout the nation. An annual gathering at Gerhard's memorial plaque in the Rubensstraat is just one of many such events.

In her younger days, Frieda lived not far from the Rubensstraat. She noticed the small group of people that gathered around the plaque each year. This stimulated her interest in the history of the war in the Netherlands in general and the story of Gerhard Badrian in particular. Who was this man? What did he do during the war? What happened in the Rubensstraat on 30 June 1944? Who were these people who gathered at the memorial? She began to read about war history and search for information about Gerhard Badrian. She would engage in brief conversations with some of the people at the memorial. None were Badrian relatives. A few were family members of men who were in the *Verzet*.

This helps explain Frieda's interest in Gerhard Badrian, but tells us nothing about how I learnt about Frieda's existence. Enter Claire Gamston.

Claire Gamston

This part of the story did not start in the Netherlands in 2014. It

Claire Gamston.

began 80 years earlier, with the birth of a baby boy named Kurt Walter Badrian in Beuthen in 1934. His mother, named Frieda Badrian on his birth certificate, placed him, aged six weeks, in the Friedenshort orphanage at Miechowitz, a suburb of Beuthen. The baby's father was not recorded on the birth certificate. Frieda was listed in the 1934 Beuthen *Adressbuch* as a single woman, described as *O.B.* (*Ohne Beruf*, i.e. unemployed). (The identity of this Frieda Badrian, i.e. her family history, is currently the subject of ongoing research. There is more than one young woman named Frieda Badrian in the records.)

In 1939, the chaplain of the Lutheran orphanage was a caring man, who knew perfectly well the extreme danger to Jewish children if they remained in Germany. He arranged for Kurt to go to England on a *Kindertransport*.

In England, Kurt was cared for during the war and eventually fostered and then adopted by a Christian family. His forename was anglicised to Courtenay and his surname became Harris, his adoptive family's name.

Courtenay married a Dutch woman and raised a family. At the

time of writing (2018), Courtenay is an 85-year old widower. His married daughter, Claire Gamston, has been helping her father for twenty years in an attempt to discover his Badrian ancestry. Claire placed advertisements in various newspapers seeking information from anyone who could tell her anything about the Badrian family. In 2008, she posted a similar request on the JewishGen Family Finder web page.

The storylines of Claire Gamston and Frieda Voorhorst intersected in September 2012, when Frieda saw one of Claire's search notices and contacted her. Their interests were of course quite different. Frieda wanted to know about Gerhard and thought that perhaps Claire was a relative of Gerhard's. (She is, but the relationship is extremely distant; their common ancestry and mine most probably date back to my great-great-great-great grandfather Menachem-Mendel Badrian, born about 1740.) Claire hoped that Frieda could shed light on Courtenay's Badrian ancestry. Frieda, being Frieda, devoted time to searching records and the two women corresponded regularly.

Claire's younger brother met Frieda in Amsterdam in November 2012. Then Claire and her husband travelled to Amsterdam the following year, primarily to visit her mother's relatives; they visited the Rubensstraat memorial plaque, timing the trip to be there on 4 May, Remembrance Day. Exactly a year later, in May 2014, they repeated the visit, in order to meet Frieda face-to-face for the first time.

On 3 May 2014, while deeply immersed in my new project, researching my Badrian family history, I saw Claire's notice on the JewishGen website. I contacted her. This triggered a rapid exchange of emails in which we each described our non-overlapping interests: hers in the family history of her father, mine in the Badrian family in the Netherlands. Not surprisingly, we couldn't help each other very much.

Except that Claire gave me one small, brilliant, crucial idea. She mentioned that someone in the Netherlands named Frieda Voorhorst had been very helpful and suggested that I get in touch with her, which I did. Most of this book flowed from that suggestion.

Epistemologists might claim that rational thought can lead to new knowledge (and it certainly can), but how can we explain the extraordinary conjunction of events that connect the birth of a baby boy in Beuthen in 1934, his travels to London on a *Kindertransport* in 1939, the death by shooting of a heroic member of the Resistance in an Amsterdam street in 1944, the observation of annual commemorations at the site by a young Dutch social worker and the determination of a young woman in England to find out about her father's origins, to the body of knowledge that I would subsequently gain that led to this book? Clearly, rational thought can offer only a partial answer to this question.

Simcha von Benckendorff

This is another story of a highly improbable chain of events. It relates to the testimony of Herta Caan, the associate of Gerhard who was interned at Westerbork and told Horst Kerpen what he had to do to escape from the camp in June 1944. Herta also maintained contact with Horst after he returned to Germany in 1956, and was able to provide enough details that allowed Frieda Voorhorst and me to find out what had happened to him in the decades prior to his death in 1993.

Herta Caan, or Herta de Wolff as she became after her marriage, was born in Germany but had Dutch nationality through her Dutch father. She was interned in Westerbork as a result of her support for the Resistance. Prior to the Nazi occupation, she had worked with Gerhard in Marius Meijboom's photographic studio then established her own studio together with a colleague. For a time, the place was used by Herta, Gerhard and another Resistance colleague, Henk Pelser, to forge ID cards. The studio and its

Herta de Wolff (née Caan).

contents were seized by the Nazis in 1942. Miraculously, Herta was still alive, in her nineties and living in London at the time of my 2014 research. She later moved to Paris.

I have never met Herta, or corresponded with her directly, and knew nothing of her crucial role in the Gerhard and Horst story until I was told about it by Simcha von Benckendorff. Simcha, Hebrew for "joy" or "celebration", is usually a boy's name, but her parents chose it, very appropriately, to express their elation when their baby daughter was born in the Netherlands after the end of the war.

Henk Pelser and his wife Saartje (Sarah) were Simcha's parents. Born in the Dutch East Indies to Dutch non-Jewish parents, Henk was a young medical student in Amsterdam at the time of the war. One of his contributions to the fake ID production procedure was to occasionally steal an ID card from jackets hanging where fellow medical students had left them after changing into their lab coats. He also assisted Frans Goedhart in printing and distributing the anti-Nazi newsletter *Het Parool*. Henk's major achievement was to establish a safe route through Belgium and France which allowed him to smuggle people and information from the Netherlands to safety in Switzerland. (He was honoured for this work by Yad Vashem in 1996.)

Late in the war, he was captured by the Nazis, considered to be only a minor criminal, and sent to a camp in Germany. After liberation, he discovered that his Jewish girlfriend had survived Bergen-Belsen, nursed her back to health and they married in August 1945. Herta met the Pelsers soon after her arrival in Amsterdam in 1938. They quickly became friends and remained lifelong friends after the war.

The closer connection to the Horst Kerpen story is that Simcha's aunt, Klara Oudkerk (her mother's sister) was a social worker who was employed at the *Bergstichting* orphanage in Laren after the war. Simcha recalls childhood memories of visiting her aunt there.

Aunt Klara didn't have a computer, and in later life, if she wanted to communicate with people on email, her niece told her that she was welcome to cite her email address and she would pass on any messages to her.

In 2004, the orphanage, in cooperation with other Jewish orphanages in the Netherlands, held a reunion of former residents. Details of the event were announced on a website, and emails were sent out to a wide distribution list which was openly published on the website. Aunt Klara received an invitation, via Simcha's email address.

In 2014, a whole decade later, Frieda Voorhorst searched on the web for information about the Laren orphanage, discovered the 2004 reunion invitation, and forwarded it to me. The aunt had in the meantime passed away.

I promptly sent individual emails to everyone on the list associated with Laren, about 30 people, requesting information about Horst (or Hans) Kerpen. Not surprisingly, given a ten-year gap, most of the emails bounced. One elderly man replied, recalling a boy called Horst Kerper [sic], without further details. Others couldn't help directly but provided the names of organisations that might be helpful. (Yes, but I knew about these already).

One reply was from Simcha, whose email address hadn't changed in more than a decade. She told me that she was about to visit an old friend in London and would contact me again after that.

The friend was, of course, Herta Caan. Simcha wrote to me and told me the story. A year later, we met over dinner in Amsterdam. She also sent me a copy of her late father's book, *Henk's War*.

In a world population of more than 7.6 billion people, how many people who were involved in some way in the escape of Horst Kerpen

Simcha von Benckendorff.

from Westerbork are still alive today? What is the probability of finding such a person? I still shake my head in wonderment that any of this happened at all.

Elke Kehrmann

I'll begin the Elke Kehrmann story with a paradox. Of the four women I have mentioned, Elke's contribution to the Gerhard Badrian story was minuscule. In early 2014, she provided me with one bit of genealogical data about Hermann Badrian, part of which was incorrect, and much later (June 2018), long after all the research for this book had been completed, she sent me a copy of Gerhard's birth certificate.

Elke Kehrmann.

Yet her contribution was magnificent. Without Elke Kehrmann, I would not have begun my Badrian family history research. And without that, there would be no Gerhard Badrian story.

How did I find Elke Kehrmann? I didn't. In 2014, she found me.

The chain of events began much earlier.

Like everyone else in the world, I have two sets of grandparents, four sets of great-grandparents, and eight sets of great-great-grandparents.

I'm a Kronheimer descendant as well as a Badrian descendant.

In the original family history that I compiled in the 1960s, I listed a distant Kronheimer cousin named Hedwig as married to a man surnamed Kerman (?), the question mark reflecting a doubt about the accuracy of either the fact or the spelling.

The doubt was resolved in 1996 when Fanny, a distant Kronheimer relative, wrote to Stephen, another relative, with information that was passed on to me. Hedwig was known as Hedy and she had married Ernst Kehrmann.

Later, this information (which, quite honestly, was of no interest to me at all) was transferred from the hard-copy family tree to my Ancestry website. The information lay there, electronically undisturbed, for almost two decades.

However, it prompted Elke Kehrmann, a lady in her sixties, an amateur genealogist of Lutheran background, living in a small village in the far east of Germany, to post a message to me in 2014 enquiring about Hedy and Ernst.

I could give her no useful additional information, and in most circumstances, one might expect that this would have been the end of our correspondence.

It wasn't.

Elke had noticed that my mother's maiden name was Badrian, and without any prompting on my part – in an act of pure altruism – she began to research Upper Silesian archival material. She sent me a list of 150 nineteenth-century people surnamed Badrian.

Among them was a Hermann Badrian born in Ornontowitz, a fact that was of little interest to me at the time because I was looking for my grandfather Louis Badrian and Louis didn't appear in Elke's list. For two reasons: Louis, Hermann's older brother, wasn't born in Ornontowitz but in Sohrau whose records were kept in a different archive, and in any case, Louis wasn't named Louis at birth.

Didn't matter. Everything became clarified after later research, in some cases four years of it. What was important was that Elke's list was the springboard from which I leapt into the pool of Badrian family history. Without Elke, no properly researched Badrian tree. Without the Badrian tree, no Gerhard story, no Frieda Voorhorst, no Claire Gamston, no Simcha von Benckendorff.

5. Notes

This, the longest section of the Epilogue, contains additional material relating to selected chapters in the book: historical background, explanations, distinctions between facts and fiction, history, comments, etc.

Chapter 2

Something isn't a fact just because it's written down somewhere: This seems an obvious truism, but I had to learn this for myself in the process of becoming a genealogical researcher. Consider two simple questions: When was Gerhard born? How does one spell his first name?

For the writer of historical fiction, a character's precise date of birth is usually of little significance. If an author were to invent a character who acted heroically during World War II in the way that Gerhard did, he could have been a man in his late twenties or early thirties, but the precise year, let alone the exact date, would have been unimportant. Indeed, such a book could well be written without mentioning the hero's birthday at all.

For the genealogist, a person's date of birth is important and usually quite easy to find. Gerhard Badrian was born in Beuthen on 13 October 1905. How long did it take me to discover that? The answer may be quite surprising.

In the 1960s, when I began constructing my mother's family tree, she didn't know any of Gerhard's biodata. In 1985, when I first saw the photo of the Rubensstraat memorial plaque, I learnt when

Gerhard died, but still did not know his date of birth. Twenty years later, the internet allowed me access to Yad Vashem records. A page of testimony dedicated to Gerhard, entered by a woman in Los Angeles, listed several biographical details about him, including a statement that he was born on 13 October 1906.

The serious research that began in 2014 showed that almost every "fact" in this testimony was incorrect. The Los Angeles woman who submitted the testimony many decades earlier should be commended for being the only person to commemorate Gerhard, but she clearly didn't know him very well.

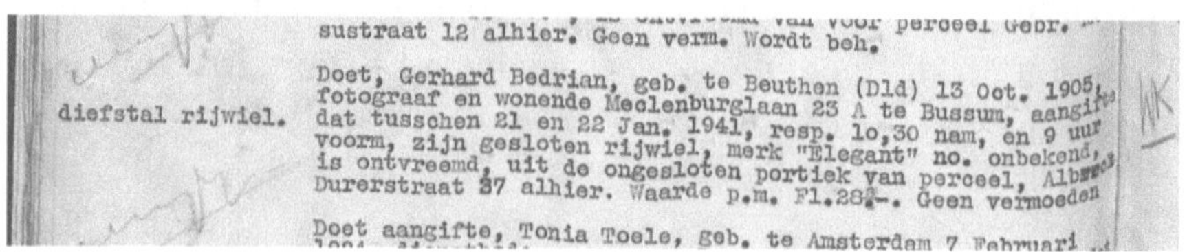

Police report of stolen bicycle.
I first heard about this document in 2014, and saw it in 2019, when it was sent to me by the Director of Collections at the Anne Frank House in Amsterdam. This was the first source of evidence about Gerhard's actual date of birth.

In 2014, Frieda Voorhorst examined historic Amsterdam police records and found a crime report. Someone had stolen Gerhard's bicycle. He had signed the report, which required him to insert his date of birth, 13 October 1905, a date confirmed later by other records.

The most convincing documentation, of course, is a copy of the original birth record. It may seem paradoxical, but the sighting of this record of the first event in Gerhard's life was actually the last piece of evidence encountered in the writing of this book. In May 2018, Elke Kehrmann sent me a copy of the Beuthen record housed in the Berlin national archives.

What's in a name?: Shakespeare poses that question in *Romeo and Juliet*. When I talked with my mother about her family history in the 1960s, she spelled his name Gerhardt – or perhaps that was my interpretation of what she said – and years later I saw several reports spelling his name that way. However, the memorial plaque in the Rubensstraat and all other Dutch references spell it Gerhard, without the hard German t at the end.

The "Behind the names: German names" website confirms the distinction. Gerhardt is distinctly German (although the Gerhard version is also used in Germany), while Gerhard is the version widely used in Dutch and Scandinavian countries.

Gerhard Joseph Badrian, birth certificate, witnessed by Haymann Badrian.

I ran with this distinction for years, and in earlier versions of the book I included brief explanatory sentences along the lines that he was named Gerhardt at birth, but at some later stage (perhaps during the World War I years when he was fostered with the de Vries family, or much later when he emigrated) he dropped the "t" and adopted the softer Dutch variant.

Until May 2018, when I saw his Beuthen birth record. The entry is unambiguous. His father had named him Gerhard. Everyone who tacked that Germanic t on the end was mistaken. It's a trivial error, of course. But academic pedant that I am, I methodically went through the earlier versions of what I had written and removed every reference to Gerhardt and every pointless "explanation" of why the spelling of his name had changed.

I had already learnt a few years earlier, and the birth record confirmed it, that his middle name was Joseph. That didn't surprise me. That would have been his Hebrew name announced at his circumcision, and it followed a longstanding Jewish tradition, widely practised in the Badrian family, of naming a baby son after a deceased grandfather. My mother never knew anything about her grandfather Joseph, not even his name, as he had died a decade before she was born and she was too young, just ten, when her father died, to have asked him questions about her grandfather.

Gerhard's father's name: Hermann is the name that appears in various Beuthen records, and that was what my mother called her uncle. In 2014, Frieda Voorhorst drew my attention to various Dutch records that gave his name as Haimann. My initial interpretation was that after emigrating to the Netherlands, Hermann wished to drop his German forename. That may well be true. However, on Gerhard's birth certificate, the father's name is already recorded (as Haymann).

⸺ ∞ ⸺

Some historical background: Beuthen (pronounced Boy'ten) is one of the oldest towns in Upper Silesia. Today it is known as Bytom and belongs to Poland.

A thousand years ago, the region was part of the first kingdom of Poland and its mines were yielding silver and lead. The town's name was first recorded as Bitom in 1136.

It was an important market town, sitting at the crossroads of north-south and east-west trade routes linking it to other parts of Europe. Over the centuries, it came under the rule of various dukes and kings, and under attack from distant invaders: the Mongols in the thirteenth century and the Swedes in the seventeenth. It became part of the Kingdom of Prussia in 1742, at the beginning of the period in which the long-lived Commonwealth of Poland and Lithuania was partitioned by the Prussian, Austrian and Russian empires, and subsequently became part of the German Empire in 1871. However, its development as a predominantly German city occurred centuries earlier, with the arrival of German settlers and the subsequent rule of the region by the Habsburg Monarchy of Austria in 1526.

Jews began to arrive in the town during the medieval period, especially in the years between 1665 and 1669, when parts of Lesser Poland were invaded by Sweden. A Jewish community began to form, consecrating its first cemetery in 1732, opening a synagogue in 1809, and building a much larger and more elegant one in 1869, by which time the Jewish population exceeded a thousand.

Throughout history, there was never a well-defined entity that a geographer could point to on a map and say, "This is Germany". In later times, one man had a fairly simple and easily-defined view of what constituted German territory. The Greater German Reich, Adolf Hitler believed, should extend to wherever German was spoken. He saw his mission in life as making that vision a reality.

Chapter 4

Early childhood: Nothing is known about Gerhard's life between the date of his birth and the later years of the World War I. The genealogical details about his uncle's family are factual; the rest of the chapter is invented.

"The only girl, Irma ..." Irma is an incidental character in this book, but since it was my mother who remembered that she had a cousin Gerhard, I considered that she deserved at least a passing mention. She was born in Beuthen a year and a half after Gerhard. A handwritten memoir written late in her life recalls happy childhood times spent together with her cousin Erna, but makes no mention of Gerhard.

The story of the *Köpenickiaden* is based on a real historical event and became widely known in Germany soon afterwards. Voigt was arrested within days and convicted, but even Kaiser Wilhelm II recognised that he had suffered unjustly, expressed the hope that his life in prison would not be too difficult, and pardoned him after he had served two years of his four-year sentence. Voigt later wrote a book about the episode, which was made into a play in 1931 (*Der Hauptmann von Köpenick*) and later still, generated several movies. A statue of Voigt dressed in a captain's uniform was erected outside the Köpenick Town Hall. Whether Gerhard had ever heard the story or (later in life) had seen the play when he lived in Berlin is unknown.

However, the association between Gerhard and the *Köpenick* story was not my personal invention. I had already become aware in 2009 of some of Gerhard's actions in rescuing people in captivity, when I first read about them on a German-language website:

> *Es gab abenteuerliche Köpenickiaden wie den … heldenhaften Juden Gerhard Badrian, der in SS Uniform Juden aus Polizeigewahrsam befreite.*

Gerhard is described here as one of several adventurous *Köpenickiaden*. I had no idea what this term meant, and all my attempts at the time to translate this odd term failed. The meaning of the rest of the sentence is clear: he was a heroic Jew who wore an SS uniform and freed Jews under police guard. (The people rescued from captivity were *Verzet* members. As far as I know, none of them was Jewish.)

The original source of the quote is a book by Walter Laquer, *Geboren in Deutschland: Der Exodus der jüdischen Jugend nach*

1933 [Born in Germany: The Exodus of Jewish Youth after 1933]. Gebundene Ausgabe (2000).

A few years later, I tried again, by googling. Success at last! I discovered accounts of the Voigt story online. Wilhelm Ruprecht Frieling has written a short book, *Der Hauptmann Von Köpenick: Die Wahre Geschichte Des Wilhelm Voigt* [The Captain from Köpenick: The true story of Wilhelm Voigt], available on Kindle.

Chapter 7

All we know about this episode is that the de Vries family had lived in Bussum prior to their moving to Amsterdam, so that placing Gerhard in Bussum during World War I is no more than a guess. Nor do we know precisely when he began to be fostered by the family, but according to skimpy accounts of the food situation in Germany during the war, the situation became serious around 1916, and so I have set the episode when he was ten.

The fostering of German children (both Jewish and non-Jewish) in the Netherlands during World War I is a documented fact, as is Gerhard's placement with the de Vries family. Rabbi Kopfstein is a real character – he served the Beuthen community for decades – but his involvement in making the arrangements with the (fictional) Rabbi Kupfermacher of Bussum is an invention. In fact, the Bussum Jewish community at the time was very small and had no rabbi (but did have a Jewish education teacher). It became an independent incorporated association only in 1918, when it acquired its first synagogue (a small disused school built in 1888), officially opened in September of that year.

How and with whom Gerhard travelled to reach the de Vries family is also unknown. However, the Prussian state railway system was already well developed by the late nineteenth century, so the long train trip across Germany was the likely way to connect with its Dutch counterparts. The alternative, a train to Hamburg and a boat to Rotterdam, was out of the question, given the English blockade of the Dutch port to German shipping.

No documentary evidence is available about the time that Gerhard spent with the de Vries family during the time of the Great War. My entirely fictional account of this period, depicting a loving couple caring for their foster-child, is an inference drawn from four much later pieces of evidence.

After Gerhard's unsuccessful attempt to establish a new home for himself and his parents in Brazil and his subsequent emigration to the Netherlands, we know that he visited the de Vries family. We know this because there is a photograph of the meeting.

About twenty years had elapsed between his first meeting with his foster-parents and this one. Clearly, they cared about each other and kept up the relationship.

Gerhard with his foster-father Jaques de Vries and foster-mother Rachel (right).

About three years later, in early 1941, Jaques de Vries died. Gerhard placed this condolence notice in the Amsterdam Jewish newspaper, the *Algemeen Handelsblad* (4 April 1941) It reads:

> Herewith I fulfil the sad duty to announce the passing of my foster-father, Mr Jaques S. de Vries. They who knew him, will realise what this loss means to me. G. Badrian

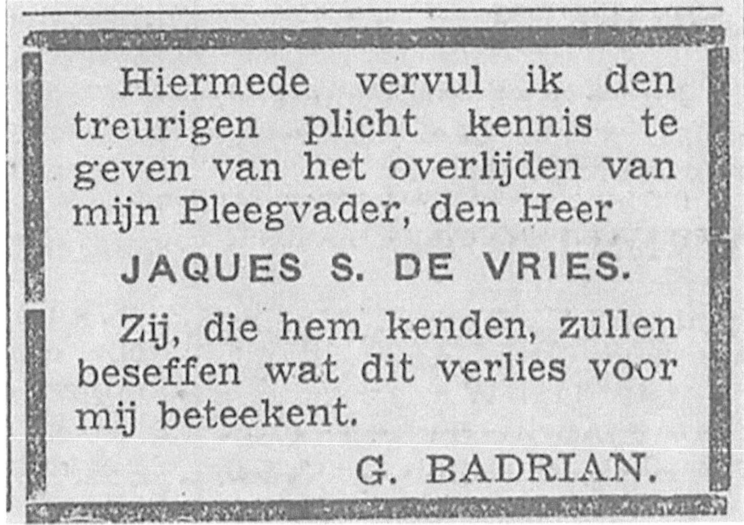

Condolence notice, 1941.

Another year passes, and the Nazis are growing ever more brutal. Gerhard makes arrangements for his foster-mother Rachel de Vries and her sister, to go into hiding. They survive the war.

And finally, at the end of the war, the Netherlands is liberated and a memorial plaque honouring Gerhard is mounted on the exterior wall of the Rubensstraat building where Gerhard was shot dead. Rachel de Vries is there and says a few words at the dedication ceremony. A newspaper in Amsterdam reported the event.

This is a family that cared deeply about each other.

Chapter 9

We know from several publications that Gerhard lived for a few years in Berlin. Remarkably, however, this entry in the Berlin 1930 *Adressbuch* is the only documentary evidence, obtained quite late (November 2018) that shows his occupation and address.

Chapter 10

The marriage certificate of Hans Kerpen and Erna Badrian in the

```
Badrian, A., Kaufm., Wilmersdf., Augustastr.26 E.
—  A., Dr., Rechtsanw. u. Notar, O 2, König-
   straße48 T.Wohn Charlottenbg.,Wielandstr.34 T.
—  Adolf, Kaufm., Steglitz, Albrechtstr.130 T.2863.
—  Bernhard, Pferdehdl., Neukölln,Oderstr.3 H.II.
—  Claire Badrian Lady-Wäsche, SW 19,
   Spittelmarkt 16. 17 T. Merk. 5814.
—  Erich,Dr.,Rechtsanw.,Schönebg.,Badensche Str.
   Nr. 8 II. T.Steph. 5314 [Postscheck Kto. 52 418].
—  G ,Just.Rat u.Notar, W 8,Französische Str.55.56
   Wohn Charlottenbg., Dernburgstr 49 T.
—  Gerhard, Photograph, Wilmersdf., Detmolder
   Straße 64 I
—  Josef, Privatier, W 15, Pariser Str. 21. 22
—  Karl, Kaufm., Charlottenbg. 5, Niehlstr. 19
   T. West. 1857.
```

1930 Berlin *Adressbuch.*

Beuthen Standesbeamte (Registrar) records that Hans was born in St Pölten, Austria. His birth had been entered in the Jewish Cultural Association register in Vienna. His occupation is described as Damenschneider (ladies' tailor); the couple's address is Dyngosstrasse 29 in Beuthen, in the same street as other members of the extended Badrian family.

Chapter 12

We know that Gerhard lived in Berlin for many years and that Marius Meijboom had studied for a time in that city. We also know that in the late 1930s/early 1940s Marius employed Gerhard in his flourishing business in Amsterdam. However, the coffee shop scene is fictional; there is no evidence that the two men had actually previously met in Berlin. Equally inventive is the suggestion that Gerhard's decision to move to Berlin was influenced by my mother.

Chapter 13

My uncle Rudi Badrian, later known as Reuven, became a citizen of the new state of Israel. I met him in my boyhood when he visited

Melbourne, and later in Israel. His son Arye provided me with the photograph of Gerhard's memorial plaque.

Chapter 15

Gustav Zweigelt is of course a fictional character, but the name is not arbitrary. Wikipedia has published an A-Z list of known members of the Nazi Party. The first name in the list is Gustav Abb, the last Fritz Zweigelt (https://en.wikipedia.org/wiki/List_of_Nazis). The name therefore literally bookends the army of political operators, murderers, thugs and swindlers whose loyalty to the Third Reich made this entire evil episode of modern history possible. *Zweigelt* ("Two-money") seems a particularly apt name for a swindler.

Chapter 16

The Mecklenburglaan address is documented in several Dutch and German records. A search of Google Maps Street View shows that the substantial building still stands.

Chapter 17

The history of Austria during the Nazi period is a side story to the central theme of the book. Gerhard Badrian and Hans Kerpen would of course have known each other, but I doubt that they would have met frequently. I expect Gerhard would have come home to Beuthen to attend Hans and Erna's wedding in 1930 and perhaps again

Mecklenburglaan 23A, Bussum.

after the birth of his nephew. Gerhard lived in faraway Berlin and I surmise that they would not have met very often after that.

Austria, however, is an important element in the Badrian family story.

Hans Kerpen was an Austrian citizen, or was, until the Nazis stripped him of his citizenship and rendered him stateless. Incidentally, by Austrian law prior to the Nazi period, a child's citizenship was determined by that of the father, so until he became equally stateless, son Horst was also an Austrian.

As Hans was born in the provincial town of Sankt Pölten and his parents remained there, it was not surprising that, to escape the horrific conditions in Germany, Hans decided to return to his home country prior to the Anschluss of 12 March 1938. At that stage, Austria was still an independent nation. At the time of the Anschluss Gerhard was already living in Bussum, so the two men would never have met again.

Sadly for Hans (and his parents), the horrors of Nazi Germany soon afflicted the Jews of Austria as well. For years, Hitler and his leadership circle had been eyeing Austria and planning to make it part of Germany. In the mid-1930s, membership of the Nazi Party in Austria had been growing steadily, and by early 1938 the nation's political system had been shrewdly manipulated to allow Hitler to take over the country without a shot being fired.

The *Anschluss* – annexation of Austria – allowed the Wehrmacht to cross the border unhindered. Hitler could now take control of the whole country and realise his dream of becoming the supreme leader of a Greater German Reich. No doubt the first reports of the *Anschluss* would have pleased the *Führer* greatly. Austrians had lined the streets, waving Nazi flags and cheering the incoming cavalcade of army trucks and tanks.

Within a day of the *Anschluss*, Nazi thugs were openly at work, beating Jews in the streets, forcing them to do humiliating work, smashing shop windows. There was no opposition. Antisemitism was not merely condoned, it was encouraged.

Antisemitic policies that had been developed over a period of years in Germany could now be implemented in just a few months. Expelling Austria's Jews (and confiscating their assets) was a key item on the agenda.

The leadership circle in Berlin established a new organisation in Vienna, the Centre for Jewish Emigration. A bright and capable young officer was chosen to be in charge, and promoted to *Obersturmführer* in recognition of the importance of the work. His name was Adolf Eichmann.

A standard procedure in Nazi-occupied countries was to centralise the location of the region's Jews. People in outlying areas were forced to sell their real estate and businesses to approved Aryan buyers and move to ghettos, or allocated areas of a major city. The Kerpen family had to relocate to Vienna.

My initial research into Hans Kerpen's ultimate fate led me to an entry in the German *Gedenkbuch* (memorial book), the register of Holocaust victims, which asserted that "on 24 November 1938, he died while fleeing in France". This was seriously misleading. A later entry is more accurate, noting that in December 1939 Hans was in the Dachau concentration camp. He then fled to France and was deported from Drancy to Auschwitz on 11 September 1942.

That still left a gap in the chronology of almost three years. I sought more information from the Austrian Embassy in Canberra and the UNESCO International Tracing Service, the archive of records of the Nazi period held at Bad Arolsen in Germany. The Embassy referred me to their Ministry of Foreign Affairs in Vienna, who put me in touch with an organisation called the General Settlement Fund. The GSF was set up to handle compensation claims from families of Austrian victims of the Holocaust. The GSF referred me in turn to the *Israelitische Kultusgemeinde* (IKG), the Jewish Community Association in Vienna.

IKG's historian, David Winterfeld, sent me a copy of the actual *Auswanderungsfragebogen* – Emigration Questionnaire – that Hans had filled in some time during 1938. The date is unclear, because the month, written in Roman numerals, had been over-written. It could be VI or VII. Whatever month it was, Hans completed it some months after the *Anschluss* of 12 March that year.

The questionnaire, apparently innocuous, provides stunning evidence of Nazi malice and deviousness. Lacking the staff required to conduct a census of Austria's 165,000 Jews, Eichmann coerced the Jewish community to do the work itself, on the pretext that his office was there to facilitate the process of emigration. The office would therefore obtain everyone's address, and the information for deciding who needed more "encouragement" to leave the country.

The responses inform us that Hans had left Germany and gone to his father's family in St Pölten (a moderate-sized regional town). The address of the family home was Lederergasse 8. (Google Maps confirms that the address still exists today. It is close to the town's former synagogue.)

Hans describes himself as *geschieden* (divorced). A dash in the line asking him how long he has lived in Vienna indicates that he has only just arrived from St Pölten. He describes his training as a *Zuschnieder* (cutter) and his occupation as a self-employed ladies' tailor, only he doesn't have a job. Asked how much he earns each month, he responds, *Kein Einkommen*, no income. Asked whether he has the necessary documents to allow him to emigrate, he replies, "yes". (On the other hand, he doesn't have a valid passport.) Where would he go? "England, Holland, North America, France". If he emigrates, he hopes to be able to practise his occupation. Asked what means he possesses to facilitate his emigration, he replies *Reisegeld*, travel money.

Clearly, he wasn't able to leave Austria in sufficient time to please the SS, so a few months later the Nazis arrested him, placed him in "protective custody" – another example of their masterly misuse of language – and sent him under guard to the Dachau concentration camp.

After his release from Dachau, perhaps early 1940, Hans fled to France, at that stage not yet invaded by the Wehrmacht. He survived there for three years. French Wikipedia notes that in October 1939, a month after the outbreak of the war, but prior to the German invasion of France, Camp de Saint-Sulpice-la-Pointe, in the south of France, was used to house Belgian refugees. A year later, it was transformed into a prison for "undesirables". By 1941, it was housing "Communists, trade unionists, anarchists" as well as German Christians deprived of their nationality, presumably for opposing the Nazis. Foreign Jews began to be interned there from 1942.

According to Bad Arolsen, Hans was at first placed in Camp de Saint-Sulpice as a refugee. Later, he was "deported on order of the *Befehlshaber de Sicherheitspolizei Frankreich* [the Commander of the Gestapo in France] from Camp de Saint-Sulpice (date unknown) to Camp Drancy".

The records are, however, not entirely clear about Hans' location prior to deportation from Drancy. Another report in the Bad Arolsen archives refers to a deportation list from Camp Rivesaltes to Camp Drancy, although the correspondence from Bad Arolsen notes that Hans' name on this list had been crossed out, implying that he was no longer there at the time of that deportation.

We do not know what happened after Hans was deported from Drancy. He might have tried to escape from the train and been shot. He might have been gassed shortly after arrival at Auschwitz. A report in the *Kalendarium der Ereignisse im Konzentrationslager Auschwitz-Birkenau 1939–1945* notes that of the 1000 Jews on Transport 31, 300 men were selected for Organisation Schmelt, a massive slave labour program that resulted in most prisoners being worked to death. Perhaps Hans was one of them, perhaps not.

So the date and manner of Hans' death are unknown. All we know is that he was never heard from again.

The story of Gerhard Badrian and his family circle, as previously mentioned, exemplifies micro-history, the telling of major events as they relate to ordinary people. Adolf Eichmann and Hans Kerpen of course never met and never knew of each other's existence, yet Eichmann's work, first as the SS officer in charge of the Central Office for Jewish Emigration in Vienna, and later as Reinhard Heydrich's successor as the manager of the Final Solution program throughout Europe, was responsible for implementing the procedures that led to Hans Kerpen's death.

Although we don't know the precise details of Hans Kerpen's death in 1942, the story of Eichmann's end, in contrast, is well known. Eighteen years later, the Israeli Shin Bet captured him in Argentina in 1960, abducted him and put him on trial in Israel in 1961.

What the journalists in the court room and millions of TV viewers saw, as they stared at the man in a glass cage, was not what they might have expected. This didn't look like an evil monster, a participant in the murder of innocent millions. What they saw, in the words of the *TIME* magazine journalist covering the trial, "was a thin, balding man of 55 who looked more like a bank clerk than a butcher: a thin mouth between protruding ears, a long, narrow nose, deep set blue eyes, a high, often wrinkled brow. He looked puny ..."

Eichmann's major line of defence was that he was merely a loyal servant of the Reich, following orders. The Israeli Supreme Court bench was unimpressed. He was executed by hanging just after midnight on 1 June 1962.

Chapter 18

Details of the farewell event, held on 19 March, were reported in a Jewish community newsletter that circulated around Beuthen and surrounding towns. The extract did not mention the year of publication, but a Hebrew calendar identifies the dates of Purim in various years, and 19 March fell two days after Purim in 1938. The Wolfram Alpha website confirmed that in 1938, 19 March was on a Saturday. The mention of Hermann's 42 years of service to the community indicated that he had arrived in Beuthen around 1896 as a young man (aged 21), before his marriage to Frieda. The March 1938 date of the event is consistent with the Dutch data noting their arrival in Bussum in April of that year.

The news item gave Rabbi Professor Dr Golinski his full set of titles, but did not mention his first name. The 1937 Beuthen

Adressbuch lists him, without titles, as Ludwig Golinski and his occupation as community rabbi. He and his wife Frida are recorded in the May 1939 census as living at Friedrich-Wilhelm-Ringstrasse 1, the same address they had in 1937. (The destroyed synagogue was in the same street.) The couple's names are not asterisked, i.e. they are not identified as Holocaust victims, implying that even at this late stage they were able to escape from Germany. The United States Holocaust Memorial Museum lists a Ludwig Golinski as a prisoner in Bergen-Belsen, but this was a man in his early twenties, not the rabbi who was born in 1879.

Chapter 19

A 1997 doctoral thesis submitted to the University of Utrecht by Petra de Regt provides some of the evidence of the professional relationship between Gerhard and Marius. Titled *Gevluchten fotografen* [Refugee photographers], it describes the lives of 23 refugees who worked as photographers in the Netherlands during the war. Gerhard Badrian was one of them. The thesis notes that he had spent some time in Berlin. A few young Dutch photographers were also attracted to Berlin and it is possible that Gerhard began friendships there that were continued in later years in the Netherlands.

According to the de Regt thesis, Gerhard became a close friend of Frans Meijer, who later would also join the Resistance. Meijer introduced Gerhard to the photographer Marius Meijboom (1911–98) who employed him (and many others) in his studio. The business grew, and in 1938 it moved a larger building at Keizersgracht 568.

Marius had also spent some time in Berlin. He studied at the Bauhaus to further his professional experience in art and design. I have no evidence that Marius and Gerhard first met in Berlin.

Marius found Gerhard to be an amiable colleague. De Regt quotes Marius: "I offered Badrian a partnership. He was a very good photographer and a sensitive artist, an honest but tough businessman who developed into a business leader. He began working on advertisement photography, which was new at the time. It was great

Keizersgracht 568 in 2015, formerly Marius Meijboom's studio.

working together. He was reliable as a craftsman and as a human being."

Another piece of evidence also indicates that Gerhard was very skilled. A PK in the Amsterdam archives, covering the 1937–43 period, records that as well as being a photographer, he was a *leraar fotografie*, a photography teacher.

A Dutch website (fotografen.nl) records Marius Meijboom's attitudes and actions during the war:

Directly after the German invasion Meijboom fell under suspicion for having Jewish employees. In 1942 he was arrested for providing photographs for forged identity cards. His studio was closed for a while, but subsequently carried on by his wife, the photographer Margreet van Konijneburg.

Meijboom was released at the end of 1943. In the final months of the war he was involved with a group who took illegal photographs of the German occupation. A selection of these photographs was exhibited in Meijboom's studio after the liberation. The group adopted the name of the show, "The Camera in Hiding" (*De Ondergedoken Camera*). ["The Hidden Camera" is the usual English translation.]

Marius was no ordinary commercial photographer. After the war, he was appointed to take the official portraits of the Dutch Royal Family. The website features biographies of leading Dutch photographers and describes Marius Meijboom as "the uncrowned king of commercial photography". He was primarily a studio photographer who also took fashion photographs. However he was "best known for his photographs of the Dutch Royal Family".

—❧—

Gerhard had begun to pay regular premiums towards a life insurance policy while in full-time employment with Marius Meijboom. In March 1942, now in hiding at an unregistered address, he stopped paying. The insurance company cancelled the policy. The file notes that the policy was cancelled because of "Jew non-payment".

In 2016, I wrote to the company, *Stichting Individuele Verzekeringsaanspraken Sjoa*, and it agreed to pay compensation to Gerhard's closest relatives, i.e. Horst's living descendants in Germany.

Chapter 21

The evidence that Erna was living in Teltow immediately prior to her migration to the Netherlands comes from her Dutch *persoonalkarte* record. Horst's placement in the *Waisenhaus* (orphanage) in Pankow-Berlin is from the DOKIN records.

The Jewish orphanage in Berlin was founded in 1882. In one of the sad ironies of history, its original purpose was to

Jüdisches Waisenhaus (Jewish Orphanage),
Berlinerstrasse 120, Pankow-Berlin.

house refugee children who had fled to Germany from the antisemitic pogroms in Russia following the assassination of Emperor Alexander II. The original building was later destroyed by fire and a new building was erected on the same site in 1913. The orphanage was closed down in 1940 and the building fell into disrepair. It was acquired and restored by a charitable foundation in 1999 and now houses a school and a district library.

Chapter 23

The details of Horst's emigration from the Berlin orphanage and his early years in the Netherlands were revealed as a result of a short burst of research in 2014. Horst's PK covering both the pre-war and post-war periods was held in the Amsterdam city archives, but would not be released under privacy regulations. It was made available only after the archive was supplied with evidence (from the Fulda city authority in Germany) that Horst had died in 1993. Armed with that evidence, Frieda Voorhorst was able to obtain a copy of the PK.

The record showed that Horst's first address in the Netherlands was RT 1 Quarantainestr. RT is the abbreviation for Rotterdam and the street name obviously included the Dutch word for "quarantine", so I googled "Rotterdam Quarantine" and that led to discovering the history of the Quarantine Station on the Port of Rotterdam and its pre-war conversion into a refugee absorption centre.

An accompanying photograph of the building was credited to DOKIN, which meant nothing to me at the time. Further investigation led to the explanation of the acronym. It stands for **Duitse Oorlogskinderen In Nederland** (German War Children in the Netherlands). DOKIN is an ongoing organisation which continues its research into the lives and deaths of the children who left Nazi Germany (and Austria) for the Netherlands. Its website is maintained by Miriam Keesing.

—⁓—

The transportation of about 10,000 Jewish children to England via

Quarantine Station, Rotterdam.

Kindertransport prior to World War II is a well-known story. What is much less widely known is that a substantial number, about 1800, were also sent to the Netherlands.

The revelation of the Dutch *Kindertransport* story was principally due to Miriam Keesing's dogged research. A report on her work, titled *Tracing Holland's Forgotten Kindertransport*, was written by Paul Berger and published in the online *Forward* magazine in its 8 June 2011 issue.

Around 1997 Miriam discovered a photograph of a "sad-looking boy" in an album compiled by her late father. Her mother and her father (who was Jewish) had left the Netherlands for Cuba in 1942. A conversation with her aunt identified that the boy's name was Uli Herzberg, a German-Jewish refugee who had stayed with her parents for a time, and was subsequently looked after by a neighbour. In 1943 Uli was arrested and deported to Sobibor, where he was murdered.

Around 2008, Miriam decided to follow up this discovery by carrying out systematic research in the Dutch archives of what happened to other German (and Austrian) refugee children. Her investigations led to her finding that Uli had a brother, still alive, in the USA, who told her about other immigrant children. She wondered how many there were. Three years of persistent study led to the answer, and to the extensive collection of documentation now known as DOKIN.

—⁂—

Without Miriam's work, I would have known nothing of Horst Kerpen's life between 1939 and 1942.

I found Horst Kerpen's name on the DOKIN website. The file was private, but I quickly obtained access after explaining the reasons for my interest. Within an hour, I had obtained a list of the addresses of all the places where Horst (or Hans – he used both names) had stayed between 1939 and 1942. (Horst is a distinctively German name, while Hans is common in several European countries.) Accompanying the DOKIN list was a set of documents, a treasure trove of micro-history that, together with the PK card, provided details of a part of his life story that had previously been a totally blank canvas. The fact that he had arrived on a *Kindertransport* was revealed through the DOKIN documents.

This was the start of my ongoing correspondence with Miriam Keesing. She explained that Horst and Erna must have arrived in the country separately. Had they come together, they would have been placed together in family accommodation.

Further crucial discoveries about other events in Horst's life were made as a result of the DOKIN research.

The names and Berlin addresses of the twelve *Kindertransport* children are in the DOKIN records. I was able to trace the eventual fate of some of the families left behind. For example, Margret Fischbein's mother Margot and older sister Eleonore emigrated to Belgium. Both were eventually captured and deported to Auschwitz on different dates. Heinz Martin Hirschberg's father Leonhard was deported to Theresienstadt and later to Auschwitz.

Chapter 24

The description of the environment in the Gouda orphanage is derived from a 2011 interview in the DOKIN files of 70-year-old Harry Ebert, who recalled childhood memories of learning Dutch, playing soccer, swimming, and going for a visit to a local railway engineering workshop.

Chapter 26

A detailed account of the Gleiwitz incident can be found at:
http://worldwartwo.filminspector.com/2014/03/gleiwitz-incident.html

The article explains that Hitler coveted a slice of land known as the "Polish Corridor", a narrow parcel which physically divided Germany into two parts, separating the "homeland" of the Prussian military aristocracy from Berlin. The League of Nations had given the land to Poland following World War I in order to grant them access to the sea. Hitler intended to invade this area as well as the rest of Poland, but he knew that attacking without clear justification would upset the citizens of his country and amplify the repercussions from other nations.

Poland, however, had done nothing to antagonise Germany, so Hitler needed a pretext to invade the country. He called on his faithful party comrade, Heinrich Himmler, to plan a series of co-ordinated deceptions, of which the Gleiwitz incident was the major component.

In mid-August 1939 Reinhard Heydrich, then head of the secret police, appointed *Sturmbannführer* (Major) Alfred Naujocks to head the Gleiwitz operation. The dead body left at the radio station, dressed in a Polish uniform, was that of Franciszek Honiok. He was a political prisoner in a concentration camp, rendered unconscious and delivered to the Gleiwitz site by SS agents, then given a lethal injection and shot.

Gleiwitz is a mere 18 kilometres from Beuthen. The Badrian family's home town was ten minutes' drive down the road from the action that launched World War II.

The Gleiwitz radio station (together with its transmission tower) is today a museum in what is now Gliwice in Poland.

Chapter 27

The description of the Amsterdam *Burgerweeshuis* is based on the recollections of Ya'acov Friedler in his unpublished memoirs in the DOKIN records. He stayed there for a year in the 1939-40 period. Horst's eleven-day stay, in contrast, was mercifully short.

The Ministry correspondence relating to Hans' foster home refers only to a Mr D. Frank. As mentioned in the book, Frank is a common surname in the Netherlands. I found a David Frank at the Hilversum address mentioned in the Ministry letter. The entire family was subsequently captured and murdered. David was deported first, to Auschwitz in September 1942, and his wife Marianne and their two sons, aged thirteen and seven, were taken to Sobibor in May 1943.

Chapter 31

After the war, Lentz was rewarded with three years' free accommodation in prison in return for the help he gave the Nazis. In contrast, in France, a man named René Carmille had a similar responsibility in the central records office. If he found a record card identifying a Jew, he made the card disappear. It is noteworthy that the proportion of Jews in France who perished in the Holocaust was about a third of that in the Netherlands. Carmille's subversive resistance was discovered. He was arrested by the Nazis and died in the Dachau concentration camp.

Chapter 34

Gerrit van der Veen's last sculptural work now stands in Utrecht.

The information about the location of the PBC headquarters in Frans Meijer's home on the Amsteldijk was found in post-war correspondence held in the files of another member of the *Verzet*, the police detective Cor Verbiest (more about him later).

Café Eijlders, located in a narrow lane

Gerrit Jan van der Veen.
Memorial plaque.

close to the Leidseplein, a large intersection in central Amsterdam, was a well-known bar and café in wartime and still operates today. In his autobiography, published in 1971, founder Johan Eijlders describes the genesis of the café.

It opened in December 1940, a few months after the German occupation. It quickly became a haunt frequented by intellectuals, artists, musicians, students, and theatre- and concert-goers. Among this varied group of patrons were numerous opponents of the Nazi regime. Leaders of (banned) student associations and members of the Resistance used the café as a meeting place.

The founder reports that in 1943 he was required to place a sign prohibiting the entry of certain groups of people. Eijlders dutifully mounted the sign using a rubber suction cup, left it there for a while, then moved it so that it was now behind a stove. The Gestapo on one occasion arrested him on suspicion that he was hiding weapons in his café. (As he survived the war, presumably they didn't find any.)

Chapter 35

Henk van der Tweel (1915–97) was a physics graduate who completed a master's degree in 1941. His advanced post-graduate studies were interrupted by the war. His scientific and technological skills were of great benefit to the PBC in the work of forging documents. Named Louis Kleerekoper at birth, van der Tweel was the alias he adopted in the *Verzet* while working with Gerrit van der Veen.

Van der Tweel was Jewish. At one point he was arrested by the Nazis, but he had a fake ID asserting that he was born in Suriname, a Dutch colony on the north-eastern coast of South America. This false birthplace had two advantages: the Nazis had no way of checking whether the information was accurate, and circumcision was a common practice in the tropical colonies for non-Jews as well as Jews. (But the Nazis didn't check.)

He continued to use his cover name after the war. He worked with colleagues to develop an early electro-encephalograph and an electro-cardiograph, and became a distinguished professor of medical physics at the University of Amsterdam.

Late in life, his memoirs were drawn upon to produce a biography, *Van hoofd en hart* [Of head and heart]: *Henk van der Tweel 1915–1997*, edited by Annelies Strackee-Kater and Marjolein van der Tweel. Amsterdam (1999), mentioned in the earlier *Sources* section. Published posthumously, the book included descriptions of his involvement in the Resistance. It contained crucially important information relating to significant episodes in Gerhard's life.

Cor Verbiest was one of the policemen involved in the Resistance who helped the PBC. If someone came in requesting a replacement for a lost ID card, he would ask a few innocuous questions and authorise the request.

—⁂—

Altering ID cards required a complex set of technical skills. The *persoonsbewijs* (PB) was printed on special watermarked paper.

The grid pattern of the watermark was made with a special ink. If illuminated with ultraviolet light from a quartz lamp, the grid pattern disappeared. Personal information typed onto the PB could be removed with acetone, but the acetone then caused the surface of the watermarked paper to smudge. The original photograph on the PB was glued to the paper and could not be dissolved by steaming. Acetone would dissolve the glue, but again would smudge the card. The photograph was partly covered with a rubber-stamped imprint which had to removed and later reproduced.

The grid pattern of the watermarked paper.

Equipment used by the PBC.

Chapter 36

The Trio's members and Cokkie Dirksen are fictional characters, but are based on real people. A group of three people known as the *Driemanschap* ("Triumvirate") helped save numerous Jews and other potential victims of the Nazis. One of the three was a young woman named Elisabeth van Lohuizen, who ran a guesthouse in the countryside near Epe that sheltered people in hiding. We know about her exploits because she kept a diary which came to light after her death when her granddaughter examined Elisabeth's effects, and turned the diary into a book.

Elisabeth knew Gerhard and Anne-Marie well, and even had photographs of them mounted in her diary. Gerhard's photo has his cover name of Bernhard handwritten on the photo. A brief diary entry dated 9 July 1944 records her sadness on receiving the news that he had been shot to death on 30 June.

Elisabeth's diary makes no mention of Rachel de Vries and her sister. Although I was comfortable to invent episodes in the book that were plausible in the sense that they contributed to the telling of the story – the scene involving *Sturmbannführer* Schlosser and his men is pure fiction – I drew the line at writing blatant falsehoods. I simply don't know whether the *Driemanschap* hid Rachel and her sister. But some good people like Cokkie Dirksen and the Trio did, and this chapter is meant as a tribute to them, whoever they were.

Chapter 38

After his arrest in January 1942, Frans Goedhart (1904–90) was sentenced to death for his "crime" of expressing opposition to the glorious Thousand-Year Reich. Fortunately, he

Frans Goedhart, in 1955.

managed to escape from captivity. He survived the war, developed *Het Parool* into a major regular newspaper and became a prominent politician.

Chapter 42

The photo of Horst taken at the home of Tanny Tromperts' parents and stored in a family album for 75 years is the earliest image that we have of him, and the only one of him as a child. I saw it for the first time only in 2017: it was one of the later pieces of documentary evidence obtained for this book. Before then, no one in the Badrian or Kerpen family had any idea of what Horst looked like as a child.

Erna's PK card records her as living in Hilversum from March to October 1939 and then living at the de Groot home in Hunzestraat, Amsterdam, for a month, although from the evidence it would seem that she subsequently worked for this family over a much longer period without living there.

In 2017, Frieda Voorhorst contacted and later met Tanny, an 84-year-old widow. One of a large family, she lived during childhood with her parents, Pieter and Klazina Tromperts, at Trompenburgstraat 6 in Amsterdam. The street runs parallel to, and about a block away from, the Amstel river. The Tromperts were not Jewish, but the area had a large Jewish population. A big playground was designated as an open-air Jewish market during the early years of the war. (Anne Frank's family lived in this neighbourhood.)

Horst would visit the Tromperts' home frequently. The photograph was taken there. Horst's age is inscribed on the back in a mixture of languages: 11 *jahr* (German for "year") *oud* (Dutch for "old"). Tanny thinks Erna wrote this. That makes sense: someone fluent in Dutch would have written *11 jaar oud*.

After their childhood friendship, Horst and Tanny were suddenly parted. The horrors of the war kept them separated for more than a decade. But they had not forgotten each other. After the war, they met again as young adults in Amsterdam.

Chapters 45, 46

The arrest of Gerhard's parents, observed from the street by the two men, is documented in Frans Meijer's post-war recollections. The location of the intended hiding place is unknown. There is no mention in Elisabeth van Lohuizen's diary of any plan to bring Hermann and Frieda to Epe.

Chapter 49

Details of Gemmeker's social circle are described in the archives of the United States Holocaust Memorial Museum.

The photograph of Gemmeker with his guests at a pre-Christmas party in 1942 was taken by Rudolf Werner Breslauer in the week before Christmas 1942. Pictured from left to right are: Frau Winkelkaemper (secretary of Ferdinand Hugo Aus der Fünten), *Haupsturmbannführer* Ferdinand Hugo Aus der Fünten (Head of the Central Office of Jewish Emigration in Amsterdam), Elisabeth Helena Hassel-Muellender (Gemmeker's mistress) and Gemmeker. The three women at right are unidentified. At the time this photo

SS-Obersturmbannführer Albert Konrad Gemmeker (centre) entertains guests visiting Westerbork for the Christmas holidays.

was taken, Gemmeker had only been commandant of Westerbork for two months. He arranged for a banquet to be held at Westerbork just prior to Christmas to celebrate his new position.

The photographer, of German-Jewish descent, fled to the Netherlands with his family. They were captured in 1942 and interned at Westerbork. Gemmeker ordered Rudolf to take still photographs and movies for propaganda purposes. His usefulness allowed the family to survive for two years, but in 1944 they were deported to Theresienstadt and then a month later to Auschwitz. The German *Gedenkbuch* records that he, his wife Bella and two sons Max and Stefan were killed. Wikipedia notes that their daughter Ursula survived.

References to Gemmeker's two unsuitable predecessors as camp *Kommandant* are drawn from information on the Westerbork Memorial Museum website. Erich Deppner, appointed 1 July 1942, was cruel and incompetent. He made impromptu decisions that caused panic among the inmates of the camp. One day, he ordered that the quota for deportation be filled by putting children on the train without their parents.

He was replaced on 1 September by Josef Hugo Dischner, an alcoholic who frequently beat inmates with a whip. He lasted for six weeks. Gemmeker, described as a "gentleman criminal", replaced him on 12 October.

Gemmeker clearly was highly regarded by his superiors, as he remained in the position until 11 April 1945, when he cleared out just in time to avoid capture by the Canadian liberators of the camp who arrived the next day.

On the train trip to Sobibor, the replacement of the Dutch police guards at some intermediate point in the journey by SS officers was deliberate Nazi policy. The Dutch police were not to travel to Sobibor; only SS personnel were allowed to know what happened to the passengers at the end of the journey.

Chapter 50

The principal destination of the trains from Westerbork was Auschwitz. About two-thirds of the deportees were taken there. Most of the rest, nineteen trainloads containing 34,313 Dutch Jews and Jewish refugees from other countries, were sent to Sobibor. Unlike Auschwitz, where some arrivals were placed in slave labour camps, Sobibor was solely an extermination camp. Only eighteen Jews sent to Sobibor from the Netherlands survived.

The map, together with recollections by Sobibor survivors, statements by Nazi war criminals at their post-war trials, and information from Westerbork website material based on survivor recollections provided the basis for my description of Hermann and Frieda's final hours of life.

Fritz is a fictional character. I do not know whether a euthanasia *Klinik* actually existed at Sobibor. There was one that carried out such a function at Treblinka, a death camp I visited in 2015. I assume that the Nazis at Sobibor must have had an established procedure for dealing with the occasional disabled or seriously ill arrival who was unable to walk through the camp.

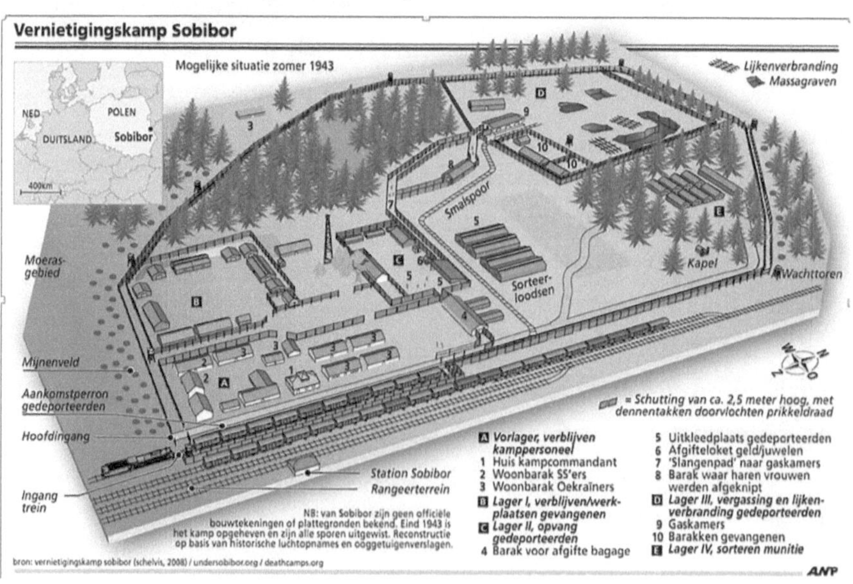

Map of the Sobibor extermination camp.

Ruth is also a fictional character, but her name commemorates one of the young women known to have been selected on arrival at Sobibor by a gang of SS officers and taken to their quarters in The Forester House where they were subjected to orgies and gang rape before they were shot. The name Karl Ludwig is documented as one of the war criminals who committed these atrocities.

The shearing of the women's hair at Sobibor, standard practice at other extermination camps as well, is also documented. One of the *sonderkommandos* was a fifteen-year-old Jewish boy, Tomasz (later Thomas) Blatt, who was selected to do this work; his parents had already been murdered in the gas chamber. Tomasz escaped from Sobibor in the mass break-out in October 1943. His writings about the camp provided background material for the 1987 film *Escape from Sobibor*. He died in 2015.

Hermann Michel and Erich Bauer are among the list of war criminals at Sobibor who were tried and convicted after the war. Bauer, who became known as the *Gasmeister*, was found guilty of participation in mass murder. He also lived in the Forester House but stated that he did not take part in sexual crimes, and testified against his former colleagues.

Chapter 52

Otto Treumann was a man with highly specialised skills. A German Jew, born in Fürth, Bavaria, in 1919, he studied in gymnasien (senior high schools) in his home town and then in Nuremburg, where he developed a keen interest in graphic design. His parents and much older brother migrated to the Netherlands in 1934, and Otto followed a year later. He furthered his education in his area of interest by studying for a year at the Grafische School and then for four years in the Nieuwe Kunstschool in Amsterdam.

During the Nazi occupation, Otto was arrested twice but released. He then went into hiding and joined the *Verzet*. His skills in graphic design, coupled with his extensive knowledge of German Gothic fonts and German handwriting, were developed to a high level in

Otto Treumann.

the PBC, where he became an expert forger of Nazi documents. His repertoire included forging identity cards, ration coupons and the signatures of high-level Nazi officers.

Given an official document containing, for example, a Gestapo logo (i.e. containing a swastika and text), he could make a precise large-scale copy. This would then be used by a printer to manufacture a metal die of correct size to be inserted into a printing plate. The high-quality forgeries were crucial to the success of the PBC's operations, including some in which Gerhard was a key figure.

Whether Gerrit appointed Gerhard as Otto's assistant, where Otto's studio was located and whether Gerhard actually forged Nazi documents himself are all fictional inventions.

Otto successfully eluded the Nazis and lived a long and productive life as a foremost graphic designer, working for numerous leading companies, including the Israeli national airline, El Al. He won several awards and honours. The Frans Duwaerprijs (named after the *Verzet* printer executed in 1944), was awarded by the City of Amsterdam in 1956. In 1970 he was bestowed with the equivalent of a knighthood by the Dutch Royal Family.

After the war, he was interviewed and filmed by Pieter Fleury as part of a series of eight short biographical portraits titled *Oorlogsgetuigen* [War Witnesses].

He died, aged 82, in 2001. On the 92nd anniversary of his birth, the Dutch Post Office issued postage stamps bearing some of his designs.

Chapter 53

I have no information about the whereabouts of Erna and Horst during the late 1942 and early 1943 period. After Erna extracted Horst from the *M'gadlei Y'tomim* orphanage in November 1942 until his incarceration in Westerbork in June 1943, nothing is known. He may have been with his mother, or hidden somewhere else.

Some documentation about Erna is available. ITS (International Tracing Service) records at Bad Arolsen note that she was taken to the slave labour camp at Vught on 24 February 1943.

A house registration card for the Mecklenburglaan 23A address in the town records of Naarden-Bussum contains no helpful information. Each card is normally a cumulative record over time of the various residents at a particular address. This particular card shows Erna as the first entry, so we can learn nothing about the previous occupants. They would have included her parents, who had resided at the Mecklenburglaan address since 1938 and would have been entered in the records long before this card's initial entry was made in 1941. We know that the Jews were forced to move from Bussum to the Jewish quarter in Amsterdam around 1942, so none of the family would have then been at this address.

Erna's entry notes her occupation and that she had moved from Blaricum to Bussum on 27 January 1941. The VOW (*Vertrokken, onbekend waarheen,* departed, unknown destination) entry of 11

INWONENDEN

(VERWANTEN, KOSTGANGERS, DIENSTPERSONEEL, ENZ.)

Inw. bij nr.	NAAM, eerste voornaam voluit en eerste letter van elk der volgende voornamen	Betrekking ¹)	Datum aangifte in	Datum aangifte uit	Vorige woonplaats of adres ²)	Nieuwe woonplaats of adres ²)
1	Badnian,Erna S	H1/dHuish	27Jan41	11Mrt43	Blaricum	VOW
6	*Haliaanda, Joh.H*	z.b.	14/7 44	1Aug44	*Amerongen*	Mecklenburglaan 19
6	*Haliaanda(Elisabeth* pens.h.	14/7 44	1Aug44	*Amerongen*	idem
4	van Nieuwhove,Maria C(Wed van H J Hopman)	zonder	6Dec44	13Feb45	Asd	Asd
9	*de Roos, Maria J. (Wed.7.g.Mom)*	*moeder*	28.1.46	4Dec50	*Heemstede*	Heemstede

Residents (relatives, lodgers, service personnel, etc.) card.

March 1943 may indicate that the civil administration in the town didn't know where she was, but the Nazi headquarters certainly knew: she was in Vught, where she would remain until her transport to Westerbork in June. The 11 March date is chilling, because on this day, her parents were on the train heading for Sobibor.

Horst may have remained hidden during the February/June period, or he may have been captured and taken to Vught, but there is no evidence to shed any light on this question.

Chapter 54

Yehoshua and Hennie Birnbaum, the carers in the Westerbork orphanage, were an Orthodox Jewish couple who were born in Poland, migrated as young children to Germany, married in Cologne, moved to Berlin, and had five children there. In 1938 the Nazis deported the family back to Poland. While Hennie was pregnant with their sixth child, the couple sent their five children to live with an aunt in the Netherlands. Hennie was unable to secure entry to the Netherlands, but boarded a train when highly pregnant and told the Dutch authorities on arrival that she was going into labour. She was taken to a Catholic hospital.

Yehoshua was granted permission to enter the country provided he agreed to go to the new refugee camp being built at Westerbork. The couple and their children were reunited. In 1939 they were allowed to leave the camp and went to live in Leeuwaarden.

After the German invasion in 1940 they were sent back to Westerbork, where they took on the responsibility of running the orphanage in Barrack 35. They did everything possible to protect the children and keep them from being deported. They even created false baptism certificates, as well as other papers alleging some children were the illegitimate offspring of German soldiers.

(Information extracted from a much more detailed biography on the United States Holocaust Memorial Museum website: https://collections.ushmm.org/search/catalog/pa1174399)

Although I have no documentary evidence, it is plausible to

speculate that someone linked to the PBC might have helped with the creation of fake baptism certificates.

—⁘—

In 1945, after liberation, Adrian van As was appointed by the re-established Dutch government to be the camp commandant.

Adrian and Bertha were subsequently honoured by Yad Vashem for their efforts in saving Jews during the Holocaust. Both have since passed away.

There is an Australian link to this story. The couple later migrated to Sydney where Adrian wrote a book, *In the Lion's Den*, about his experiences in the Westerbork camp. He was a regular speaker at schools where the B'nai B'rith New South Wales' Courage to Care anti-racism exhibition was displayed. The Sydney Jewish Museum prepared a short documentary on the history of the Holocaust in which the couple are shown as examples of Righteous Among the Nations. The film was for many years screened at B'nai B'rith Courage to Care exhibitions in my home state (Victoria). This is where I first learnt about the existence of this brave couple, long before I had ever heard of Westerbork.

The statement that there is no record anywhere of Horst leaving the camp is actually consistent with Nazi records archived at the ITS in Bad Arolsen, which show Horst continuously resident in the camp from 1943 into 1944.

Our first knowledge of Gerhard's nephew's name came from Guido Abuys, the Conservator at the *Herinneringscentrum Kamp Westerbork* (Remembrance Centre of Camp Westerbork). The name was recorded as Horst or Hans. I was unsure at first whether the boy had a forename and a middle name, or two alternative names, or was the result of a difficulty in interpreting a handwritten entry. As the boy's father was named Hans, it would have been unusual in Jewish tradition to give the son the same name at the time of his birth.

However, our later interpretation was that Horst adopted the name Hans after he came to the Netherlands. Horst is a very common name in Germany but is a rare Dutch name. Hans, in contrast, is common in both countries. A young child in a foreign country occupied by German forces might have preferred to have a name that was less obviously German.

Chapter 56

The central events in this episode are all based on documented evidence, reported briefly in Henk van der Tweel's memoirs. *Verzet* member Willem Petrus (Peter) Roelofs was arrested on 19 July 1943. The note recorded by the Dutch police officer on the day of the rescue a month later and cited by van der Tweel was found in the police archives after the war. In a later recollection, Peter Roelofs mentions that Gerhard was accompanied on this occasion by his PBC colleague Hans Van Gogh.

Gerhard would have had to present an official handover document, the *Übernahmeschein*, for this ruse to have worked. I have assumed that it would have needed the signature of Rauter, who reported only to Seyss-Inquart in the Netherlands and to Himmler in Germany.

I have not seen any examples of the fake documentation that Gerhard used when masquerading as a Nazi officer. However, Frieda Voorhorst sent me a copy of a similar document. On the letterhead of the *Befehlshaber* (Commander) of SD headquarters in The Hague, it states that the *Beamte* (Officer) Willem Johannes Hoogenboom is *berechtigt* (authorised) to collect prisoners and bring them to the SD. In passing, it is worth noting that there was obviously nothing remarkable about a Dutchman serving in the SS. Numerous NSB members did so. "SS Officer Hoogenboom" was none other than

Gerhard's colleague Kobus ("Ko") den Hartogh. The printed letter-head displays the Gestapo logo of the eagle with outstretched wings with a circle containing the swastika in its claws. Fastened to the letter is a photograph of "Hoogenboom" with two rubber stamp impressions on the letter overlapping the photo. After the war, Ko was a regular attender at the annual memorial service at the plaque in the Rubensstraat. Seventy years after Gerhard's death, Ko's daughter continued the tradition after her father passed away.

The fact that the PBC had a vast collection of fake rubber stamps is based on incontrovertible evidence: the Gestapo inventory of seized material found in the PBC office a few days after Gerhard was ambushed. Some of these rubber stamps were fakes. Others were genuine: as mentioned in the book, one Dutch manufacturer was sympathetic to the Resistance and when the Gestapo ordered a rubber stamp, a copy was made at the same time and passed to the *Verzet*.

There is no evidence that Gerhard actually struck Peter's face, but a similar event occurred during the rescue of another member of the *Verzet*, who was rounded upon by Gerhard, then slapped and abused for his unshaven face and unkempt appearance. Presumably this was a Resistance member who didn't know Gerhard personally; the *Verzet* member recounted later that he was terrified about what would happen to him at the hands of this man.

Chapter 58

Gasthuis, literally meaning "guesthouse", is an old Dutch word from the Middle Ages which originally referred to a shelter for travellers, often attached to monasteries. Sometimes they were known as *hospitales*. The meaning of *Gasthuis* evolved over the years to encompass both connotations, i.e. a shelter for the traveller or a shelter for the sick.

—∞—

The German newspaper *Die Zeit*'s edition of 27 December 1985 published a letter by Richard Stern of Amsterdam, in which he reminisces about wartime events in his city. He mentions Mia Hergesell and her marriage to an unnamed police detective (i.e. Cor Verbiest), The detective is described as *untergetauchten*, literally "diving under", i.e. "undercover". Mr Stern acknowledges the great help he received from Mia as a result of the couple's connection with the Badrian Group (she was active in the PBC). Gerhard is described as:

> … a German-Jewish photographer who was a leader in the active Resistance who operated as "Major Westerman" in German uniform and had a German Werhmachts-Opel.

I have never encountered any description of a Resistance action carried out by a "Major Westerman". Richard Stern's letter tells us that there were other episodes in which Gerhard impersonated a Nazi officer.

I deliberately appropriated this name for my fictional account of Gerhard's deception in removing Horst from Westerbork in 1943.

Notes made by Frieda Voorhorst based on the Uschi radio program and conversations with relatives of *Verzet* members tell of other episodes. The Gestapo eventually became wise to the fact that the Resistance was rescuing its members from police stations, and introduced a requirement that any transfer of prisoners from police stations had to be authorised by a telephone call to head-quarters. Gerhard and his colleagues were alerted by Commissioner Voordewind if prisoners were being moved, and one story tells of him forcing the prison van to stop and demanding that certain prisoners be handed over.

Chapter 62

The photograph was taken by Dudok van Heel. Gerhard did use Marius Meijboom's studio to develop films for the Hidden Camera group, but whether he was involved in this particular image is unknown. The event captured by the photo was explained by a Canadian historian of the Dutch Holocaust, Robert Jan van Pelt, in a *New York Times* blog by Errol Morris, in the sixth of a series of articles titled "Bamboozling ourselves".

The photograph captures graphically the change in the Nazi murder rate. A year earlier, at the time of Hermann and Frieda's capture, hundreds of victims were taken to the *Schouwburg* daily, and one to two thousand were transported each Tuesday from Westerbork to the death camps. By March 1944, almost three-quarters of the Jewish population had been murdered. Small round-ups like the one depicted in Dudok's photograph continued for another six months. The last train, on which Anne Frank was a passenger, left in September.

The Dutch website https://sites.google.com/site/oorlogsvermisten/home provides estimates of the number of victims during the Nazi occupation period. Based on census figures from various years, the total population of the Netherlands was about 9 million. An estimated 210,000 people died during World War II, about 2.3 per cent of the population.

The pre-war Dutch Jewish population was about 126,000, around 1.4 per cent of the population. By 1938, about 17,000 refugees had swelled the Jewish population, i.e. to a total of 143,000. Later arrivals would increase this total. Another source estimates that 30,000 refugees had arrived by the time of the German invasion of May 1940.

The website records 105,000 known Holocaust victims, most of them deported to Auschwitz or Sobibor. It notes that the records are not necessarily complete, so that this figure would be an underestimate.

The 1947 census records 14,346 Jews living in the Netherlands. This figure might also be an underestimate, as some survivors may have successfully hidden their identity and continued to do so after the war. Other survivors, with the help of the Resistance, may have escaped to safe countries, e.g. Switzerland, generally by a circuitous route.

What these figures tell us is that about 75 per cent of the Jewish population (Dutch citizens and refugees) perished in the Holocaust.

After Poland, where the victims of the Nazis and their collaborators numbered 90 per cent, the Dutch figures are the second-worst in Europe. This statistic is probably not widely known.

—m—

Simcha von Benckendorff helped her father Henk Pelser to write a book about his wartime experiences. She consulted with several historians who explained that the Nazis were very keen to acquire the Dutch colonies as well as incorporating the Netherlands into the German empire. This was to be achieved by the region being ruled by a civil administration consisting of dedicated Nazis who were strongly motivated to implement Hitler's genocidal ambitions. Other occupied European countries were ruled by generals whose major concern was military control rather than implementing racist political ideology.

An article by Pim Griffionen and Ron Zeller, "Comparing the Persecution of the Jews in the Netherlands, France and Belgium, 1940–1945: Similarities, differences, causes", in Peter Romijn et al., with an introduction by Wichert ten Have, *The Persecution of the Jews in the Netherlands, 1940–1945: New Perspectives* (Amsterdam: Amsterdam University Press/Vossiuspers UvA/NIOD, December 2012. ISBN: 9789056297237), examines the causes of the widely differing death rates in great detail.

Yes, the death rates were appalling, but it is worth noting that the Netherlands also produced the second highest numbers (after Poland) of non-Jewish people recognised by Yad Vashem for saving Jews during the Holocaust. Of the 27,000 people honoured by Yad Vashem, 25 per cent were Polish, and 21 per cent were Dutch.

Also worth recording is that the list of 105,000 victims is based on deportation and extermination records, and therefore does not contain the name of Gerhard Badrian. His name is, however, recorded in other Dutch memorial sites relating to the war.

Chapters 65–8

Riete Gompertz.

Riete Gompertz (1919–2010), aka Rita Horvat on her false ID, was a Holocaust survivor who lived to an advanced age. The evidence she provided about the Herengracht, the Weteringschans and Westerbork episode was crucial for my account of what happened to Horst Kerpen at the time of these events.

Riete's survival was miraculous. Had the Nazis known that she actually had four Jewish grandparents, she would have been deported to an extermination camp. However, as her father had converted to Christianity in childhood, Riete was classified as a Protestant. Having been *gedoopt* (baptised) in childhood, under the distinctly different rules that applied under the Nazi regime to children of mixed marriages in the Netherlands, this protected her from extermination. (After the war, she described herself as a "Protestant Jew".)

Naturally, her involvement in the Verzet – she helped the PBC with their forgery of ID cards – was an additional source of danger, but quite likely the Nazis had no knowledge of her involvement. She was arrested simply because she was an *illegaal*, hiding (with a false ID) in a safe house. Top-level leaders of the Resistance were executed. Senior operatives such as Bob Groothand or Anne-Marie Deij were deported to Ravensbrück concentration camp in Germany, where they survived. Riete's punishment, internment at Westerbork, was relatively mild. Adult prisoners sent to Westerbork were classified as P (*Prioriteit*, meaning deportation and extermination) or S (*strafgeval*, punishment for criminal activity). Riete Gompertz was an S. The Nazis made use of her skill as a young artist: she was set to work painting signs around the camp.

Prisoners were permitted to write and receive correspondence once a fortnight, and from a letter in the Dutch archives, written by Riete to her mother five days after her arrival, together with her statements in a TV documentary made decades later, it was possible to construct, for the first time, an accurate timeline of events in Horst Kerpen's life between his capture at the Herengracht safe house, his imprisonment in Weteringschans, the failed assault by the PBC on the prison, and Riete and Horst's transfer together to Westerbork on 9 May 1944.

I already knew about the Herengracht raid in 2014 from Henk van der Tweel's book, and, as mentioned earlier, it was this description of the (unnamed) nephew of Gerhard Badrian who was captured and later rescued from Westerbork that provided the very first evidence that Erna had a son who was alive in Amsterdam in 1944. That, of course, was an exciting discovery!

The book contains an English translation as well as the original Dutch text. The description of the raid was derived from an account provided by Peter Roelofs, who recalled that in March 1944, among the people captured was (in the English version) "a cousin of Gerhard Badrian". (The word in the original Dutch text was *neefje*. *Neef* can mean either a male cousin or a nephew; the *je* suffix is a term of endearment meaning "little" or "dear".)

A detailed account of the raid on the Weteringschans can be found in Wikipedia. That description correctly describes the motivation for the raid as the desire to free imprisoned leaders of the *Verzet*. It quite understandably makes no mention of Horst, and when I first read this material, I did not know that Horst had spent time in the high security prison. (Try, if you will, to picture the mental state of a thirteen-year-old boy who has endured orphanages, foster homes, a previous stay in Westerbork and the murder of his mother and grandparents, now locked up for more than a week in a jail with armed guards and dogs.)

The quote of Gerhard's words as he brought his severely injured leader to his colleague's home appears in Henk van der Tweel's memoirs.

—⁊—

I have described the mode of transport from Weteringschans to Westerbork as a prison van.

At the peak of the deportation period, from late 1942 to late 1943, trains were used to transport hundreds of Jews daily from Amsterdam to the transit camp. I have assumed that for small numbers, a motor vehicle would have been used.

"The young woman who had cared for the children the previous year wasn't there anymore." This is actually true. Yehoshua and Hennie Birnbaum, the young couple who had been in charge of the Westerbork orphanage for several years, both before and during the Nazi period, had, sometime between 1943 and 1944, been sent by Gemmeker to Bergen-Belsen concentration camp in Germany, together with their children. Miraculously they survived, although they suffered terribly in the late stages of the war and afterwards. The biography of the family mentioned earlier describes their travails.

Hennie and Yehoshua Birnbaum sit together after the war and look at a photograph.

Chapter 69

The copy of the *Meldezettel* of 7 June 1944 from the Westerbork records, with its specific naming of "Hans" Kerpen as missing from the camp the previous day, was another exciting piece of evidence that confirmed the rescue episode reported in the van der Tweel book. I obtained this in 2014.

However, the combination of the van der Tweel description and the *Meldezettel* evidence raised a challenging time line problem. If the Herengracht raid took place in March 1944, and Horst was admitted to Westerbork on 9 May 1944, where was he in the intervening weeks?

The question puzzled me for two years. The answer was provided by the Riete Gompertz material. It illustrates yet again the point that something is not a fact merely because it's written down. There is an error in Peter Roelof's account of the Herengracht raid, namely, the date he assigned to the episode, March 1944. It was this "fact" that led to my problem about the time line. The Herengracht raid actually occurred at the end of April.

"Nitpicking!" might well be your immediate reaction. What does it matter? March, April, May, who cares?

The error can be easily explained. Peter Roelofs wasn't there when it happened, and he was recalling, maybe years later, his memory of the event to van der Tweel. Such memories are often inaccurate. Surely Peter's tiny error is forgivable. But Riete, who was there when it happened and wrote about it soon afterwards, provides more reliable evidence.

Frieda Voorhorst obtained a copy of the Amsterdam police records of the period. On 29 April 1944, Hendrika Groothand (Bob Groothand's half-sister) and Riete (with a false identity) were, among others, in police custody. The record does not mention Horst Kerpen, so presumably he was imprisoned somewhere else, perhaps in another police station. The prisoners spent only one night in the police station cells. (The fictional meeting of Lippert's prisoner dispatch committee reflects my attempt to explain the change in procedure to shorten dramatically the time spent by captives in local police stations.)

Riete's first letter to her mother is dated Sunday 14 May. She writes that she arrived at Westerbork the previous Tuesday, i.e. she was interned on 9 May, and that she spent nine days in the Weteringschans prison, i.e. she was imprisoned there from 30 April. The date of 9 May is exactly the same date as recorded on the 7 June *Meldezettel* recording Horst's escape from the camp. Riete describes two boys named Hans and Henk, notes that neither was classified as S or P, and that Henk was placed in the Westerbork hospital barracks while Hans was housed in the orphanage.

The Herengracht episode therefore occurred at the end of April, and not in March. None of this matters if one is writing fiction. It does if one is writing history.

The precise number of captives taken at the Groothand house is unknown. Some were Jews who were deported and killed. Others survived. Three baptised Jews were sent to Theresienstadt. The Groothand sisters also survived. Bob was not present at the Herengracht house, but was already in custody elsewhere under a false name. She was transported, along with her sister Iep and her half-sister Rika, to Ravensbrück, a concentration and slave-labour camp for women 90 kilometres north of Berlin.

For their work in saving Jews, Bob (formal name Johanna), Iep (Maria) and Rika (Hendrika) were honoured by Yad Vashem.

> GROOT DE LAMBERTUS &
> JANNETJE
> GROOTHAND SISTERS MARIA,
> JOHANNA & HENDRIKA

From the Wall of Honour, Righteous among the Nations, Yad Vashem.

As the *Meldezettel* was a daily publication, the issue number 464 on 7 June 1944 allows a simple deduction that issue number 1 was produced on 2 March 1943. This was a Tuesday, the date on which the first train to Sobibor left Westerbork. Hermann and Frieda were on the second train, a week later. Clearly, the daily roll call and printed record was a policy introduced under Gemmeker's watch.

Chapter 71

I have given the vegetable-truck driver the fictitious name of Herbert Blau. In a conversation with Simcha von Benckendorff, Herta tried to recall the driver's surname and thought it was something like Blüte.

For the typical reader of *The Unsung Family Hero*, I expect that the episode in which Gerhard contacts Herta Caan to arrange the escape of his nephew from Westerbork might rightly be considered as just one of several similar actions that he carried out as a member of the Resistance. Significant, certainly, but far less dramatic: no impersonating a brutish, loud-mouthed senior Gestapo officer here, no waving of forged papers in the face of a police captain, no driving off in a fake Wehrmacht car to take a *Verzet* colleague to a safe house, no (failed) assault on a high-security prison, no carrying of a severely wounded leader to (alas temporary) safety. All that was needed was a series of messages to a helpful colleague inside Westerbork, a cooperative vegetable truck driver and a planned route to a safe house afterwards. Quiet work, undramatic, but completely effective. Gerhard wasn't even there.

For me as author, however, this episode captures the spirit of why the word *Family* appears in the title of the book. Through his work in the PBC, he, along with his colleagues, saved countless numbers of people, Jews and others, by providing them with high-quality fake IDs. His masquerades saved a few captured Resistance colleagues. There may have been more: we only know about the episodes that survivors wrote about afterwards. But the 1944 Westerbork episode is different. It's personal. In this one, Gerhard intervenes to save someone in my extended family. That made it very special for me.

Chapter 72

Gerhard had promised Herta that he would rescue her from Westerbork as soon as he could make all the necessary arrangements. It was a promise that he was sadly unable to fulfil.

As 1944 rolled on, the Nazi war machine began to fall apart, under huge pressure from the Soviets in the east and the Allies from the West. Deportations to Auschwitz ceased in September, and the extermination camp was liberated in January 1945. Two months later, in April, Canadian forces liberated Westerbork. Herta Caan survived the war.

Gemmeker had already left for Amsterdam where he pretended that he was merely working in administration. He was subsequently arrested and imprisoned at Westerbork, which became a temporary internment camp for Nazi officials and members of the NSB.

Chapter 73

During my visit to the Netherlands in 2015, Frieda Voorhorst arranged for the two of us to meet with Dr Jan Verbiest, a retired medical practitioner, the son of the late police detective Cor Verbiest. Frieda had previously been in contact with Jan, but had not met him in person. We first met outside the Rubensstraat apartment, and later walked the short distance to his home. He then took us a few doors further along the same street to his late parents' home. His father had died in 2010, but the home was now unoccupied, his mother having died only a year before our visit. Jan was in the midst of sorting through his father's vast collection of reports, documents and photographs relating to the wartime period.

Jan shared several recollections about his father's work in the *Verzet*. In the weeks following our meeting, he gave Frieda permission to look through the material. The recollections and notes in the files together provided several important pieces of information that found their way into the writing of my book. Some web research provided me with additional background about the remarkable policeman.

Perhaps one small fact is more telling than anything else: for 70 years after the war until his own passing, Cor kept a photo of Gerhard on his desk at home.

One outcome of our meeting and Frieda's subsequent work was that some weeks later I received an interesting memento in the mail: one of the blank ID cards that Gerhard and his *Verzet* colleagues stole from the National Printing Works in the Hague in April 1944.

The beautiful photo of Anne-Marie Deij in my book also came from Cor's files.

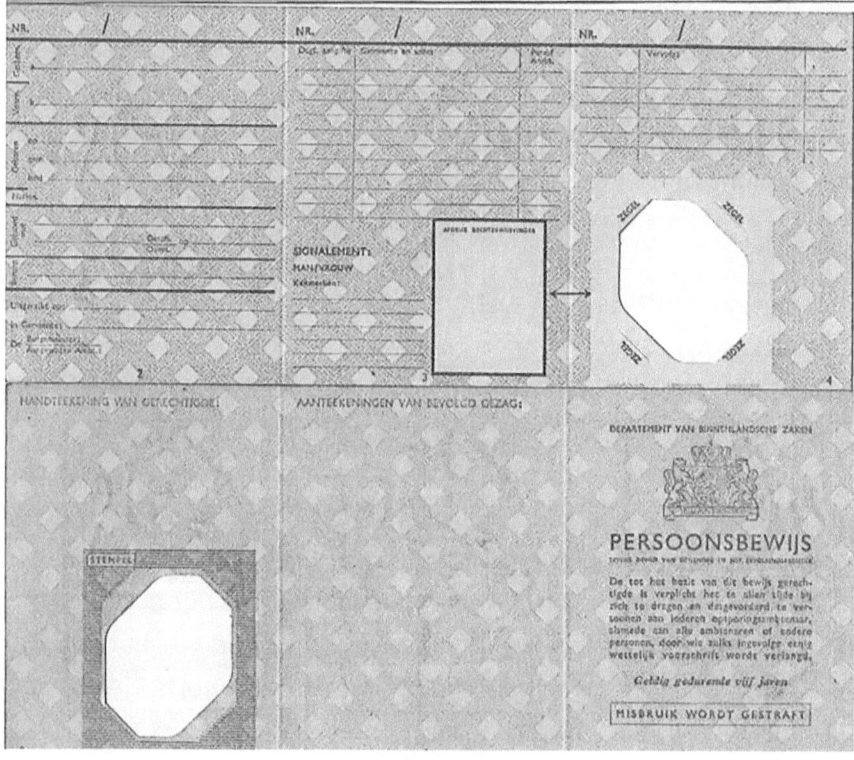

Blank PB card.

Detective Cornelis (Cor) Verbiest (alias "George"), was based in Amsterdam. His familiarity with police intelligence provided him with advance notice of raids and his police badge was a useful asset during various resistance actions. He would help *Verzet* members to get around checkpoints in the city. One example, which I did not mention in my book, was on the return trip to Amsterdam after the raid in The Hague.

A 1999 PhD thesis by A.J.J. Meershoek, *Dienaren van het gezag: De Amsterdamse politie tijdens de bezetting* [Servants of the Authority: The Amsterdam police during the occupation] notes that early in 1944, Commissioner Voordewind, at the time chief of the criminal investigation branch, put Verbiest in touch with the *Verzet*. Verbiest's contact was Gerhard Badrian. Gerhard met Voordewind occasionally. Such was the level of support that Verbiest must have had from his chief that some of the actions in which Verbiest and Gerhard participated were carried out during working hours! In my book, I have put the Voordewind–Verbiest-Badrian connection earlier. There are hints in Cor's file notes that he already knew of the location of the PBC headquarters in the Amsteldijk in 1943.

—⁂—

Cor was born in Goeree Overflakkee, south Holland in 1918, the seventh of eleven children of a farming couple. In 1936 he left the farm to live in Amsterdam, joined the police force and was mobilised in the army. After May 1940, when the Dutch army was disbanded, he was appointed as a detective, based at police headquarters in Amsterdam.

In November 1940, he married Johanna Petronella Swinkels, but the marriage did not last. While working in the police force, he joined the *Verzet* and became acquainted with Gerrit van der Veen.

Through this connection, he met Mary Charlotte (Mia) Hergesell, actively engaged in forging identity documents, whom he would marry in 1944.

One of Cor's responsibilities was to implement a Nazi order to confiscate radios. Jan told us that police were required to collect them from stores that sold or repaired them. Cor would telephone a storekeeper before his visit to inform him that he would come

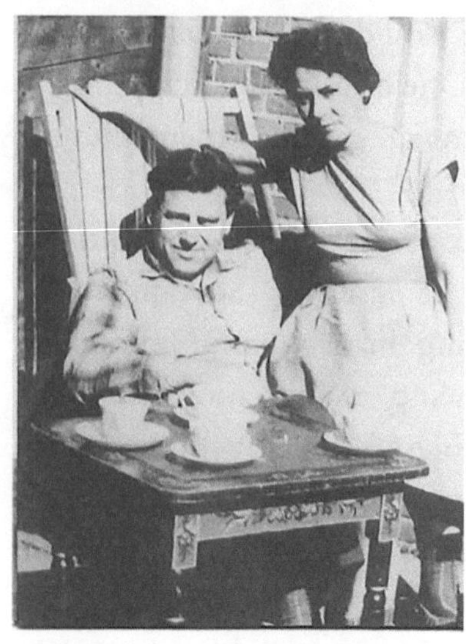

Cor and Mia Verbiest.

Cor Verbiest.

around at a particular time to collect the radios, thus giving the owner ample opportunity to hide some of them away. If by that stage the owner hadn't quite grasped the meaning of the advance message, Cor would tell him something like, "No, that one's in quite good condition, I'll just take these."

Jan explained that members of the public who had lost their *persoonsbewijzen* (PB, identity cards) were required to report the loss to the police before obtaining a replacement.

Sometimes these losses were not genuine: the owner might have allowed someone to use it as the basis for an altered, false ID. Cor's approach was to simply ask a few gentle questions and tell the owner to be on their way. (Gerhard's last PK card contains two listings, in November 1941 and February 1943, of reissued PBs. A plausible inference would be that he "lost" them deliberately.)

I have used both of these anecdotes in my telling of the story.

Cor's position in the police gave him access to advance information of Nazi raids aimed at confiscating Jewish property, and he was sometimes able to warn potential victims.

After the arrest of Gerrit van der Veen in 1944, he and Mia had to go into hiding for a while. After the war, Cor was active in founding a department to aid in the recovery of stolen Jewish goods and their return to the few survivors.

In 1946, he held a press conference to call out members of the police force who were war criminals. He submitted a report recommending some policy changes in the police force, but his proposals were ignored. Years later, in 1960, Cor was appalled when a senior policeman who had actively supported the Nazis was appointed as his superior, and he promptly resigned from the force.

Later in life, he organised a local museum in Sommelsdijk (in the region where he was born), telling of the history of Jews in the area. He believed that far too little had been done to help people who had been persecuted by the Nazis. Cor considered that the youth knew almost nothing of what had happened during the war. He and Mia regularly attended the annual memorial service for Gerhard on the Rubensstraat.

Cor died on 26 September 2010, aged 92, the last of the eleven siblings. Mia passed away in November 2014.

—◊—

The files were also helpful to me in obtaining a few details about how Horst Kerpen was hidden in the 1943–44 period, between his first rescue from Westerbork and his subsequent recapture in the Groothand house. In a note made many years after the war, Kobus den Hartogh told Cor that after the mid-1943 escape from Westerbork, Horst had been hidden briefly in the PBC headquarters on the Amsteldijk, but this was considered to be an unsafe location. After this, two women are mentioned in the notes. Trudy van Witsenburg hid Horst for a time in her home at Minervalaan 7, not far from the Rubensstraat. In September until about December, Horst was cared for by Jopie Gaffen, somewhere on the Keizersgracht, the same street where Marius Meijboom had his studio.

Cor Verbiest's files and notes made by Frans Meijer tell us something of the history of the period just prior to the Rubensstraat ambush. Gerhard and Anne-Marie (Cor's notes reveal that she called him by a pet name, Gerd) thought about leaving Amsterdam for a while and going to the country town of Epe. Gerhard was having severe problems with his back and left arm, and a physician, Dr Groen, strongly advised taking a break for a few weeks. Gerhard, however, declined to accept the advice. The arrest of Gerrit van der Veen meant that Gerhard could not leave, as he was now even more involved in the leadership of the PBC.

The name of the town, Epe, had no significance for Frieda or me at the time. In any case, Gerhard decided not to go there, and so the question of why Epe was mentioned was of little importance. A year later, however, Frieda discovered the *van Lohuizen Diary*. As mentioned earlier, Elisabeth van Lohuizen and her husband ran a guesthouse in Epe that sheltered people in hiding. They and a third person formed the *Driemanschap*. Gerhard had known the couple for at least three years. My fictional description of Cokkie Dirksen and the Trio in Groningen adheres fairly closely to the factual situation in Epe. The reference to 72 of their 90 guests surviving is based on a statement in the *Diary*.

Chapter 77

The Rubensstraat ambush is mentioned in Cor Verbiest's files. A Dutch woman, E. Swemers-de Jongh, was a witness to the event. After the war she lived in Stockholm and testified at Betje Wery's trial on charges of Nazi collaboration. In notes of her testimony, Mrs Swemers stated: "I was in the bathroom [in Wery's apartment in the Rubensstraat building]. Then I heard Betje Wery coming home with some other people. While I was getting dressed I peeked through the curtains. I saw a young lady [Anne-Marie], a young man [Frits Boverhuis] and a bald man [Gerhard]. They left the house and I heard shooting. I saw the bald man lying on the ground. SD people were coming from everywhere. I was very scared, still thinking Betje Wery was loyal, so I thought this house would be raided too. Betje Wery came upstairs and said, 'This is my doing. This man took many lives.'" Assuming that the witness statement is accurate, this was clearly an attempt by Wery to demonstrate to the SD officers that she was certainly loyal: but loyal to the Nazis, not to the Dutch people.

(Information from Dr Jan Verbiest and Frieda Voorhorst; additional biographical information from:

https://demirandabuurt.wordpress.com/2010/12/27/
een-pinguin-bij-het-graf-van-cornelis-verbiest/

and

http://collections.ushmm.org/search/catalog/irn517427)

Chapter 85

The information that Horst had been admitted as a resident in *De Bergstichting* (The Berg Foundation) in Laren in 1946 provided the first piece of documentary evidence that Horst was a Holocaust survivor. The information came from Guido Abuys at the Westerbork Remembrance Centre, and was confirmed by ITS records at Bad Arolsen.

The registration card contains some anomalies. Two alternative dates of birth are listed. His first admission to the transit camp is listed ("8-6-43 Wbk"), but his two escapes in 1943 and 1944 are not.

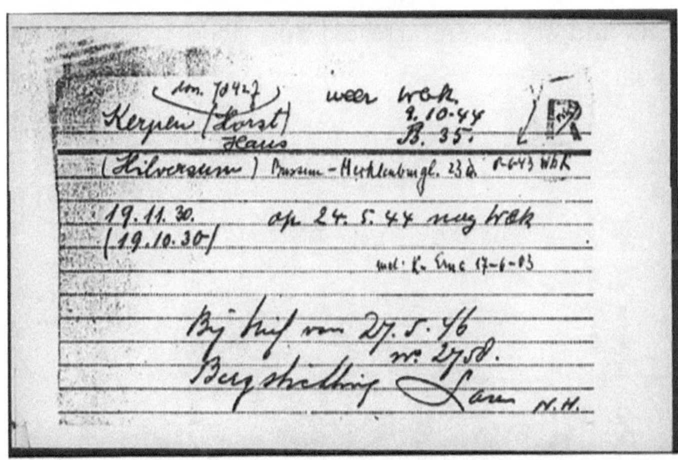

Horst's registration card at Westerbork.

There is an unexplained entry at the top ("weer Wbk 9-10-44 B 35") implying that he was in the Barrack 35 orphanage again (for a third time!) a few months after his escape. I have been unable to find any verification of this. If the entry is true, he must have escaped again, as he was not listed as being in the camp when it was liberated by Canadian forces in April 1945. The late 1944 to 1945 period was less dangerous than previously. Sobibor had been demolished after a mass escape of prisoners in late 1943, and the last transport for Auschwitz left in September 1944. The Allies and the Soviet forces were steadily advancing to liberate western Europe.

—m—

The *Bergstichting* was established in 1909 as a shelter for Jewish orphans and also for children from distressed families who had been placed there by court order. "Berg" means "mountain" but the Netherlands, as everyone knows, is as flat as a pancake. The orphanage was actually named after a wealthy German-born fashion designer Albert (Sally) Berg (1857–1924), who in middle age donated the estate to the foundation. In 1940, 106 boys and girls aged between four and 21 were accommodated there. In early 1943, all residents were ordered to relocate to an address in Amsterdam, and on April 7 residents and staff were arrested and deported. The non-Jewish

The Berg Foundation, Laren.

director Jan Reitsema (1894–1968) tried to protect the pupils and staff as much as possible, and about 70 residents survived the war by being hidden, or by being supplied with non-Jewish identification.

(Information from http://www.communityjoodsmonument.nl and other sources.)

An account of the heroic and imaginative efforts of Mr Reitsema to save the majority of the children can be found in http://www.groningen4045.nl/portretten/jan-reitsema-adorp

After liberation, he returned to take charge of the orphanage at Laren and was there during the immediate post-war years when Horst Kerpen was a resident.

Jan Reitsema retired in 1960. He was honoured by Yad Vashem in 1964. In 1971, after his death, the orphanage buildings were demolished and in 2017, a monument was erected on the site, commemorating the 48 children and four adults who were murdered by the Nazis. The surrounding parkland was named *Reitsemaplantsoen* on the same day.

Chapter 86

British bombing attack on Gestapo HQ in Euterpestraat, 26 November 1944. Continued attack with incendiary bombs resulted in the total destruction of the building.

Renaming of Euterpestraat as Gerrit van der Veenstraat, 18 May 1945. The event took place on the corner with Rubensstraat; the building in the picture is Rubensstraat 26.

Chapter 89

A few years later, the government proposed an amnesty for Nazi war criminals convicted in the war crimes trials. This provoked widespread protests.

A photograph, taken in Arnhem in 1952, illustrates the extent of the opposition. Lages remained in jail.

Willy Paul Franz Lages.

However, he didn't die in jail. *Levenslang*, life imprisonment, wasn't *levenslang* after all. In 1966, elderly and described as seriously ill, he was freed "on humanitarian grounds" and allowed to return to Germany. There he received medical treatment. He died five years later, a few months before his seventieth birthday. Aus der Fünten, one of the two remaining prisoners in Breda – in fact the only two Nazi war criminals still in

1952 protest against amnesty for Willy Lages.

captivity in Europe – lasted two decades longer. Released in January 1989, he was deported to Germany and died in April, six months short of his eightieth birthday.

Chapter 90

The pathways along which the two photos of Horst (as a child and as a young adult) travelled to reach the pages of this book is another story of unlikely chains of events, and also a story about the internet and modern social media.

One path was laid down by Frieda Voorhorst, who compiled a brief version of the Gerhard Badrian story and uploaded it to her Facebook page.

The other pathway began in the memory lanes of Tanny Tromperts' mind, as she occasionally looked through her photo albums. This triggered memories of her childhood friend Horst whom she met again in the mid-1950s. She knew he had gone to Germany soon afterwards, but she never heard from him again. She wondered what had happened to him.

In 2016, she contacted a Dutch TV station that produces a regular series called *Spoorloos* [Without a Trace], based on stories of people who vanish and others who try to find them, but they didn't express any interest in her story.

Undeterred, she then talked with Dirk Veenhuizen, a longstanding family friend who was interested in genealogy and history. He had already completed a project about four German Jewish children who had arrived as refugees in 1938. Tanny invited him to find out what had happened to Horst. He made electronic copies of the two photographs. His searches soon led him to Frieda Voorhorst's Facebook page about Gerhard Badrian.

The two pathways intersected in February 2017. Dirk contacted Frieda, who got in touch with Tanny, first by phone and then in person. Soon afterwards, Dirk and I were exchanging emails.

A later event occurred in July 2018, when Horst's son Robert and his wife visited Amsterdam to meet Frieda Voorhorst for the first time to see some of the significant places in Horst's life. The visit included a meeting with Tanny Tromperts.

No man is an island, either in space or in time. Gerhard Badrian's death in 1944 was still generating consequences almost 75 years later.

Chapter 93

"There are moments when you can't tell a story anymore, when you have to face an ending."

The quote about endings that heads the final chapter is taken from the last sentence of an article published in the Melbourne newspaper, *The Age*, on 7 January 2019. Dr Malcolm Angelucci is a linguist at the University of Melbourne. He and his partner Majella Thomas created a 10-kilometre-long poem, inscribed on the central white line of a bicycle track that winds through various northern Melbourne suburbs. The quote is the final stanza of the poem.

In an appropriate conjunction of literacy and literal meaning, the bike track ends at the entrance to the Fawkner General Cemetery.

6. Image credits